EXAM PREPARATION
AND STUDY GUIDE

Real Estate Principles, 10e

and

Real Estate

An Introduction to the Profession, 10e

**EXAM PREPARATION
AND STUDY GUIDE**

Frank A. Holden, Jr.

Real Estate Principles, 10e

and

Real Estate

An Introduction to the Profession, 10e

Charles J. Jacobus

THOMSON

SOUTH-WESTERN

Australia · Canada · Mexico · Singapore · Spain · United Kingdom · United States

THOMSON

SOUTH-WESTERN

Exam Preparation and Study Guide to accompany
Real Estate: An Introduction to the Profession, 10e, and Real Estate Principles, 10e
Charles J. Jacobus

VP/Editorial Director:
Jack W. Calhoun

VP/Editor-in-Chief:
Dave Shaut

Executive Editor:
Scott Person

Associate Acquisitions Editor:
Sara Glassmeyer

Developmental Editor:
Arlin Kauffman

Production Project Manager:
Amy McGuire

Senior Marketing Manager:
Mark Linton

Manager of Technology, Editorial:
Vicky True

Senior Technology Project Editor:
Matt McKinney

Web Coordinator:
Karen Schaffer

Senior Manufacturing Coordinator:
Charlene Taylor

Printer:
Thomson West
Eagan, MN

Art Director:
Chris Miller

Cover Designer:
Pop Design Works

Cover Image(s):
© Getty Images

For permission to use material from this
text or product, submit a request online
at http://www.thomsonrights.com.

For more information about our
products, contact us at:

Thomson Learning Academic Resource
Center

1-800-423-0563

Thomson Higher Education
5191 Natorp Boulevard
Mason, OH 45040
USA

Contents

Preface   *ix*

Basic Test-Taking Tips   *xi*

CHAPTER 2   NATURE AND DESCRIPTION OF REAL ESTATE   1
Tests of a Fixture   5
Lot Types   6
Subdivision Plats   6
Rectangular Survey   8

CHAPTER 3   RIGHTS AND INTERESTS IN LAND   9
Land Area Problems   15

CHAPTER 4   FORMS OF OWNERSHIP   16
Ownership Situations   21

CHAPTER 5   TRANSFERRING TITLE   24
Deed Situations   29

CHAPTER 6   RECORDATION, ABSTRACTS, AND TITLE INSURANCE   31
Short Answer Questions   36

CHAPTER 7   CONTRACT LAW   38
Contract Situations   43

CHAPTER 8   REAL ESTATE SALES CONTRACTS   45
Math Problems   50

CHAPTER 9   MORTGAGE AND NOTE   51

CHAPTER 10   DEED OF TRUST   57

CHAPTER 11   LENDING PRACTICES   61
Finance Problems and Situations   66

CHAPTER 12   THE LOAN AND THE CONSUMER   69

CHAPTER 13   SOURCES OF FINANCING   73

CHAPTER 14   TYPES OF FINANCING   79

CHAPTER 15   TAXES AND ASSESSMENTS   83
Property Tax Problems   88
Gain on Sale Problems   89

CHAPTER 16   TITLE CLOSING AND ESCROW   91
Settlement Problems   96
Settlement Worksheet   97

CHAPTER 17   REAL ESTATE LEASES   100
Property Management Problems   106

CHAPTER 18   REAL ESTATE APPRAISAL   107
Appraisal Problems   113

CHAPTER 19   LICENSING LAWS AND PROFESSIONAL AFFILIATION   115

CHAPTER 20   THE PRINCIPAL–BROKER RELATIONSHIP: EMPLOYMENT   121
Commission Calculations   125

CHAPTER 21   THE PRINCIPAL–BROKER RELATIONSHIP: AGENCY   127

CHAPTER 22   FAIR HOUSING, ADA, EQUAL CREDIT,
AND COMMUNITY REINVESTMENT   132

CHAPTER 23   CONDOMINIUMS, COOPERATIVES, PUDS,
AND TIMESHARES   137

CHAPTER 24   PROPERTY INSURANCE   143
Insurance Problems   146

CHAPTER 25   LAND-USE CONTROL   147

CHAPTER 26   REAL ESTATE AND THE ECONOMY   152

CHAPTER 27   INVESTING IN REAL ESTATE   156
Investment Problems   161

ANSWER KEY   **165**

Chapter 2   165
Chapter 3   167
Chapter 4   170
Chapter 5   172
Chapter 6   174
Chapter 7   176
Chapter 8   179
Chapter 9   181
Chapter 10   183
Chapter 11   184
Chapter 12   186
Chapter 13   188
Chapter 14   190
Chapter 15   191
Chapter 16   194
Chapter 17   196
Chapter 18   198
Chapter 19   201
Chapter 20   203
Chapter 21   204
Chapter 22   206
Chapter 23   207
Chapter 24   209
Chapter 25   210
Chapter 26   212
Chapter 27   213

GLOSSARY   217

Preface

WELCOME to the latest edition of *Exam Preparation & Study Guide,* a self-paced exam preparation supplement to the texts *Real Estate Principles* and *Real Estate: An Introduction to the Profession,* by Charles J. Jacobus. Effective use of this book and the questions contained in it will significantly increase your overall comprehension of the material in the textbook. Additional exposure to the material and increased retention will improve your confidence and help alleviate "exam anxiety." These factors combined should markedly improve test scores. To ensure maximum benefit from this book, we recommend the following:

Use the book more than once.   Write your answers on a separate sheet of paper. This will make scoring easier, and leave the questions and answers unmarked for additional "practice" retakes. Writing your answers directly into the *Study Guide* will cause you to focus automatically on the previously marked answers the next time you practice; thus minimizing the benefit of retesting.

Practice all question types.   Even though you may be preparing for "just" a multiple choice exam, you can greatly enhance your comprehension by completing the other question formats as well. We've included "story" problems, math problems, fill in the blanks, practice forms, plats and other diagrams to help you approach topics from a variety of angles. A thorough comprehension of the subject will improve your ability to answer multiple choice questions.

Practice taking timed tests.   Duplicate the testing situation by practicing the questions under pressure. This is one of the best ways to overcome "exam anxiety." Try to answer fifty questions within thirty minutes. Missed items quickly pinpoint weak areas of understanding and help you focus your attention on them for additional study.

Research wrong answers.   Reread misunderstood material in the textbook. Determine why the correct answer is valid. To avoid memorizing the questions, do not reread the ones you answered correctly. Memorizing may cause you to miss subtle wording differences on the exam, thereby causing you to answer incorrectly.

Pace your studying.   Immediately test yourself after class discussion. Look up wrong answers. Remember that last minute "cramming" before a final exam or the state licensing exam may cause you to panic when confronted with difficult material or to become overly tired during the exam.

Limit your study time.   Most people more easily recall the first and last part of whatever they study, while the middle material becomes a little muddled. It is better to study for ten to twenty minutes with breaks rather than for a solid hour.

7. Answer all questions.   Eliminate as many of the choices as possible, and then guess. Wrap up by reading each question and only the answer you chose, then ask yourself, "does this completed sentence make sense?"

8. About changing answers, . . . DON'T.   Unless you find an obvious mistake, such as an incorrectly recorded answer or misread question, do not change your original response. First guesses are correct more often than changed answers.

Real Estate Principles, 10e

and

Real Estate

An Introduction to the Profession, 10e

Nature and Description of Real Estate

2

After successful completion of the questions in this chapter, you will be able to:

1. Define real estate, land, air and subsurface rights, improvements, appurtenances, and fixtures.
2. Define personal property.
3. Define terms dealing with water rights such as percolating water, riparian rights, and littoral rights.
4. Describe land by using the metes and bounds method, the rectangular survey system, or by a recorded plat.
5. Describe the land in terms of vertical measurements.
6. Define the physical and economic characteristics of land.

1. The definition of land includes the surface of the earth, air space above, and
   A. anything affixed to land with the intent of being permanent.
   B. all appurtenant buildings.
   C. emblements.
   D. shrubs, ponds, and streams and other natural attachments.

2. W conveyed land to R by means of a deed which described the land but made no mention of buildings or improvements. Does this deed convey ownership of the buildings and improvements to R?
   A. Yes, because anything left on the property will be conveyed at closing.
   B. Yes, because buildings and improvements are considered appurtenant to the land.
   C. No, buildings and improvements are classified as personal property.
   D. No. Buildings and improvements must be conveyed by a separate bill of sale.

3. Things that the law considers to be permanently attached to the earth are called
   A. fixtures.   C. surface rights.
   B. emblements.   D. subsurface rights.

4. Property which is NOT considered to be real estate is called
   A. littoral property.   C. riparian property.
   B. personal property.   D. private property.

5. In determining whether an article of personal property has become a fixture, which of the following tests would NOT be applied?
   A. Manner of attachment
   B. Cost of the article
   C. Adaptation of the article to the land
   D. Existence of an agreement between the parties

6. In remodeling their home, the W's put the items described below in the home. Once in place all would be fixtures EXCEPT
   A. an Oriental throw rug in the front entry hall.
   B. the built-in dishwasher.
   C. the antique, leaded glass chandelier.
   D. custom fitted wall-to-wall carpet installed over plywood subflooring.

7. A tenant rented a commercial building for the operation of a printing shop. He installed shelves which are fastened to the walls, and printing equipment which is bolted to the floor. Are these now the property of the landlord?
   A. Yes, because they are installed in a permanent manner.
   B. Yes, because their removal will damage the property.
   C. No, because they are not specifically adapted to the property.
   D. No, because trade fixtures remain the property of the tenant if removed before the expiration of the lease.

8. Which of the following is personal property?
   A. Fixtures
   B. Emblements
   C. Shrub planted in the ground
   D. Air rights

9. Easements, rights-of-way, and condominium parking stalls are examples of
   A. emblements.
   B. trade fixtures.
   C. riparian rights.
   D. appurtenances.

10. The right of an owner to use water from a stream for his own use is called a(n)
    A. emblement.
    B. riparian right.
    C. littoral right.
    D. percolating right.

11. H owns a farm which borders on one bank of a creek. He wants to use water from the creek for irrigation. Is he entitled to do so?
    A. Yes, because of the doctrine of capture.
    B. Yes, because he has riparian rights to use water from the creek.
    C. No, because the water belongs to both the state and federal government and not any private owner.
    D. No, because his land borders on only one bank of the creek.

12. Underground water that is not confined to a defined subsurface waterway is called
    A. appropriated water.
    B. percolating water.
    C. table water.
    D. littoral water.

13. The term "water table" refers to
    A. the level at which water will be located.
    B. the difference between the high and low water marks in a stream.
    C. sea level at high tide.
    D. sea level at low tide.

14. The lease on a rented house identified the property as 645 West Maple Avenue, Grand-view, Anystate. Assuming this to be the correct address of the property, is this legal means of identifying the property in the lease?
    A. No, because it does not contain a complete legal description of the property.
    B. Yes, it is sufficiently accurate for use in a residential lease contract.
    C. No, because if the street name or number were ever changed, the property could not be identified.
    D. No, because all contracts dealing with real estate must contain a complete legal description by metes and bounds or government rectangular survey.

15. Which of the following has been utilized as a monument to designate the corner of a parcel of land in the metes and bounds description of the land?
    A. Iron pipe driven in the ground   C. Woodpile
    B. Shed   D. Utility pole

16. The term "point of beginning" refers to
    A. a permanent reference marker.
    B. the nearest corner of the parcel from the reference mark.
    C. a benchmark.
    D. the intersection of a principal meridian with its base line.

17. As measured from north, an angular bearing of 135 degrees would be equivalent to which of the following in a surveyor's description of the same angle?
    A. S 45 degrees W   C. N 45 degrees E
    B. N 45 degrees W   D. S 45 degrees E

18. A surveyor was called upon to make a metes and bounds survey of an irregularly shaped parcel of land. Which of the following statements would be correct?
    A. A surveyor may conduct his survey without physically visiting the parcel.
    B. A surveyor must always travel in a clockwise direction in making the survey.
    C. The angular bearing of all boundary lines would be measured from north.
    D. The corner where the survey begins is identified as the point of beginning.

19. In the rectangular survey system of land descriptions, which of the following run in an east-west direction?
    A. Principal meridians   C. Longitude lines
    B. Guide meridians   D. Standard parallels

20. East-west lines in the government rectangular survey system are known as
    A. base lines.   C. meridians.
    B. guide meridians.   D. quadrangles.

21. In the U.S. public land survey system, each 24-by-24 mile area created by the guide meridians and correction lines is called a
    A. survey.   C. township.
    B. quadrangle.   D. range.

22. In a diagram of a township, section 10 lies directly south of section
    A. 3.   C. 16.
    B. 4.   D. 15.

23. A township is
    A. six miles square.   C. six square miles.
    B. one mile square.   D. one square mile.

24. A line of townships running in a north-south direction in a rectangular survey is known as a
    A. section.
    B. range.
    C. base line.
    D. township.

25. 43,560 is the number of square feet in a(n)
    A. acre.
    B. section.
    C. township.
    D. tier.

26. How many square miles are there in a section?
    A. 1
    B. 6
    C. 36
    D. 640

27. The NW 1/4 of the NW 1/4 of the NW 1/4 of a section of land contains
    A. 10 acres.
    B. 20 acres.
    C. 40 acres.
    D. 80 acres.

28. The system of land description which identifies land by reference to a recorded plat may be referred to by any of the following terms EXCEPT
    A. recorded survey system.
    B. lot-block-tract system.
    C. recorded map system.
    D. assessor's parcel system.

29. A formal land description by reference to documents other than maps can be based on
    A. a recorded deed.
    B. an unrecorded mortgage.
    C. an assessor's parcel number.
    D. the town tax map.

30. Several states use a state-sponsored set of intersection survey points based on latitude and longitude that is known as a
    A. grid system.
    B. survey system.
    C. plat map.
    D. geologic survey system.

31. The point, line, or surface from which vertical height or depth is measured in a vertical land description is called a
    A. plat.
    B. datum.
    C. point of reference.
    D. grid.

32. When describing subsurface mineral rights, the datum chosen can be
    A. a plat reference.
    B. the surface of the parcel.
    C. a grid reference point.
    D. the assessor's parcel number.

33. In describing an air lot, the description will include
    A. the subsurface area.
    B. elevation of the air lot over the parcel.
    C. topological map references.
    D. tax map references.

34. A contour map shows
    A. topographical features of the land.
    B. political boundaries.
    C. mineral deposits.
    D. public highways.

35. Which of the following is an economic characteristic of land?
    A. Immobility
    B. Indestructibility
    C. Nonhomogeneity
    D. Scarcity

36. A generally recognized physical characteristic of land includes
    A. scarcity.
    B. modification.
    C. nonhomogeneity.
    D. situs.

5. A property owner may receive compensation for damages to the remaining land after a portion of the land has been taken through condemnation. These types of damages are called _____ damages.
   A. compensatory
   B. partial
   C. fee simple
   D. severance

6. The right of government to place reasonable restrictions on the use of land is known as
   A. a restrictive covenant.
   B. police power.
   C. escheat.
   D. estate.

7. All of the following are examples of a government's exercise of its police power EXCEPT
   A. rent controls.
   B. building codes.
   C. zoning laws.
   D. restrictive covenants.

8. A property owner who suffers from a government's exercise of its police powers
   A. may request inverse condemnation of his property.
   B. will not be compensated for his loss.
   C. will receive consequential damages from the government.
   D. is entitled to severance damages.

9. A property owner who fails to comply with a government's exercise of its police power may be subject to
   A. confiscation of his property.
   B. civil and criminal penalties.
   C. escheat of his land to the state.
   D. involuntary condemnation.

10. Property owned by a person who dies intestate without heirs will escheat to the
    A. city.
    B. city or county.
    C. state or county.
    D. federal government.

11. A person who is without heirs may avoid having his property pass to the state upon his death by
    A. leaving a valid will containing instructions for the disposition of his property.
    B. granting a life estate to another for the duration of his life.
    C. granting an easement to his church.
    D. giving a license to his church.

12. Which level of government has the responsibility for protecting the rights of property owners against confiscation by foreign governments?
    A. Federal
    B. State
    C. County
    D. City

13. A property owner who holds fee simple title to land will have all of the following "sticks" in his bundle of rights EXCEPT the right to
    A. occupy and use it.
    B. restrict the use of the land.
    C. devise it by will.
    D. violate building, health, and safety codes.

14. Which of the following rights in land may be held by a private owner?
    A. Refusal to sell to the government
    B. Rejection of a claim for taxes
    C. The right to disinherit one's heirs
    D. Repudiation of zoning laws

37. Because a parcel of land cannot be precisely substituted for another, it is said to be
    A. nonfungible.
    B. indestructible.
    C. in demand.
    D. scarce.

38. Area preference in the location of land is described as
    A. fixity.
    B. situs.
    C. sunk costs.
    D. surface rights.

39. It has been said that the three most important factors when buying real estate are "location, location, and location." To what characteristic of real estate does this statement refer?
    A. Scarcity
    B. Modification
    C. Indestructibility
    D. Situs

SECTION 2.2: Tests of a Fixture

Indicate whether the following articles on the property would be classified as fixtures or personal property.

1. Mailbox on post in ground
   A. Fixture
   B. Personal property

2. Custom-fitted storm windows
   A. Fixture
   B. Personal property

3. Perennial shrubbery
   A. Fixture
   B. Personal property

4. Dining room chandelier
   A. Fixture
   B. Personal property

5. Kitchen cabinets
   A. Fixture
   B. Personal property

6. Warm air furnace
   A. Fixture
   B. Personal property

7. Table fan, plugged in
   A. Fixture
   B. Personal property

8. Tree
   A. Fixture
   B. Personal property

9. Child's backyard swing set
   A. Fixture
   B. Personal property

10. Barn
    A. Fixture
    B. Personal property

11. Fence around barnyard
    A. Fixture
    B. Personal property

12. Garden tractor
    A. Fixture
    B. Personal property

13. Crops in vegetable garden
    A. Fixture
    B. Personal property

14. TV antenna installed
    A. Fixture
    B. Personal property

15. Kitchen sink
    A. Fixture
    B. Personal property

16. Installed cable system
    A. Fixture
    B. Personal property

SECTION 2.5: Rectangular Survey

1. The NE 1/4 of the SW 1/4 of the SE 1/4 of Section 12 is identified as parcel
   A. L.   C. U.
   B. W.   D. F.

2. How many acres are in parcel H?
   A. 10   C. 30
   B. 20   D. 40

3. The N 1/2 of the SE 1/4 of the NE 1/4 of Section 12 is identified as parcel
   A. L.   C. B.
   B. K.   D. M.

4. What are the dimensions of parcel X?
   A. 2640' x 1320'   C. 1320' x 660'
   B. 660' x 330'   D. 1320' x 1320'

5. The total acreage of parcels Q and Y is
   A. 160 acres.   C. 20 acres.
   B. 40 acres.   D. 80 acres.

6. Locate and shade in the E 1/2 of the NW 1/4 of the NW 1/4 of Section 12. This is identified as parcel
   A. A.   C. D.
   B. B.   D. F.

7. Locate and shade in the N 1/2 of the SE 1/4 of the NE 1/4 of Section 12. This is identified as parcel
   A. K.   C. M.
   B. L.   D. N.

8. The NW 1/4 of the SE 1/4 of the SW 1/4 of the SE 1/4 of Section 12 is identified as parcel
   A. U.   C. M.
   B. W.   D. V.

9. Locate and shade in the parcel described as follows: Beginning at the NE corner of Section 12, westerly for a distance of 1320 feet, to the point of true beginning, thence on course S 45 degrees W to the NW corner of the SW 1/4 of the NE 1/4, thence southerly for 1320 feet, thence easterly for 1980 feet, thence northerly for 330 feet, thence easterly for 660 feet, thence northerly for 330 feet, thence westerly for 1320 feet, thence northerly for 1980 feet to the point of true beginning.

   Land described here is located in parcels
   A. F, E, J, L, and M.   C. E, J, L, and N.
   B. D, E, J, K, L, and M.   D. E, J, L, and M.

Rights and Interests in Land

After successful completion of the questions in this chapter, you will be able to:

1. List the rights that government has in land.
2. Describe the fee simple bundle of rights including the difference between title and deed.
3. Define encumbrances, easements, encroachments, deed restrictions, and liens.
4. Differentiate between the various types of liens.
5. Analyze and compare the var freehold estates and understa usage.
6. Explain the differences among estates.
7. Define personal interests such and chattels.

1. The system under which persons are given the right to own land is know
   A. feudal system.   C. chattel system.
   B. allodial system.   D. fee system.

2. Under the feudal system of land ownership, the responsibility for prov ment services and determining land use was held by
   A. vassals.   C. the king.
   B. lords.   D. parliament.

3. By which of the following processes may a government acquire ownershi held land?
   A. Condemnation   C. Police power
   B. Rent control   D. Taxation

4. A government may exercise its power of eminent domain to take private lic use through the process of
   A. condemnation.   C. assemblage.
   B. appropriation.   D. allocation.

15. The term "estate" refers to
    A. the quantity of land as shown on a plat of the property.
    B. one's legal rights in the land.
    C. the value of one's property, real and personal, upon one's death.
    D. the location of one's property in the subdivision.

16. The holder of a life estate in land derives his rights from
    A. the fee simple title holder.   C. a leasehold estate.
    B. the laws of inheritance.   D. governmental rights in the land.

17. The term "title" as used with reference to land refers to
    A. the legal description of the property.
    B. a person's evidence of ownership of the land.
    C. the tax record for the property.
    D. a person's relationship to the previous owners.

18. An impediment to title to real property is called a(n)
    A. encumbrance.   C. intrusion.
    B. appurtenance.   D. domain.

19. All of the following constitute an encumbrance on the title to real property EXCEPT a
    A. will conveying the property to the owner's heirs upon death of the owner.
    B. restrictive covenant in the deed to the property.
    C. mortgage.
    D. lease.

20. A right of use and enjoyment held by one person in the lands of another for a special
    purpose is called a(n)
    A. easement.   C. license.
    B. encumbrance.   D. encroachment.

21. Which of the following easements could be created without a written document?
    A. Utility easement   C. Easement appurtenant
    B. Easement by prescription   D. Flood control easement

22. An easement acquired by continuous use is called an easement by
    A. subscription.   C. condemnation.
    B. necessity.   D. prescription.

23. M sold the back half of his lot to K, and gave K a permanent easement across his land in
    order for K to have access to the road. Which of the following statements is true?
    A. The easement is an easement in gross.
    B. The easement is an easement appurtenant.
    C. The servient estate is held by K.
    D. The dominant estate is held by M.

24. Utility easements are
    A. easements appurtenant.
    B. an encumbrance to the dominant estate.
    C. commercial easements in gross.
    D. an appurtenance to the dominant estate.

Forms of Ownership

LEARNING OBJECTIVES

After successful completion of the questions in this chapter, you will be able to:

1. Explain the characteristics and benefits of sole ownership.
2. Summarize co-ownership including joint tenancy, tenancy in common, and tenancy by the entireties.
3. Define and explain the significance of the four unities, of joint tenancy.
4. Discuss the advantages and disadvantages of community property.
5. Define trusts.
6. Discuss the various types of partnerships and corporations.
7. Discuss limited liability companies.

1. Ownership in severalty occurs when
   A. two or more people have identical interests in the same property concurrently.
   B. husband and wife share ownership of the same property.
   C. property is owned by one person.
   D. two or more persons own the same property in any form of title.

2. Among the advantages of ownership of real property in severalty is
   A. freedom of choice as to the use or disposition of the property.
   B. the ability to defeat a spouse's claim of dower or curtesy rights.
   C. freedom to avoid special assessments levied by the local government.
   D. the ability to limit activity on an adjacent property.

3. All of the following are true of a tenancy in common EXCEPT
   A. all tenants hold an undivided interest in the entire property.
   B. each tenant may have a separate deed to his/her share, or share one deed.
   C. the tenants may dispose of all or part of their shares without the agreement of the other tenants.
   D. there is a right of survivorship among the tenants.

4. Two women wish to purchase a condominium unit as co-owners. One woman will hold a 60% interest and the other a 40% interest. Both are single and each wants the other to inherit her share automatically upon death. How can they accomplish this?
   A. By taking title as tenants in common with a 60-40 interest split and naming each other in their respective will to inherit the interest upon death.
   B. By taking title as joint tenants with the right of survivorship.
   C. By taking title as a partnership, with a 60-40 split in interest.
   D. By taking title as joint tenants and naming each other as heirs in their respective wills.

5. A tenant in common may NOT
   A. claim a portion of the property for his own use.
   B. convey his interest by will.
   C. use his share of the property as collateral for a mortgage loan.
   D. sell his share without the agreement of the other tenants.

6. X, Y and Z own property as tenants in common. X owns 20%, Y owns 30%, and Z owns a 50% interest. Z needs to raise cash, and offers to sell M a 25% interest of half of his 50% interest.
   A. He cannot because tenants in common may not dispose of their interests without agreement of all the other tenants in common.
   B. He can, but he must sell M his entire interest, not just a portion of it.
   C. A tenant in common may dispose of all or part of his interest without the consent of the other tenants in common.
   D. A tenant in common may dispose of all or part of his interest without consent of the other tenants in common if he has successfully bought a suit for partition.

7. The difficulty in disposing of undivided interests and liability for debts against the property are regarded as hazards of
   A. in severalty ownership.
   B. co-ownership.
   C. Real Estate Investment Trusts.
   D. condominium ownership.

8. Three people are going to purchase an investment property as co-owners, and will take title as joint tenants. Which of the following statements is correct?
   A. Each may convey his share to his heirs in his will.
   B. Each will receive a separate deed for his share.
   C. All will have equal interests in the property.
   D. Each will enjoy limited responsibilities for debts incurred on the property.

9. The surviving co-owner may automatically inherit the deceased co-owner's share when property is held as a
   A. tenancy in common.
   B. joint tenancy.
   C. limited partnership.
   D. corporation.

10. All of the following are true of joint tenancy EXCEPT
   A. unities of time, title, interest, and possession must be present.
   B. new joint tenants may be added without forming a new joint tenancy.
   C. survivorship exists among joint tenants.
   D. a husband and wife may hold title as joint tenants.

11. M wants to leave her real estate to her nephew Z, but still wants the flexibility to change her mind in the future. She can accomplish this goal with a
    A. will naming her nephew as recipient of her real estate.
    B. joint tenancy with her nephew.
    C. tenancy in common with her nephew.
    D. court-ordered petition.

12. If any unity of joint tenancy is broken, the law will regard the estate as
    A. a tenancy by the entireties.   C. a tenancy in common.
    B. community property.   D. an estate in severalty.

13. X, Y and Z own a property as joint tenants. X wants to sell his interest to M. In the absence of documents creating a new joint tenancy,
    A. M will become a tenant in common with Y and Z.
    B. Y, Z, and M become tenants in common each with 1/3 interest in the property.
    C. Y, Z, and M must create a partnership when M acquires X's interest.
    D. Y, Z, and M become tenants by the entireties.

14. Tenancy by the entireties is based upon
    A. French colonial law.
    B. the premise that husband and wife are one legal unit.
    C. the premise that interest in marital property should be based on each partner's contribution to the acquisition.
    D. community property theories.

15. A married couple own their home as tenants by the entirety with the right of survivorship. Which of the following statements would be true regarding their ownership?
    A. Upon death of their spouse, the survivor automatically becomes a tenant in common.
    B. Each spouse has a disposable interest in the property during the lifetime of the other.
    C. Should they be divorced, they would become joint tenants in the ownership of the property.
    D. In most states, a creditor cannot force the sale of the property unless the creditor is the creditor of both spouses.

16. Two men want to purchase an investment property as co-owners. If they hold title as joint tenants, will either spouse inherit his share upon his death?
    A. Yes, because of the right of survivorship which exists among joint tenants.
    B. Yes, because a joint tenant's share passes to his heirs upon death.
    C. No, because the spouses were not named as joint tenants on the deed.
    D. No, because joint tenancy defeats a spouse's dower rights.

17. If tenants by the entireties divorce, barring any other agreement,
    A. they become tenants in common with each other.
    B. divorce does not affect the status of the title to the property.
    C. the ex-wife takes title in severalty.
    D. the ex-husband takes title in severalty.

18. The basic concept of community property law is that
    A. husband and wife are merged into one by marriage.
    B. husband and wife are equal partners.
    C. husband and wife are separate owners in severalty.
    D. the husband owns everything in the entirety.

19. A married couple live in a community property state. Which of the following would most likely be considered their community property?
    A. Property which is inherited by either spouse.
    B. Property conveyed as a gift to either spouse.
    C. Property purchased after they were married.
    D. Property owned by either spouse prior to their marriage.

20. After his marriage to W, H took title to real property in severalty, using marital funds to make the purchase. The property is located in a community property state. In order for H to sell this property, W must
    A. be given her share as separate property.
    B. surrender her dower rights in the property.
    C. sign the deed as grantor.
    D. receive her share of the property by partition.

21. Under community property law, a husband is considered to be a co-owner in any property purchased from the wife's earnings
    A. even though his name does not appear on the deed.
    B. if the property is acquired before the marriage with joint funds.
    C. if the wife names the husband as an heir in her will.
    D. only if he is named in the deed.

22. A married couple owns their home as tenants in common in a community property state. Upon the husband's death, which of the following will be true?
    A. The wife will inherit his share through her right of survivorship.
    B. By will, the husband may devise his share to anyone.
    C. The wife's dower rights will be vested immediately.
    D. The property will belong to the wife in severalty.

23. In community property states, property not held as community property is designated as
    A. private property.   C. separate property.
    B. personal property.   D. sole property.

24. Three women have formed a partnership to purchase real estate. Two of the women want to restrict their liability, naming the third as the general partner. What type of ownership did they create?
    A. Syndicate   C. Joint venture
    B. General partnership   D. Limited partnership

25. In order to hold property in the name of the partnership, a list of the partners must be published in each county and state where the
    A. partnership does business.   C. partners reside.
    B. partnership owns property.   D. partnership owns investments.

26. In a general partnership
    A. each partner has limited financial liability.
    B. each partner pays individual taxes on their share of partnership earnings.
    C. only the partnership pays taxes, not individual partners.
    D. the financial liability to each partner does not exceed the level of the investment of each in the partnership.

27. Which of the following would sometimes prove to be a negative factor in the corporate form of ownership?
    A. Limited personal liability
    B. Liquidity of investment
    C. The ability to acquire an ownership interest with small capital investment
    D. Tax considerations

28. An individual investor who is seeking the partnership advantages of capital aggregation and pass-through of profits, but who wishes to avoid unlimited financial liability, would join a
    A. joint venture.   C. general partnership.
    B. limited partnership.   D. association.

29. Management of a limited partnership is performed by the
    A. limited partners.   C. corporate officers.
    B. general partners.   D. property management firm.

30. The limited partnership is a popular way to own real estate because of
    A. unlimited liability.
    B. minimum management responsibility.
    C. greater control on progress of the investment.
    D. its liquidity.

31. Before investing in a limited partnership, one should
    A. acquire copies of deeds to all property one owns.
    B. investigate the past performance of the general partners.
    C. divest of interest in all other partnerships.
    D. investigate the other investments of the limited partners.

32. A joint venture differs from a partnership in that
    A. a joint venture is formed to carry out a single project.
    B. a joint venture cannot bind the other joint tenants to a contract.
    C. parties to a joint venture have rights of survivorship.
    D. parites to a joint venture may not be relatives.

33. Which of the following usually offers the most liquid form of property ownership?
    A. Limited partnership   C. Sole ownership
    B. Joint tenancy   D. Stock in a corporation

34. A business entity owned by stockholders who possess shares of stock as evidence of their ownership is
    A. a general partnership.   C. a corporation.
    B. a limited partnership.   D. condominium ownership.

35. The possibility of double taxation on income is a negative factor in the
    A. corporate form of ownership.
    B. limited partnership form of ownership.
    C. major corporations only.
    D. general partnership form of ownership.

36. Protection from personal liability is an advantage of
    A. corporate ownership.   C. joint tenancy.
    B. general partnership ownership.   D. sole ownership.

37. The day-to-day operations of a corporation are the responsibility of its
    A. stockholders.   C. partners.
    B. board of directors.   D. corporate officers.

38. A man wants to set up a trust to provide income for his minor children, to take effect after his death. What form of trust would this be?
    A. Inter vivos trust   C. General trust
    B. Testamentary trust   D. Corporate trust

39. A limited liability company
    A. may not be organized by anyone under 21 years of age.
    B. frees the manager or member from debts or liabilities of the company.
    C. may be a corporation or partnership.
    D. must include "Inc." or "LTD." in its name.

SECTION 4.2: Ownership Situations

1. Charlie and Mabel, a married couple, owned their home as tenants by the entireties. What events would take place in each of the following situations?
    A. In order to raise cash for his business, Charlie sold their home, acting alone. Mabel later refused to sign the deed. What is the status of this sale?

    _____

    _____

    B. The deed to this property reads "Charlie and Mabel, husband and wife, as tenants by the entireties." If it were located in a state where survivorship is automatic, what action would be necessary for Mabel to receive the fee in severalty upon Charlie's death?

    _____

    _____

    C. If Charlie and Mabel get divorced, what type of tenancy would be established, assuming a settlement that awarded the property to one spouse in severalty?

    _____

    _____

    D. If title were granted as in C above, and one person did not wish to continue co-ownership, what possibilities are available to him/her?

    _____

    _____

    E. If the property was not subdivided, how else could the interests of the parties be separated?

    _____

    _____

F. Suppose Charlie incurred a debt in the form of a bank loan, but without his wife's signature on the note. If Charlie were to default on the loan, could the property be attached for the satisfaction of the debt?

_____

_____

2. Suppose that Charlie and Mabel lived in a community property state. After marriage, they purchased their home. Mabel was not employed and had no funds of her own. The home was purchased entirely from funds produced by Charlie at his employment. Would this be separate or community property?

A. Upon her parents' death, Mabel inherited real property which was situated in the same state. Would the inheritance be community property or would this be Mabel's separate property?

_____

_____

B. Suppose that Charlie died before Mabel. When his will was read, it was found that he had left his interest in their home to his sister. Would this be a legal provision of the will? Would Mabel have any dower rights in the property?

_____

_____

C. When his parents died, Charlie inherited some cash, which he used to purchase investment property. If he took title in his name alone, would it be community property or separate property? Would Mabel have any dower rights?

_____

_____

3. O and W, each of whom is married, purchase a parcel of investment property as joint tenants in a state in which survivorship is presumed among joint tenants. Title is taken in this manner. This is not a community property state.

A. Upon the death of either tenant, who would acquire the interest of the deceased tenant? Could this be defeated by will?

_____

_____

B. What rights, if any, would a widow of the deceased tenant have in the property? Why?

_____

_____

4. Brown, Jones, and Smith, each of whom was married, purchased a parcel of investment property for $50,000. Brown paid $10,000, Jones paid $15,000, and Smith paid $25,000. They took title in those proportions on the deed.

A. What type of tenancy would be established and why?

_____

_____

B. What proportionate shares of the property would each tenant hold?

_____

_____

C. If there were a rental property containing five units, how would ownership of the individual units be divided? Why?

_____

_____

D. Should Smith want to sell a portion of his share to Green, could he do so without the agreement of Jones and Brown? If so, what would be the relationship of Green to the other tenants?

_____

_____

E. If one of the owners should die, what disposition would be made of his share, if he died intestate?

_____

_____

F. Suppose the property were in a community property state, and Brown had purchased his share with funds earned from his employment. Would this be community property or separate property? If he should die intestate, to whom would his share be given?

_____

_____

G. How would the earnings of the property be divided for tax purposes?

_____

_____

5. Give a brief explanation of how a real estate investment trust is operated.

_____

_____

A. What term is used to describe investors in a REIT?

_____

_____

B. How are the earnings of a REIT taxed?

_____

_____

C. Failure of a REIT to follow the rules for its operation may have what effect on the tax situation of its investors?

_____

_____

Transferring Title

After successful completion of the questions in this chapter, you will be able to:

1. Explain the essential elements of a deed.
2. Describe the various covenants and warranties.
3. Explain the different types of deeds, such as general warranty, special warranty, bargain and sale, and quitclaim deeds.
4. Define other types of deeds such as gift deeds and guardian deeds.

5. Explain how real estate is conveyed after death.
6. Define adverse possession, easement by prescription, and ownership by accession.
7. Describe how property is transferred by public grant and dedication.

1. The law requiring that transfers of real property ownership be in writing is known as the
   A. Law of Evidence.
   B. Statute of Liberties.
   C. Statute of Frauds.
   D. Statute of Limitations.

2. The actual act of transferring ownership of land is known as a
   A. grant.
   B. devise.
   C. demise.
   D. curtesy.

3. Which of the following are essential to the validity of a deed?
   A. The grantor must be of legal age and sound mind.
   B. The grantee must be of legal age and registered.
   C. The grantee must sign the deed.
   D. The deed must be recorded to be valid.

4. One day after the birth of his first son, R signed a deed conveying real estate he owned, to his son. The consideration recited in the deed was stated as the love that R felt for his son. Which of the following statements is true?
   A. The deed is invalid because R cannot convey property to a minor.
   B. The statement of love constitutes valuable consideration.
   C. The child's mother must sign the deed for it to be valid.
   D. The deed is invalid because no valuable consideration is identified.

5. With the words of conveyance in a deed, the grantor
   A. states that he is granting the property to the grantee.
   B. warrants that he has the right to convey title to the property.
   C. relinquishes all rights to the property.
   D. warrants that there are no encumbrances on the property.

6. Which of the following may NOT be conveyed by deed?
   A. Fee simple estate   C. Easements
   B. Life estate   D. Leasehold estate

7. Which of the following property descriptions would be acceptable in a deed?
   A. The property located at 123 Maple Street in Baltimore
   B. The property identified as lot 3 section F on the town of Smithville Tax Map
   C. The property identified as Lot 24 on the recorded plat of Smithville Acres, book 17, page 894
   D. The property at the northwest intersection of the Bryant and Gessner roads in the town of Smithville

8. If only air or mineral rights are being conveyed by deed,
   A. the legal description of the land will be omitted.
   B. words of conveyance will be omitted.
   C. the deed need not be signed by the grantor.
   D. the deed still must contain all essential elements.

9. In order to convey title to real property, a deed must be signed by the
   A. grantee.   C. agent.
   B. grantor.   D. buyer.

10. In order to convey title, a deed must be
    A. delivered by the grantor and accepted by the grantee.
    B. registered.
    C. acknowledged.
    D. witnessed by two competent adults.

11. A grantee is assured that he will not be disturbed by someone else claiming an interest in the property by the covenant of
    A. seizin.   C. further assurance.
    B. quiet enjoyment.   D. warranty forever.

12. The grantee is assured that the title to property is not encumbered by unpaid taxes, judgments, etc., by the covenant
    A. of warranty forever.   C. of seizin.
    B. of further assurance.   D. against encumbrances.

13. If additional documents are necessary to perfect the grantee's title, this would be required by the covenant
    A. of seizin.   C. against encumbrances.
    B. of further assurances.   D. of warranty forever.

14. The covenant which is the absolute guarantee that the title and rights to possession of the property are as stated in the deed is the covenant
    A. of seizin.   C. against encumbrances.
    B. of quiet possession.   D. of warranty forever.

15. Deeds are usually acknowledged to
    A. make them valid.
    B. provide constructive notice.
    C. make them enforceable.
    D. make them admissible to the public records.

16. In addition to the minimum requirements of a deed, all five covenants and warranties are found in all of the following deeds EXCEPT a
    A. general warranty deed.
    B. special warranty deed.
    C. warranty deed.
    D. full covenant and warranty deed.

17. The deed considered to be the best deed a grantee can receive is a
    A. general warranty deed.
    B. special warranty deed.
    C. bargain and sale deed.
    D. quitclaim deed.

18. As used in a deed, the word "appurtenances" means
    A. rights that pass with the conveyance.
    B. a deed wherein a full set of covenants and warranties is lacking.
    C. the place where the deed is signed and notarized.
    D. a combination granting clause and habendum.

19. The phrase "the grantee's heirs and assigns forever" indicates the conveyance of a
    A. fee simple estate.
    B. life estate.
    C. leasehold estate.
    D. less-than-freehold estate.

20. The word "assigns" in a deed refers to
    A. anyone to whom the grantee may later deed the property.
    B. creditors of the grantee.
    C. the grantor.
    D. the grantor's heirs.

21. A grantor who does not wish to convey certain rights of ownership
    A. must note the exceptions in a separate instrument.
    B. may not do so, as a deed conveys the entire premises.
    C. may note the exceptions in the deed.
    D. must convey the entire premises and have the grantee reconvey the right to be retained by the grantor.

22. The description of the land in a deed
    A. automatically includes all buildings on the land.
    B. conveys buildings only if described in the deed.
    C. conveys only the land.
    D. does not convey subsurface rights unless so stated in the deed.

23. The exact form and wording of a deed are
    A. critical to its validity.
    B. set by federal statutes.
    C. determined by state law.
    D. flexible as long as all essentials are present.

24. In a grant deed, the grantor is responsible for encumbrances
    A. of future owners as well as his own.
    B. during the period of time he possessed the property.
    C. of previous owners as well as his own.
    D. of current owners of adjacent properties.

25. A deed wherein the grantor convenants and warrants the property's title against defects occurring during the grantor's ownership and not against defects existing before that time is a
    A. bargain and sale deed.
    B. grant deed.
    C. special warranty deed.
    D. quitclaim deed.

26. A quitclaim deed conveys
    A. the grantor's interest in the property at the time of conveyance.
    B. any rights that the grantor may acquire in the future.
    C. any rights that the grantor acquired when the property was conveyed to him.
    D. only those rights specifically requested by the grantee.

27. Quitclaim deeds are often used to convey
    A. title as a gift.
    B. the grantor's interest without imposing any future obligations to defend the title upon the grantor.
    C. title to a blood relative.
    D. condominium ownership.

28. Gift deeds usually take the form of
    A. sheriff's deeds.
    B. bargain and sale deeds.
    C. warranty deeds.
    D. grant deeds.

29. In what type of deed must the grantor state the legal authority that permits the grantor to convey the property of a minor?
    A. Gift deed
    B. Life estate deed
    C. Sheriff's deed
    D. Guardian's deed

30. You would expect to find the word "remise" and "release" in a
    A. warranty deed.
    B. special warranty deed.
    C. grant deed.
    D. quitclaim deed.

31. Which of the following could be used to convey title upon mortgage foreclosure?
    A. Sheriff's deed
    B. Grant deed
    C. Quitclaim deed
    D. Guardian deed

32. A deed used to correct an error in a previously executed and delivered deed may be called a
    A. correction deed.
    B. deed of condemnation.
    C. gift deed.
    D. fixed deed.

33. A court of law with the power to admit and certify wills is called a
    A. probate court.
    B. surrogate court.
    C. district court.
    D. either surrogate or probate court.

34. Title inherited from a person who dies intestate is known as
    A. title by division.
    B. a devise.
    C. title by intestate succession.
    D. a condemnation.

35. The term "escheat" refers to
    A. the passing of title to real property to the state when no will or heirs can be found for a decedent's estate.
    B. title acquired through undue influence or duress.
    C. title granted to a citizen by the government.
    D. title conveyed to the government as a result of condemnation.

36. A handwritten will signed by the testator but not witnessed is known as a(n)
    A. nuncupative will.   C. oral will.
    B. holographic will.   D. formal will.

37. Title acquired by unauthorized occupation of another's land is known as title by
    A. dereliction.   C. adverse possession.
    B. accretion.   D. squatter's rights.

38. In order to successfully claim title by adverse possession, the claimant must meet all the following requirements EXCEPT
    A. actual possession of the land.
    B. open and hostile possession.
    C. continuous possession for the statutory period.
    D. occupancy of the land with the permission of the owner of record.

39. J has been farming his deceased father's land and paying property taxes on it for so long that everyone in town has come to assume that J owns it. A document in the public records seems to indicate that J is the owner, but there is no deed or other conveyance from his father. Which of the following is true?
    A. J has color of title to the farm.
    B. J is a tenant at sufferance.
    C. Anyone buying the farm from J should have all of J's relatives sign the deed as grantors.
    D. J owns the property if he has paid the property taxes.

40. When a person assumes, through adverse possession or assignment, the rights of a previous adverse possessor, it is known as
    A. tacking on.   C. adversity.
    B. prescription.   D. probate.

41. An easement acquired by prolonged adverse use is acquired by
    A. implied grant.   C. prescription.
    B. necessity.   D. condemnation.

42. An owner can break a claim of adverse possession by
    A. destroying the property in question.
    B. giving the trespasser permission.
    C. ignoring the trespasser.
    D. keeping accurate records of the trespasser's movements.

43. The process of increasing land due to the gradual deposition of waterborne soil is known as
    A. reliction.   C. accretion.
    B. avulsion.   D. alluvion.

44. When a waterline permanently recedes, exposing dry land, the process is known as
    A. avulsion.   C. correction.
    B. reliction.   D. easement.

45. Land acquired through accretion or reliction is known as ownership by
    A. accession.   C. assemblage.
    B. appurtenance.   D. alluvion.

46. A conveyance of land by a government to a private citizen is known as
    A. dedication.   C. public grant.
    B. prescription.   D. private grant.

47. Land may be transferred from the public domain to private ownership by
    A. dedication.
    B. a land patent.
    C. warranty deed.
    D. gift deed.

48. A voluntary gift of private land to the public is known as
    A. alienation.
    B. dedication.
    C. reliction.
    D. annexation.

49. When a landowner, by act or ward, shows that he intends that land be dedicated, even though no written dedication has been made, it is known as
    A. a public devise.
    B. a public bequest.
    C. statutory dedication.
    D. common law dedication.

50. Forfeiture can result when a grantee fails to
    A. meet a condition or limitation imposed by the grantor.
    B. make mortgage payments.
    C. pay the interest.
    D. acknowledge the deed.

SECTION 5.2: Deed Situations

Each situation described below would be resolved by a certain type of deed. Examine the situation and determine the type of deed best used in each instance. Justify your selection by showing why the features of that deed apply.

1. S was named in the will of her late brother to settle his estate. In order to raise money for taxes, it was necessary to sell a parcel of real estate which he had owned. Title would be conveyed by means of a(n) _____ deed.

   Justification: _____

2. C's real property was sold at a court-ordered foreclosure sale. The property was located in a state which allowed C one year to pay the debt and redeem the property. For a consideration, C agreed to give up this right to the purchaser at foreclosure. He would do so by means of a(n) _____ deed.

   Justification: _____

3. S voluntarily sold his home through normal marketing procedures. Title would probably be conveyed by means of a(n) _____ deed.

   Justification: _____

4. G wishes to convey property to his daughter as a gift. He is willing to warrant that he has not encumbered the property, but will not give any further warranties of title. In this situation, title would probably be conveyed in a(n) _____ deed.

   Justification: _____

5. A husband and wife purchased a home in your state through normal marketing procedures. In this situation they would normally ask for a(n) _____ deed.

   Justification: _____

6. Discuss and give several pitfalls in the use of preprinted deed forms for the transfer of real estate ownership.

_____

_____

7. Why would a grantee be willing to accept a deed with fewer covenants than those found in a warranty deed?

_____

_____

8. Identify and discuss one of the more important differences in the transfer of real estate ownership by grant and by will.

_____

_____

9. Define and illustrate the term "color of title."

_____

_____

Recordation, Abstracts, and Title Insurance

LEARNING OBJECTIVES

After successful completion of the questions in this chapter, you will be able to:

1. Summarize the need for public records and explain the requirements for recording.
2. Describe the typical public records organization.
3. Differentiate between an abstract and a chain of title.
4. Explain the purpose and application of title insurance.
5. Describe a quiet title suit.
6. Discuss the Torrens System.

---

1. The Statute of Frauds established the requirement that
   A. written deeds be used to show transfers of ownership.
   B. all deeds be recorded in the public records.
   C. a system of public records be established.
   D. anyone claiming ownership of land visibly occupy the land.

2. Notice provided by recording an instrument in the public records is
   A. real property notice.
   B. actual notice.
   C. constructive notice.
   D. county court notice.

3. An investor is considering the purchase of a 100-unit apartment building that is fully occupied. Which of the following would be true?
   A. The investor should search the public records for copies of the tenant's rental agreements.
   B. No chain of title report is needed because the property is an income property.
   C. The tenants are charged with inquiring as to the rights of the new owner.
   D. By their presence, the tenants are giving constructive notice of their right to be there.

4. Once a person is aware of another's rights or interest in property, that person is said to have
   A. constructive notice.
   B. legal notice.
   C. inquiry notice.
   D. actual notice.

5. The public recorder's office
   A. serves as a central information station for documents pertaining to interests in land.
   B. is an agency of the federal government.
   C. is an agency of the state government.
   D. is accessible to attorneys only.

6. Instruments affecting land transfers are recorded in the jurisdiction in which the
   A. parties to the instrument maintain legal residence.
   B. land is situated.
   C. instrument is created.
   D. tax rate is lowest.

7. Documents are recorded by
   A. placing the original document on file in the recorder's office.
   B. submitting the original document which is photocopied and placed on file.
   C. posting a photocopy of the original document on the property.
   D. posting the name and mailing address of the owner on the property.

8. An unrecorded deed to land is binding upon
   A. the parties to the deed.   C. the public generally.
   B. subsequent purchasers.   D. subsequent lenders.

9. R conveyed property to S by a deed dated June 1. S did not record the deed nor take possession of the property. On June 10 the same year, R conveyed the same property to T, who properly searched the records and visited the property. T promptly recorded his deed and took possession of the property. Later, S claimed ownership based on his earlier deed. Will S's claim be recognized?
   A. No, because S did not provide legally required notice of his ownership and did not take possession.
   B. No, because priority is given to the deed with the later date.
   C. Yes, because of the earlier date on his deed.
   D. Yes, because R's conveyance to S constituted fraud.

10. Priority of a recorded instrument is determined by the date of
    A. acknowledgment.   C. the instrument.
    B. delivery to the grantee.   D. recordation.

11. Which of the following would NOT usually be placed on record?
    A. Mortgage on the property   C. Deed to the property
    B. Month-to-month rental agreement   D. Option to purchase the property

12. Records in the public recorder's office may be inspected by
    A. attorneys only.   C. only government personnel.
    B. the general public.   D. court staff only.

13. A prospective purchaser of real estate is presumed by law to have inspected the
    A. building systems.
    B. public records pertaining to the land.
    C. insurance policies covering the real estate.
    D. financial status of the current owner of the real estate.

14. Deeds and other instruments which affect land titles should be recorded
    A. immediately after execution and delivery.
    B. within five business days, excluding Sunday.
    C. just prior to putting the property up for sale.
    D. only if the owner contemplates selling the property.

15. The purpose of having a person's signature acknowledged is to
    A. construct a paper trail for transfer tax purposes.
    B. make the document admissible to the public records.
    C. notify family members directly of the signature.
    D. provide a seal from the notary public, without which the property may not be financed.

16. In completing a title search, which of the following would an abstracter do first?
    A. Check the grantor index to ascertain that the present owner had not previously conveyed to someone else.
    B. Check the grantee index to verify the present owner's claim of title.
    C. Check other public records such as court records, lien indexes, judgment rolls, and lis pendens index.
    D. Trace the chain of title back to the original sale or grant of the land.

17. Instruments are recorded in the public records in what order?
    A. Alphabetical order, based on the grantee's last name
    B. Chronological order, as received for recordation
    C. According to the date of the instrument
    D. Alphabetical order, based on the grantor's last name

18. When one has traced the ownership of a parcel of land to the beginning of its recorded history, without reference to any encumbrances or other documents affecting the title, the result is a(n)
    A. abstract of title.   C. chain of title.
    B. history of title.   D. record of title.

19. Among the sources which have to be checked to establish an unbroken chain of title would be
    A. criminal court records.   C. county income records.
    B. title insurance records.   D. judgment rolls.

20. The name of the borrower would be filed alphabetically in the
    A. mortgage index.   C. lis pendens.
    B. mortgagor index.   D. lender's index.

21. Which of the following would not ordinarily be checked in searching a title to a parcel of land?
    A. Judgment records   C. Chattel mortgage records
    B. Lien records   D. Lis pendens index

22. A lis pendens index is
    A. an index of existing leases on property.
    B. an index of pending lawsuits.
    C. a tract index.
    D. a chain of title.

23. A person who searches land titles as an occupation may be known as a(n)
    A. abstracter.
    C. title surveyor.
    B. title paralegal.
    D. court officer.

24. A summary of all recorded documents affecting title to a parcel of land is called
    A. a chain of title.
    C. a title report.
    B. an abstract of title.
    D. a title insurance policy.

25. In the normal course of events, when an abstract of title is sent to an attorney for examination, the attorney will render a(n)
    A. opinion of title based on the facts contained in the abstract.
    B. certificate of title which guarantees the title to be as recorded in the abstract.
    C. survey of title based on the abstract.
    D. title insurance policy commitment.

26. S, an abstracter, prepared the abstract on property being conveyed to B. Should B's title later prove to be defective, S could be held liable if the title defect was based on
    A. a forged deed in the chain of title.
    B. a spouse's unextinguished dower rights.
    C. an unrecorded deed to the property.
    D. a mistake due to negligence in searching the title.

27. Protection against incomplete or defective records of the title to land can best be obtained by securing
    A. an abstract of title.
    C. an attorney's opinion.
    B. title insurance.
    D. a title searcher's opinion.

28. Protection against a loss occasioned by which of the following would NOT be covered by title insurance?
    A. Forged deeds, or deeds by incompetents
    B. Unextinguished dower or curtesy rights
    C. Claims by undisclosed or missing heirs
    D. Destruction of improvements by a tornado

29. Title insurance companies were originally organized to provide protection for
    A. the buyer of real property.
    C. the real estate agent.
    B. the seller of real property.
    D. attorneys and abstracters.

30. Before a title insurance company will issue a title insurance policy on a property,
    A. the property must be physically inspected by a representative of the title insurance company.
    B. a title report must be prepared showing the apparent condition of the report.
    C. the improvements on the property must be insured.
    D. the deed of conveyance must be prepared.

31. Which of the following would commit an insurance company to issue a title policy?
    A. Preliminary title report
    C. Lawyer's opinion
    B. Binder
    D. Abstract of title

32. B purchased real estate from H without making a visual inspection of the land for signs of notice. The American Title Insurance Company insured the title. B later discovered that H had previously conveyed the land to S who was in possession at the time of B's purchase, but had not recorded his deed. Is B's potential loss covered by the title insurance company?
    A. Yes, because the title insurance protects against any defect in the title.
    B. Yes, because the title insurance company should have made a visual inspection of the land for signs of actual notice.
    C. No, because the title insurance never protects against unrecorded deeds.
    D. No, because the title insurance policy would not protect against claims which could have been disclosed by a visual inspection or inquiry of persons in possession.

33. You are standing in the backyard of a house that is offered for sale. You want to buy the house, but the fence surrounding the backyard appears to encroach onto the land of the next door neighbors. Which of the following would normally disclose such an encroachment?
    A. Abstract of title
    B. Standard title insurance policy
    C. Attorney's opinion of title
    D. Current survey

34. The premium for a title insurance policy is
    A. paid annually.
    B. paid semiannually.
    C. a single premium, paid upon issuance.
    D. included in the monthly mortgage payment.

35. Which of the following is true of a lender's policy of title insurance?
    A. The face amount of the policy is always equal to the acquisition cost of the property.
    B. The coverage increases as the loan is amortized.
    C. It makes exceptions for claims that could have been anticipated by a physical inspection of the property.
    D. It is assignable to subsequent holders of the mortgage loan.

36. A title insurance policy issued for the protection of a lender who has taken real estate as collateral for a loan is called
    A. a lender's policy.
    B. mortgage insurance.
    C. an owner's policy.
    D. a borrower's policy.

37. When both an owner's and a lender's policy of title insurance are purchased simultaneously,
    A. the cost will be the total of normal premiums for both policies.
    B. the combined cost is slightly more than for an owner's policy alone.
    C. there is no extra charge for the lender's policy.
    D. the cost of the lender's policy is deducted from the owner's policy.

38. Should a title insurance company elect to fight a claim in court, the legal expenses incurred will be
    A. deducted from the coverage under the policy.
    B. assumed by the title insurance company without affecting the coverage.
    C. shared by the insured and the insurance company.
    D. paid by the insured.

39. A homeowner had a title insurance policy in the amount of $30,000 on his home. A claim was filed against the property, and the title insurance company paid out $10,000 to settle the claim. The coverage under the policy would continue at
    A. $10,000
    B. $20,000
    C. $30,000
    D. $40,000

40. Marketable title to real estate is title which is
    A. absolutely free of any possible defect.
    B. free of reasonable doubt as to ownership.
    C. issued by a court after completion of a quiet title action.
    D. insured by a title insurance company.

41. The purchase of title insurance eliminates the need for
    A. casualty insurance.
    B. a survey of the property.
    C. constructive notice.
    D. none of these.

42. Which of the following would usually provide the greatest assurance to an owner that the title to his property is marketable?
    A. Attorney's certificate of title
    B. Owner's policy of title insurance
    C. Preliminary title report
    D. Mortgagee's policy of title insurance

43. Regarding a quiet title suit, all of the following are true EXCEPT
    A. it is a judicial proceeding.
    B. it removes all claims to title other than the owner's.
    C. it quiets those without a genuine interest in the property.
    D. it can be used to clear up a disputed title.

44. Because of a controversy over how a will was probated, several parties are claiming small interests and one person a major interest in a single parcel of land. The major owner wants to sell but the title companies have refused to insure the title. The major owner's alternatives are to
    A. negotiate and obtain quitclaim deeds from the minor owners.
    B. file a quitclaim title suit.
    C. take possession of the property.
    D. lease the property from the title insurance company pending legal resolution.

45. A Torrens certificate of title is more meaningful than an attorney's certificate of title because the
    A. Torrens certificate is founded on judicial decision.
    B. Torrens certificate is founded on an opinion of the condition of the title.
    C. attorney is being compensated for his opinion.
    D. Torrens system is streamlined.

46. A quiet title suit is necessary for a
    A. Torrens certificate.
    B. marketable title act.
    C. title search.
    D. abstract.

47. Title insurance policies are issued to protect against something
    A. happening in the distant future.
    B. happening in the foreseeable future.
    C. which happened in the past.
    D. which happened in the past 40 years.

SECTION 6.2: Short Answer Questions

1. How does a property owner give notice to the world of his claim of ownership?

   _____

   _____

2. What must be accomplished to make an instrument admissible to recordation? Name three officials who are authorized to perform this act.

_____

_____

3. Name five sources (kinds) of records other than indexes of recorded deeds that may have to be checked in completing a title search on a parcel of land.

_____

_____

4. Explain the basic differences in coverage afforded by an owner's title insurance policy versus a mortgagee's policy.

_____

_____

5. How does a casualty insurance policy differ from a title insurance policy?

_____

_____

6. Name and explain briefly three reasons for the popularity of title insurance.

_____

_____

7. Explain what is meant by "marketable title." Name two ways in which an owner who holds less than marketable title can overcome doubts regarding its marketability and make a sale of the property possible.

_____

_____

8. What is the mortgage electronic registration system (MERS)?

_____

_____

Contract Law

1. M agreed orally to purchase a used car from C provided M could get a bank loan for a part of the purchase price. M gave C money as an earnest money deposit. Was this agreement an expressed contract?
   A. Yes, because it resulted from the stated intent of the parties.
   B. Yes, because C accepted the earnest money deposit.
   C. No, because the agreement was not in writing.
   D. No, because it was based upon a contingency.

2. An implied contract may arise from
   A. an oral agreement.
   B. a written agreement.
   C. the actions of the parties.
   D. the actions of the attorneys.

3. A contract based upon a promise exchanged for a promise is a
   A. unilateral contract.
   B. implied contract.
   C. partial contract.
   D. bilateral contract.

4. F listed his home for sale with broker H. H agreed to advertise the property and to hold an "open house" weekly until a buyer was found. F agreed to pay a commission of seven percent if a purchaser was found. This agreement constituted a
   A. bilateral contract based on good consideration.
   B. unilateral contract based on good consideration.
   C. bilateral contract based on valuable consideration.
   D. unilateral contract based on a valuable consideration.

5. A contract based upon one party's promise in exchange for an act from the other party is classified as a(n)
   A. bilateral contract.
   B. unenforceable contract.
   C. executed contract.
   D. unilateral contract.

6. A unilateral contract is enforceable against
   A. both parties.
   B. the offeror.
   C. the offeree.
   D. neither party.

7. An agreement in a contract in which one or both parties agree not to act in a certain manner is known as
   A. forbiddance.
   B. forbearance.
   C. forgiveness.
   D. forfeiture.

8. A lender agreed not to foreclose on a delinquent mortgage loan provided that the borrower agree to a new repayment schedule. This agreement constituted a(n)
   A. voidable contract.
   B. implied contract.
   C. contract for forbearance.
   D. deed limitation.

9. A contract which binds one party but not the other is
   A. unenforceable.
   B. void.
   C. voidable.
   D. illegal.

10. A contract which is legally insufficient is classified as
    A. voidable.
    B. void.
    C. unavoidable.
    D. illegal.

11. D and M are going to Europe for a month and want to give someone at home the authority to sign certain real estate settlement papers for them while they are gone. They would do this by appointing a(n)
    A. attorney-in-fact.
    B. power of attorney.
    C. attorney.
    D. lessee.

12. An attorney-in-fact derives his powers from
    A. the state bar association.
    B. a power of attorney.
    C. judicial appointment.
    D. popular election.

13. W, who is moving to another city, wants to give his agent, broker Z, the power to sign a sales contract and deed to real estate which he wants to sell. Which of the following statements would be correct?
    A. W could not give Z a written power of attorney to act for him in this manner.
    B. W could appoint Z by means of an oral power of attorney.
    C. Z can sign the contract and deed as a result of the listing agreement.
    D. The power of attorney would have to be written, acknowledged, and recorded.

14. A person who executes a contract for a corporation must derive that authority from
    A. the corporations' registered agent.
    B. the state corporation commission.
    C. the corporate board of directors.
    D. a court of competent jurisdiction.

15. H installed a built-in microwave oven in his home. When he sold the home to R, he did not mention that the oven was not included in the sale. R expected it to be included. This contract of sale is a legally valid contract because
    A. once installed, the oven became a fixture and therefore part of the property.
    B. H had agreed to the inclusion of the oven.
    C. H's actions constituted fraud.
    D. a meeting of the minds was present.

16. S listed his home for sale through broker W. Purchaser P agreed to all the terms of the listing and signed a purchase agreement. This agreement constituted a contract when
    A. P signed the purchase agreement.   C. W handed the offer to S.
    B. W accepted the signed offer from P. D. S signed the purchase agreement.

17. In his will, P, Sr. left his farm to P, Jr. The farm had never been surveyed, but P, Jr. had always understood that it contained 110 acres. P, Jr. sold the land to W, representing it to contain 110 acres. W had it surveyed and found that it contained only 100 acres. Which of the following statements would be true?
    A. P's statements to W constituted fraud.
    B. P's statements to W constituted innocent misrepresentation.
    C. Either W or P could declare the contract void.
    D. Only P could declare the contract void.

18. Mutual agreement is missing when a contract is made
    A. with a minor.   C. under duress.
    B. after business hours.   D. verbally.

19. If a contract is signed under duress,
    A. the aggrieved party may subsequently declare the contract void.
    B. either party may declare the contract voidable.
    C. the aggrieved party must declare the contract voidable.
    D. the aggrieved party must execute the contract.

20. A real estate agent who takes advantage of an elderly property owner's ignorance of the value of his own property in order to induce him to sell below market value would have committed
    A. undue influence.   C. menace.
    B. duress.   D. a mistake.

21. An act intended to deceive the other party in a contract is
    A. duress.   C. mistake.
    B. menace.   D. fraud.

22. A contract based on fraud is
    A. void.   C. voidable by either party.
    B. voidable by the injured party. D. unenforceable.

23. A real estate licensee who committed a fraudulent act in order to make a sale
    A. may be subject to criminal penalties.
    B. may be subject to suit for civil damages.
    C. may have his/her license revoked.
    D. may be subject to all of the above.

24. Broker N listed a home for sale wherein the seller stated that the existing loan was assumable by the buyer. N told this to prospective buyers, and in time a sales contract was executed. However, the lender refused to allow the assumption to take place. As a result of this, the
    A. seller can rescind the sales contract.
    B. buyer can rescind the sales contract.
    C. broker will lose his license.
    D. broker can be sued for fraud.

25. A contract made as a joke or in jest is precluded from becoming a valid contract because it lacks
    A. contractual intent.
    B. acknowledgment.
    C. competent parties.
    D. valuable consideration.

26. A contract based upon an unlawful objective would be
    A. binding.
    B. enforceable.
    C. void.
    D. voidable.

27. L borrowed money from M at a rate of interest which exceeded the usury ceiling in their state. After making only two payments, L stopped making any more payments on the loan. Could M bring legal action to collect the loan balance?
    A. No, because M completed partial performance by making two payments.
    B. No, because a contract that requires the breaking of a law cannot be enforced.
    C. No, because the principal balance on the loan is an uncollectible debt.
    D. No, because the charging of usurious interest rates constitutes fraud.

28. L agreed to purchase real estate from G, and gave him an earnest money deposit at the time the agreement was made. Which of the following constituted the consideration in this contract?
    A. Earnest money deposit
    B. Total amount to be paid for the property
    C. Listing price
    D. Commission amount

29. All of the following are examples of valuable consideration EXCEPT
    A. barter of goods for services.
    B. gift of property to a friend.
    C. even trade of one property for another.
    D. sale of property for less than market value.

30. In contract law, a "mistake" refers to
    A. ignorance of the law.
    B. innocent misrepresentation.
    C. poor judgment.
    D. ambiguity in negotiations.

31. A contract which is in the process of being carried out is
    A. executed.
    B. executing.
    C. executory.
    D. executrix.

32. All of the following must be in writing in order to be enforceable EXCEPT a
    A. contract to purchase real estate.
    B. mortgage.
    C. month-to-month rental agreement.
    D. lease for 13 months.

33. The rule that permits oral evidence to complete an otherwise incomplete written contract is the
    A. Uniform Commercial code.
    B. rule of specific performance.
    C. parol evidence rule.
    D. statute of frauds.

34. An assignment
    A. releases the original contract parties from further liability to the contract.
    B. is a special form of power of attorney.
    C. can be used to transfer a right or interest.
    D. is used when an estate sale is necessary.

35. When a lessee in a rented property assigns his lease to another party, he assumes the role of
    A. assignor.
    B. assignee.
    C. sublessee.
    D. mortgagor.

36. Substitution of a new contract and a new party for a previous one is known as
    A. innovation.
    B. assignment.
    C. subrogation.
    D. novation.

37. R has been leasing warehouse space for two years under a five-year lease. Business has been good and R wants to build his own warehouse. He also wants to be fully relieved from liability under the present lease agreement. This can be accomplished by
    A. assignment.
    B. unilateral rescission.
    C. contractual divorce.
    D. mutual rescission.

38. If the objective of a contract becomes legally impossible to accomplish,
    A. the law will consider the contract discharged.
    B. a lawsuit for specific performance is appropriate.
    C. a lawsuit for money damages is appropriate.
    D. liquidated damages would be appropriate.

39. In a state which had enacted the Uniform Vendor and Purchaser Risk Act, G sold his home to M, who took possession prior to settlement. After moving in but before settlement took place, the house was destroyed by a tornado. Which of the following statements is true?
    A. The loss will be borne by G.
    B. The loss will be borne by M.
    C. M is entitled to a refund of the money already paid.
    D. M is relieved of his duty to pay the purchase price.

40. The failure of one party to a contract to perform as agreed without a valid excuse constitutes
    A. a form of consideration.
    B. a breach of contract.
    C. partial performance.
    D. duress.

41. Legal action to force the breaching party to carry out the remainder of a contract is called a suit for
    A. liquidated damages.
    B. specific performance.
    C. partial performance.
    D. breach of contract.

42. The law which limits the time in which a wronged party may file legal action for obtaining justice is the statute of
    A. frauds.
    B. limitations.
    C. novation.
    D. performance.

43. If no fraud is presumed, what is the status of a contract signed by an illiterate person?
    - A. Valid
    - B. Void
    - C. Voidable
    - D. Unenforceable

44. A seller changes his mind about selling his property before a buyer is found. What must he do with the listing contract?
    - A. Ratify the contract
    - B. Rescind the contract
    - C. Renounce the listing
    - D. Revoke the listing

SECTION 7.2: Contract Situations

1. Name three examples of implied contracts, not necessarily associated with real estate, which may be encountered in daily situations. Explain why each constitutes an implied contract.

    1. _____

    _____

    2. _____

    _____

    3. _____

    _____

2. Which of the following constitutes a unilateral contract? Explain why or why not.

    A. Marriage _____

    _____

    B. A reward poster _____

    _____

3. Each of the following situations comprises a contract which may be either valid, void, voidable, or unenforceable. Identify each situation and explain your answer.

    A. S, age 17, purchased a stereo set on an installment plan. After three months, S returned it to the dealer who advised her that she would be held responsible for the remaining payments under the installment contract. What defense, if any, would S have in this situation?

    _____

    _____

    B. In selling a parcel of real estate to a prospect, a new sales agent identified the property as Lot 1, Block 2, Section 3, Spring Valley Subdivision. The property description of the property was Lot 3, Block 1, Section 2, Spring Valley Subdivision. What is the status of this contract?

    _____

    _____

C. A homeowner agreed to sell his home to a buyer by means of a written contract of sale, drawn on a standard form. When the buyer had the title examined, an incurable defect was found which made transfer by the homeowner impossible. What is the status of this contract?

_____

_____

D. Mr. and Mrs. P made an offer to purchase property from S, a single woman. All parties were adults. Mr. and Mrs. P made an earnest money deposit of $2,000 and agreed to a down payment of $20,000 on the purchase price of $80,000, subject to their ability to secure a first mortgage loan of $60,000 on acceptable terms. A local savings and loan association agreed to make the loan on favorable terms. S signed the agreement, but subsequently changed her mind and decided not to sell. What is the status of this contract?

_____

_____

4. In the old movie "The Perils of Pauline," the villain tied Pauline to the railroad track in order to force her to sign over the deed to the family home. Suppose that Pauline had signed the deed instead of awaiting rescue by the handsome hero. Could she have later disavowed the contract? If so, on what grounds could she have done so?

_____

_____

5. A grandparent conveys property by deed to a grandchild. What would be the consideration if the conveyance was a gift? What type of consideration would this be?

_____

_____

6. O, the owner of real estate, and P, a would-be purchaser, enter into an oral agreement under which P agrees to meet O at his office next Tuesday morning at 10:00 a.m., at which time P will pay O $100,000 in cash and O will deliver to P a deed to the property.

A. O and P meet as agreed and each fulfills his part of the agreement. Is this a valid deed? Justify your answer.

_____

_____

B. The day after entering into their oral agreement, O receives another offer of $110,000 for the property. Can P hold him to their agreement? Why or why not? For what reason?

_____

_____

C. The law which covers this situation is known as

_____

Real Estate Sales Contracts

LEARNING OBJECTIVES

After successful completion of the questions in this chapter, you will be able to:

1. Explain the provisions of a typical purchase contract.
2. Explain equitable title.
3. Discuss contingencies, time limits, and breach of contract.
4. Explain the use of an installment contract and lease with option to buy.
5. Discuss alternatives to sales contracts, including binders and letters of intent.
6. Describe the exchange agreement and delayed exchanges.
7. Distinguish between licensee real estate practice and practicing law.

1. A real estate sales contract is entered into between a buyer and seller in order to give the buyer time to do all the following EXCEPT
   A. ascertain the seller holds marketable title to the property.
   B. arrange for financing.
   C. reach a firm decision to buy the property.
   D. have the title examined.

2. A properly prepared sales contract
   A. commits each party to its terms.
   B. is not enforceable in a court of law.
   C. insures the quality of title.
   D. guarantees loan approval.

3. A formal real estate sales contract, prepared at the outset by an agent using prepared forms, may be identified as any of the following EXCEPT
   A. a purchase contract.
   B. an option contract.
   C. an offer and acceptance.
   D. a purchase offer.

4. Normally found provisions of a real estate sales contract include all of the following EXCEPT
   A. a buyer's offer to purchase.
   B. a provision for an earnest money deposit.
   C. a seller's acceptance.
   D. the buyer's plan for renovation.

5. M purchased real estate from S under an agreement which called for him to pay for the property in installments, and to receive a deed upon payment of the entire purchase price. This agreement could properly be identified as each of the following EXCEPT
   A. a land contract.
   B. a contract for deed.
   C. an option to buy.
   D. an installment contract.

6. In normal real estate brokerage practice, the amount of earnest money deposit paid by the purchaser is
   A. determined by negotiation between the buyer and seller.
   B. set by state law.
   C. equal to the agent's commission.
   D. the minimum required to make the contract valid.

7. Once the buyer and seller have executed a sales contract, paperwork and details of the title transfer may be handled by any of the following EXCEPT
   A. an escrow agent.
   B. the real estate broker.
   C. an attorney.
   D. the recorder of deeds.

8. Property taxes, rent, loan interest, etc., may be divided between the buyer and seller by the process of
   A. allocation.
   B. appropriation.
   C. proration.
   D. proportioning.

9. A seller owns a house which has been rented to a tenant, and is currently in the middle of a one-year lease. The seller wants to sell the house to J. As part of his offer to purchase, J can ask the owner to
   A. terminate the tenant's lease.
   B. let the tenant continue to lease.
   C. give a 30-day notice to vacate to the tenant.
   D. raise the rent if the tenant chooses to remain in the property.

10. The inclusion of a termite and dry rot clause in a contract for the sale of real estate is
    A. optional and negotiable.
    B. often required by state law.
    C. essential to an enforceable contract.
    D. required by mortgage lenders.

11. Typically, physical possession of the property is given to the buyer
    A. upon a signing of the sales contract.
    B. before close of escrow (settlement/closing).
    C. the day of close of escrow (settlement/closing).
    D. 30 days following close of escrow (settlement/closing).

12. A contract of sale called for the loan closing cost to be paid entirely by the seller. Was this an enforceable provision of the contract?
    A. Yes, because the seller is required to pay all loan closing cost.
    B. Yes, because the loan closing cost is negotiable.
    C. No, because loan closing cost should by paid by the contractor.
    D. No, because loan closing cost should be prorated between buyer and seller.

13. A buyer signed a contract to purchase real property from the seller, subject to the buyer's ability to secure a loan for a part of the purchase price within thirty days. After diligent effort, the buyer was unable to secure the loan within the specified time. This contract is
    A. void on its face.
    C. voidable by the seller.
    B. voidable by the buyer.
    D. unenforceable.

14. If a seller fails to carry out his obligation under a typical residential contract of sale, the buyer may take any of the following actions EXCEPT
    A. sue for specific performance.
    C. sue for monetary damages.
    B. rescind the contract.
    D. demand liquidated damages.

15. A buyer made an offer to purchase property contingent on the seller's acceptance within seven days. Prior to the seller's acceptance, the buyer found another property which he liked better, and decided to withdraw his offer. He could
    A. not withdraw his offer until the seller had decided to accept or reject the offer.
    B. not withdraw his offer until the expiration of the seven day period in his offer.
    C. withdraw at any time prior to acceptance of the offer by the seller.
    D. withdraw at any time within seven days.

16. The phrase "time is of the essence" in a sales contract means that the
    A. time limits specified in the contract must be faithfully observed.
    B. parties are prohibited from giving each other an extension.
    C. contract should be executed within a reasonable time.
    D. contract is not legally binding, being considered too vague.

17. When an offer to buy is made through an agent, such as a real estate broker,
    A. there is never any need to consult an attorney for counsel.
    B. an attorney should be consulted if the buyer has any doubts or questions regarding the legal effects of the offer.
    C. the state bar association requires that an attorney be consulted.
    D. state law requires that an attorney be consulted.

18. If a buyer makes an offer, and the seller accepts part but not all of its conditions,
    A. this constitutes partial acceptance and is binding upon the buyer as if it were fully accepted by the seller.
    B. those conditions accepted by the seller are binding on the buyer.
    C. this does not constitute a rejection of the entire offer.
    D. the entire offer is considered rejected.

19. The purchase agreement used for most real estate sales is prepared
    A. in its entirety by the agent.
    B. in advance by the seller and attached to the listing.
    C. by an attorney especially for the transaction.
    D. by the agent by filling in blank spaces on a form approved by an attorney.

20. Mr. and Mrs. S entered into a real estate contract with no contingencies with Mr. and Mrs. G. If Mr. G dies before settlement takes place, all of the following are options to pursue EXCEPT
    A. Mr. and Mrs. S are obligated to carry out the contract.
    B. Mrs. G is obligated to carry out the contract.
    C. Mr. G's estate is obligated to carry out the contract.
    D. the contract is declared void at the moment of Mr. G's death.

21. A short form contract used in some states to hold a deal together until a more formal contract can be prepared is known as
    A. a rider.
    B. a binder.
    C. an addendum.
    D. an attachment.

22. A letter of intent is
    A. one which creates no liability.
    B. an agreement to enter into a contract.
    C. binding on the seller, at the option of the buyer.
    D. binding on both the buyer and the seller.

23. Who should be represented by an attorney at the meeting for the purpose of preparing a formal contract as provided for in a binder?
    A. Seller and buyer
    B. Buyer and his agent
    C. Agent and his broker
    D. Seller and his agent

24. When property is sold by means of an installment contract, the
    A. seller delivers a deed at closing.
    B. buyer is given the right to occupy the property until the contract terms have been fulfilled.
    C. buyer may not occupy the property until additional terms are met.
    D. buyer may decide not to buy the property and receive any earnest monies already paid.

25. Traditionally installment contracts used for the purchase of real estate has favored the
    A. vendor.
    B. vendee.
    C. grantor.
    D. grantee.

26. The increasing use of installment contracts for the sale of real estate has led to laws in some states designed to protect the interests of the
    A. buyer.
    B. seller.
    C. lender.
    D. agent.

27. The purchaser under an installment contract may protect his interests by requiring that
    A. the seller place a deed in escrow at settlement.
    B. the contract not be recorded in the land records.
    C. the buyer be allowed to immediately occupy the property.
    D. the seller advertise notice of the sale for three weeks.

28. A well-written installment contract will include language which specifies all of the following EXCEPT
    A. who is responsible for maintenance of the property.
    B. how taxes and insurance will be paid.
    C. who is responsible for casualty losses to the property.
    D. no restrictions can be placed on the use of the property.

29. A purchaser's right to acquire legal title to real property under the terms of a valid purchase agreement is known as
    A. naked title.
    B. equitable title.
    C. specific performance.
    D. contract title.

30. Equitable title
    A. can be transferred by sale.
    B. may not be willed or inherited.
    C. can avoid inheritance taxes.
    D. cannot be transferred by deed.

31. A buyer and a seller entered into a purchase contract for the sale of the seller's residence. From the moment the contract was signed by both parties, the
    A. legal title to the property was vested in the purchaser.
    B. equitable title to the property was held by the seller.
    C. buyer now retained an equitable interest in the property.
    D. seller retained the right to rescind the contract.

32. W holds equitable title to real property under an installment contract. W wants to sell the property to X. Can she do so?
    A. No, an installment contract does not permit any sales.
    B. No, since W does not hold legal title.
    C. Yes, by assignment of the contract from W to X.
    D. Yes, by delivering a warranty deed to X.

33. Under the terms of a lease with option to buy, the tenant is given the right to purchase the property
    A. at a price to be negotiated at the time of purchase.
    B. at any time during the option period.
    C. after expiration of the lease.
    D. at a preset price.

34. A lease-option tends to favor the
    A. optionor.   C. vendor.
    B. optionee.   D. vendee.

35. The purchase contract which accompanies a lease-option should be negotiated
    A. at the same time as the lease.   C. during the option period.
    B. when the option is exercised.   D. after the option expires.

36. Evidence that a tenant has an option to buy a property should be recorded so as to establish that the
    A. tenant has no rights except temporary occupancy.
    B. tenant's rights date back to the date of recordation.
    C. tenant is obligated to buy the property.
    D. owner is under no obligation to sell.

37. An option to buy is an example of
    A. an executed contract.   C. a unilateral contract.
    B. a bilateral contract.   D. voidable contract.

38. Landlord L and tenant T entered into an agreement in writing which gave T the right to match any valid offer which L might receive for the purchase of the property. Did this agreement constitute a lease-option on the property?
    A. Yes, because it gave the tenant the right to purchase the property.
    B. Yes, because the agreement was in writing.
    C. No, because there was no consideration.
    D. No, because the elements of an option to buy were not present.

39. Exchanging of real properties is popular among sophisticated investors because
    A. large amounts of cash facilitate trades.
    B. income taxes may be deferred on profits from the first property in the transaction.
    C. it is easier to trade properties than to finance individual purchases.
    D. trades keep the IRS out of the transaction.

40. When an owner-occupied dwelling sells for a profit, which has been owned for 24 months, taxes on the gain are
    A. due upon the sale of the original residence.
    B. not due.
    C. due in the year of purchase of the new residence.
    D. waived under the residence replacement rule.

41. Requirements for real estate exchanges include that
    A. all properties must be of equal value.
    B. only two properties may be involved.
    C. no cash is involved.
    D. any number of properties of unequal value may be involved.

42. Under the 1984 Tax Reform Act, in order to qualify for a delayed exchange, the
    A. designated property to be exchanged must be identified within 30 days of the original closing.
    B. title to the designated property must be acquired within 90 days of the original closing.
    C. property must be received before the designating party's tax return is due.
    D. property must be designated and closed within six months.

43. W wants to trade up to a larger property and at the same time defer that capital gain in his present property. He wants T's property and would like to trade directly with T. However, T wants cash, not W's property. J has cash and wants W's property. Which of the following would accomplish these goals?
    A. W trades with T who, in turn, sells to J.
    B. J buys W's property, and with the money W buys T's property.
    C. J buys T's property and trades with W.
    D. Either option A or C.

SECTION 8.2: Math Problems

1. F bought a parcel of unimproved land measuring 200' x 435.6' for $96.50 per front foot. After one year, he decides to sell the land. He already paid property taxes of $1,000 per acre. He desires to make at least a 30% profit. What is the approximate minimum sale price for F to achieve his objective?

   $ _____

2. The buildings on a 150' by 180' lot cover 25% of the lot. In order to widen roads the state buys vacant land along the front totaling 15% of the total area of the lot. How many square feet of land not covered with buildings is retained by the owner?

   $ _____

3. A subdivider is selling eight lots that are 75' by 120'. Which will give her the highest selling price?
   A. $1.50 per square foot
   B. $13,600 per lot
   C. $185 per front foot
   D. $110,000 for the entire parcel

4. A purchaser buys a lot for $11,000 and remits a $3,000 down payment. He pays $72.50 per month for ten years and ten months. How much more than the original sales price did he pay?

   $ _____

5. S, the owner of real estate valued at $77,000, allows T, the owner of a 60-acre farm, $1,500 an acre as a trade property. What is the cash difference, and to whom is it payable?

   _____ is owed $ _____

Mortgage and Note

After successful completion of the questions in this chapter, you will be able to:

1. Distinguish between lien theory and title theory.
2. Differentiate between a promissory note and a mortgage.
3. Explain clauses in the note and mortgage, especially the importance of acceleration and alienation clauses.
4. Explain hypothecation, mortgage satisfaction, estoppel certificate and deficiency judgments.
5. List debt priorities in order.
6. Explain the foreclosure process, and describe the difference between judicial and non-judicial foreclosure.
7. Explain mortgage takeovers, including subject to, assumption, and novation.

1. Evidence of the amount and terms of a borrower's debt to a lender is provided by means of a
   A. mortgage.
   B. promissory note.
   C. deed of trust.
   D. first mortgage.

2. To be accepted as valid evidence of a borrower's debt, a note must do all of the following EXCEPT
   A. be in writing, between parties having contractual capacity.
   B. state the borrower's promise to repay a certain sum of money.
   C. show the terms of payment.
   D. be recorded in the public records.

3. In order to be enforceable, a promissory note must be signed by the
   A. borrower.
   B. lender.
   C. agent.
   D. trustee.

4. A promissory note which fails to state that it is to be secured by a mortgage or deed of trust is
   A. a personal obligation of the borrower.
   B. a secured obligation of the borrower.
   C. unenforceable.
   D. may not be assigned or sold.

5. The purpose of putting the location of the execution on a promissory note is to
   A. establish applicable state laws.
   B. tell the borrower where to send the payments.
   C. allow the lender to sell the note out-of-state.
   D. create a negotiable instrument.

6. The words "or order" in a promissory note make it
   A. impossible for the lender to transfer the right to collect the note to another party.
   B. a negotiable instrument.
   C. a debt which can be assumed by another party.
   D. difficult for the lender to foreclose.

7. Under a note secured by a mortgage, the obligor is the
   A. lender.
   B. borrower.
   C. note holder.
   D. mortgagee.

8. Should a borrower fail to make payments when due, the lender may demand immediate payment of the entire balance under the terms of the
   A. prepayment clause.
   B. defeasance clause.
   C. acceleration clause.
   D. hypothecation clause.

9. Normally, which of the instruments associated with a mortgage loan is recorded in the public records?
   A. Promissory note
   B. Mortgage
   C. Purchase contract
   D. Bill of sale

10. Regarding the use of a mortgage, which of the following statements is correct?
    A. A mortgage is evidence of a borrower's debt to a lender.
    B. A mortgage hypothecates property as collateral for a loan.
    C. A mortgage must reference an earnest money agreement when serving as collateral for a loan.
    D. An owner may not occupy mortgaged property.

11. A borrower's property serves as collateral while the borrower retains the rights of possession and use of it by the process of
    A. alienation.
    B. hypothecation.
    C. pledge.
    D. acceleration.

12. Under the terms of a mortgage, the mortgagee is the
    A. obligor under the promissory note.
    B. lender.
    C. trustee.
    D. maker of the note.

13. In states which subscribe to the title theory of mortgages, the
    A. mortgage deeds title of the mortgaged property to the lender.
    B. borrower forfeits the rights of possession and use of the property.
    C. mortgage is considered a lien on the property.
    D. title is transferred to the lender only if the borrower defaults.

14. A mortgage becomes null and void when the note is paid in full under the terms of the
    A. defeasance clause.
    B. prepayment clause.
    C. alienation clause.
    D. hypothecation clause.

15. All of the following covenants will appear in a mortgage EXCEPT
    A. to pay taxes and insurance.
    B. against removal.
    C. against encumbrances.
    D. of good repair.

16. N wishes to purchase W's house for $100,000, giving her a $20,000 cash down payment and a note and mortgage for the remaining $80,000. N can expect to hypothecate which of the following with a mortgage?
    A. Lot and house
    B. House, but not the lot
    C. Lot, but not the house
    D. N's other real estate holdings

17. The clause which gives the lender the right to call in the note if the mortgaged property is sold or otherwise conveyed by the borrower is known as the
    A. acceleration clause.
    B. alienation clause.
    C. defeasance clause.
    D. foreclosure clause.

18. If all or part of a mortgaged property is taken by eminent domain, the condemnation clause requires that
    A. any money received be used to reduce the balance owed on the note.
    B. the entire loan balance be paid in full.
    C. the borrower is relieved of further financial responsibility.
    D. government must pay the note in full before condemnation.

19. When the owner paid off his mortgage loan in full, the lender gave him a satisfaction of mortgage document. Should this instrument be recorded in the public records?
    A. Yes, because recordation is required by state law.
    B. Yes, because the records would otherwise indicate that the obligation was still outstanding.
    C. No, because the mortgage was terminated by the defeasance clause once the debt was paid.
    D. No, because the note was not recorded in the public records.

20. L hypothecated the title to two equally valued properties as collateral for a $50,000 loan. When he had repaid $25,000 of the principal amount, one of the properties was removed from the mortgage obligation by means of a
    A. mortgage satisfaction.
    B. partial release.
    C. defeasance.
    D. release of mortgage.

21. E sold his home to W, subject to an existing mortgage loan. W later defaulted on the loan. Which of the following statements is correct?
    A. The lender has recourse to the assets of W for the balance due.
    B. W is jointly responsible for the loan balance.
    C. The mortgagee can look to E for the loan balance.
    D. E was relieved of liability for the loan balance when W accepted title subject to the existing loan.

22. Who may be held responsible for mortgage loan repayment when a loan is assumed as part of a real estate sale?
    A. Purchaser only
    B. Seller only
    C. Both the purchaser and the seller
    D. Agent, only if there is a default

23. When a loan is assumed, the
    A. seller can be relieved of liability by novation.
    B. buyer need not verify the loan balance with the lender.
    C. seller can avoid liability by selling "subject to" the mortgage.
    D. buyer can avoid liability through novation.

24. When a lender wants to sell a loan to another investor, the borrower may sometimes be asked to verify the loan balance by means of
    A. a certificate of novation.
    B. an estoppel certificate.
    C. a certificate of reduction.
    D. a subordination certificate.

25. The lien priority of mortgages is determined by the
    A. date of the mortgage instrument.
    B. date of the promissory note.
    C. language of the mortgage instrument.
    D. order of recordation.

26. A mortgage which is lower in lien priority than another mortgage on the same property is known as a
    A. first mortgage.
    B. junior mortgage.
    C. senior mortgage.
    D. promissory note.

27. M is preparing an offer to buy a lot on which the seller will carry back a mortgage. M wants to build a house on the lot and has applied for a construction loan, but the lender will make the loan only if it can be secured by a first mortgage. This can be accomplished by asking the seller to execute
    A. an estoppel certificate.
    B. a release of lien.
    C. a mortgage reduction certificate.
    D. a subordination agreement.

28. Most mortgage foreclosures are the result of the borrower's
    A. violation of mortgage covenants.
    B. failure to make loan payments on time.
    C. noncompliance with the terms of the mortgage agreement.
    D. violation of the alienation clause.

29. A real estate borrower who is behind in his loan payments would first take which of the following steps?
    A. Sell the property before the next loan payment is due.
    B. Wait for the lender to accelerate the loan.
    C. Wait for the statutory redemption period.
    D. Meet with the lender as soon as possible.

30. Given a choice of foreclosure methods, in a simple and straightforward case, a lender will usually prefer which method of loan foreclosure?
    A. Judicial
    B. Nonjudicial
    C. Partition suit
    D. Reconveyance suit

31. In a foreclosure action, the lender asks the court for a judgment directing that the
    A. mortgagor's interests in the property be cut off.
    B. property be sold at public auction.
    C. lender's claim be paid from the sale proceeds.
    D. all of the above be done.

32. A mortgagee informs the public of a pending foreclosure action by recording a(n)
    A. acceleration.
    B. lis pendens.
    C. estoppel.
    D. subordination.

33. The period of equitable redemption given to a borrower
    A. begins when the loan is made.
    B. ends when the property is sold at foreclosure.
    C. ends within a year after the sale.
    D. is useful during the life of the loan.

34. When a real estate mortgage is foreclosed, unpaid real estate tax liens against the property
    A. are cut off.
    B. become a lien on the personal property of the delinquent mortgagor.
    C. remain in force against the property.
    D. are added to the purchase price at the foreclosure sale.

35. When the amount received from a foreclosure sale is insufficient to pay off the mortgage loan and the other expenses of the sale, the lender may sometimes file for a(n)
    A. deficiency judgment.   C. estoppel lien.
    B. mechanic's lien.   D. statutory lien.

36. The deed given to the purchaser at foreclosure by the sheriff or other officer of the court usually takes the form of a
    A. general warranty deed.   C. special warranty deed.
    B. quitclaim deed.   D. bargain and sale deed.

37. The period of time set by state law after a foreclosure sale, during which the mortgagor may redeem the property is known as the period of
    A. equitable redemption.   C. voluntary redemption.
    B. legal redemption.   D. statutory redemption.

38. Bidders pay more at a foreclosure sale if the property is located in a state which
    A. has a short statutory redemption period.
    B. has a lengthy statutory redemption period.
    C. permits the mortgagee to occupy the property during the statutory redemption period.
    D. gives title and possession to the high bidder immediately following the foreclosure auction.

39. A borrower who feels mistreated by a power of sale foreclosure can
    A. obtain a judicial foreclosure.   C. obtain a judgment.
    B. appeal the issue to the courts.   D. obtain a lien.

40. Judicial foreclosure may sometimes be avoided by
    A. invoking the acceleration clause.
    B. the trustee who acts as an intermediary between the beneficiary and trustor.
    C. power of sale and entry and possession.
    D. beneficiary petitioning for a reconveyance suit.

41. By voluntarily giving the lender a deed in lieu of foreclosure, a delinquent borrower
    A. can avoid foreclosure proceedings.
    B. is still responsible for possible deficiency judgments.
    C. cannot avoid foreclosure proceedings.
    D. will have to make several additional payments as a prepayment penalty.

42. Mortgages which are secured by personal property
    A. are known as chattel mortgages.
    B. must be foreclosed by judicial foreclosure.
    C. are called first mortgages.
    D. are not allowed in most states.

43. When an installment contract to buy real estate goes into default, the
    A. vendee can rescind the contract.
    B. contract can be judicially foreclosed.
    C. vendor will have little legal basis to repossess the property.
    D. vendee may be liable for a possible deficiency judgment.

44. An investor borrowed $100,000 to be repaid as follows: $10,000 at the end of the 1st, 2nd, 3rd, and 4th years, and $60,000 at the end of the 5th year. The interest rate was as follows: 10.5% for the 1st year, 11% for the 2nd year, 11.5% for the 3rd year, 12% for the 4th year, and 12.5% for the 5th year. How much interest did he pay?

    $ _____

45. P took out a mortgage loan one year ago in the amount of $120,000. Since then she has made twelve monthly payments of $1,200 each and the interest paid to date on this loan is $12,000. If she asks the lender for a certificate of reduction at this time, how many dollars would it show?

    $ _____

46. A property has a first mortgage loan balance of $70,000, a second with a balance of $40,000, a third mortgage loan balance of $15,000 against it, and a fourth mortgage loan balance of $5,000 against it. At foreclosure of the first mortgage, the property sold for $88,000 and sale expenses and back taxes take $3,000 of that. Who gets what?

    First $ _____   Third $ _____

    Second $ _____   Fourth $ _____

Deed of Trust

1. S obtained a loan on real estate by means of an instrument which conveyed title to the property to a trustee. This instrument is a
   A. note.
   B. reconveyance deed.
   C. mortgage.
   D. deed of trust.

2. When a debt secured by a deed of trust is fully paid off, title is reconveyed to the borrower by the
   A. beneficiary.
   B. trustor.
   C. trustee.
   D. lienee.

3. A borrower defaulted on the obligations of his note which had been secured to the trustee by a deed of trust. Upon request of the beneficiary, may the property be sold in order to secure funds with which to satisfy the indebtedness?
   A. Yes, because of the provisions of the due-on-sale clause.
   B. Yes, because of the provisions of the power of sale clause.
   C. No, because loans on real property require foreclosure through court action.
   D. No, because of the statutory redemption period given to delinquent borrowers.

4. The quantity of title conveyed to a trustee by means of a deed of trust is
   A. fee simple absolute.
   B. fee simple conditional.
   C. naked title.
   D. a cloud on the title.

5. A difference between a deed of trust and a mortgage is that when the loan is made, the borrower
   A. delivers a note but not the mortgage to the lender.
   B. delivers a mortgage but not the note to the lender.
   C. delivers the note and deed of trust to the trustee.
   D. conveys bare title to the trustee.

6. When a deed of trust is recorded, bare title is conveyed by the
   A. lender to the borrower.   C. borrower to the trustee.
   B. borrower to the lender.   D. trustee to the lender.

7. When a deed of trust is foreclosed, title is conveyed by the
   A. borrower to the lender.   C. borrower to the trustee.
   B. trustee to the borrower.   D. trustee to the purchaser at foreclosure.

8. Which of the following clauses would be found in a deed of trust but NOT in a mortgage?
   A. Reconveyance clause   C. Acceleration clause
   B. Power of sale clause   D. Defeasance clause

9. In order for a deed of trust to be cleared from the public records, which of the following documents are delivered to the trustee?
   A. Request for reconveyance and promissory note
   B. Mortgage and promissory note
   C. Reconveyance deed and trustee's deed
   D. Trust deed and satisfaction piece

10. Which of the following documents would be recorded in the public records in order to clear an existing deed of trust?
    A. Promissory note   C. Mortgage
    B. Reconveyance   D. Request for satisfaction

11. B was the successful bidder at the foreclosure sale of a loan on property which had been secured by a deed of trust. He would receive a(n)
    A. absolute fee simple title to the property.
    B. trustee's deed.
    C. general warranty deed to the property.
    D. special warranty deed to the property.

12. Which of the following would a lender like to have in a deed of trust or mortgage?
    A. Request for reconveyance   C. Assignment of rents
    B. Court-ordered foreclosure   D. Statutory redemption

13. Which of the following instruments is the most common form of security for a loan on real estate, on a nationwide basis?
    A. Deed of trust   C. Security deed
    B. Mortgage   D. Trust deed

14. Where trust deeds are used, their popularity may be attributed to which of the following reasons?
    A. The time between default and foreclosure is shortened.
    B. There is usually a long statutory redemption period.
    C. Lack of provisions for assignment of rents clause.
    D. Title is already in the name of the beneficiary.

15. If the trustor dies before a deed of trust is paid off, the
    A. debt is automatically forgiven.
    B. debt would be an obligation of the trustor's estate.
    C. trustor's estate would be relieved of liability for the debt.
    D. debt becomes immediately due and payable.

16. If the trustee should die or be dissolved before the debt secured by a deed of trust is paid off, a successor may be named by the
    A. trustor.   C. judge.
    B. beneficiary.   D. trustee's estate.

17. Appointment of a trustee for a deed of trust can be by
    A. automatic form where the trustee is notified of the appointment and accepts.
    B. automatic form where the trustee is NOT personally notified of the appointment.
    C. accepted form where the trustee is NOT personally notified of the appointment.
    D. automatic verification by both the trustor and beneficiary.

18. A real estate purchaser can agree to assume
    A. an existing deed of trust.
    B. an existing mortgage.
    C. either a deed of trust or a mortgage.
    D. neither a deed of trust nor a mortgage can be assumed by the purchaser.

19. A deed of trust that has been subordinated can hold each of the following debt priority positions EXCEPT
    A. senior.   C. second.
    B. junior.   D. third.

20. Each of the following real estate methods requires the purchaser to give a promissory note to the lender EXCEPT
    A. mortgage.   C. land contract.
    B. deed of trust.   D. purchase money mortgage.

21. Each of the following can be foreclosed by judicial foreclosure EXCEPT a(n)
    A. mortgage.   C. land contract.
    B. deed of trust.   D. estoppel certificate.

22. When the debt is fully repaid, under which of the following financial instruments will the buyer receive a deed from the seller?
    A. Mortgage   C. Land contract
    B. Deed of trust   D. Trust deed

23. The purpose of the assignment of rents clause in a deed of trust is to
    A. preserve the value of the note's security.
    B. expedite the sale of the property at auction.
    C. protect the rights of the tenants.
    D. ensure a timely foreclosure in the event of default.

24. Generally, state laws regarding foreclosure on deeds of trust require that
    A. the lender demonstrate to the trustee that the loan is in default.
    B. the property be sold privately.
    C. lenders are not permitted to file a surplus money action.
    D. the borrower defer invoking "equity of redemption" until after the sale of the property.

25. In what order of priority are the following claims against the proceeds of a deed of trust paid after a trustee's sale under a defaulted deed of trust?

    A. Unpaid loan balance   C. Trustor

    B. Claims of junior lien holders   D. Expenses of the sale

    First   _____   Third   _____

    Second _____   Fourth _____

Lending Practices

CHAPTER

11

LEARNING OBJECTIVES

After successful completion of the questions in this chapter, you will be able to:

1. Explain the features of an amortized loan.
2. Describe types of loans including budget mortgages, term loans, and balloon loans.
3. Describe loan terms including loan-to-value ratio, equity, origination, and discount points.
4. Describe the FHA and VA programs and lending procedures.
5. Discuss conventional loans and private mortgage insurance.
6. Calculate down payment, equity, and mortgage insurance premiums.

1. A loan wherein the principal is all repaid in one lump sum payment at the end of the loan's life is known as a(n)
   A. straight or term loan.
   B. amortized loan.
   C. budget mortgage.
   D. balloon note.

2. The last day of a loan's life is known as the
   A. settlement date.
   B. maturity date.
   C. sale date.
   D. contract date.

3. A straight or term loan for the purpose of purchasing real estate will usually require the borrower to do all of the following EXCEPT
   A. execute a note or bond, promising to pay loan interest at regular intervals.
   B. make periodic payments toward reduction of the principal balance.
   C. repay the loan balance at maturity.
   D. hypothecate the real estate as collateral for the loan.

4. To determine the amount of loan payments by using an amortization table, you must know all the following EXCEPT
   A. loan-to-value ratio.
   B. frequency of payments.
   C. interest rate.
   D. amount of loan.

5. The amount of each periodic payment needed to amortize a loan in a given time can be determined by consulting a(n)
   A. loan balance table.
   C. remaining balance table.
   B. amortization table.
   D. bi-weekly repayment plan.

6. When a loan is fully amortized,
   A. each payment is applied first to payment of principal due, then to reduction of the interest balance.
   B. principal payments are scheduled so as to have the entire principal repaid by the loan's maturity date.
   C. payments apply only to interest, paying the balance in full on the maturity date.
   D. payments are divided in half and applied to interest and principal, with a large balloon payment on the maturity date.

7. Which of the following would result in the least interest expense to the borrower if all loans were made at the same annual percentage rate of interest?
   A. Amortized loan, ten-year maturity
   B. Amortized loan, five-year maturity
   C. Term loan, five-year maturity
   D. Term loan, ten-year maturity

8. A buyer borrowed money to purchase a home under terms which required him to make monthly payments which included loan amortization plus 1/12 of the insurance premium and annual real property tax. What is this type of loan called?
   A. Budget
   C. Blanket
   B. Package
   D. Open-end

9. A balloon note is characterized by
   A. equal monthly payments of principal and interest.
   B. a final payment larger than preceding payments.
   C. interest-only payments during the life of the loan.
   D. payments increasing at regular, stated intervals.

10. A major negative of balloon loan financing is that the borrower may have difficulty
    A. meeting the final payment when it becomes due.
    B. obtaining a satisfaction of mortgage after the final payment.
    C. selling the property during the life of the loan.
    D. making the payments as they increase every year.

11. A loan calling for a series of amortized payments followed by a payment at maturity that is substantially larger than previous payments is known as a(n)
    A. package loan.
    C. equity loan.
    B. partially amortized loan.
    D. graduated payment loan.

12. A borrower wants to know what portion of a 30-year, fully amortized loan would be paid off by the fourth year of the loan's life. She should consult
    A. an amortization table.
    C. a partial amortization table.
    B. a loan balance table.
    D. the loan-to-value ratio.

13. At which one of the following interest rates would earlier mortgage loan repayment be most effective in reducing the interest paid by the borrower?
    A. 4%
    C. 12%
    B. 8%
    D. 16%

14. Compared to monthly payments, biweekly payments of one-half of the monthly payment will
    A. increase the total amount of interest paid over the life of the loan.
    B. shorten the life of the loan.
    C. lengthen the life of the loan.
    D. result in a balloon payment.

15. A lender will make a loan on a residential property at an 80% loan-to-value ratio. The house is appraised at $98,000, but the actual sale price is $96,000. Which of the following statements will be true?
    A. The cash down payment will be $19,200.
    B. The loan will be in the amount of $78,400.
    C. The cash down payment will be $17,600.
    D. The loan will be in the amount of $80,000.

16. The difference between a property's market value and the debts against it is known as
    A. loan-to-value ratio.   C. L/V ratio.
    B. owner's equity.   D. effective yield.

17. As used in real estate finance, the term "point" means
    A. one percent of the purchase price.
    B. the down payment expressed as a percentage of price.
    C. one percent of the loan amount.
    D. the borrower's equity expressed as a percentage of value.

18. The loan origination fee stated to a purchaser for setting up a loan may be charged as a percentage of the loan or
    A. as prepaid interest.
    B. an itemized billing for expenses incurred by the lender.
    C. a percentage of the sale price, whichever is less.
    D. a monthly fee over the life of the loan.

19. When a lender charges discount points to make a loan, the
    A. yield to the lender will decrease.
    B. yield to the lender will increase.
    C. yield to the lender will not change.
    D. cost of the loan to the borrower decreases.

20. Discount points on mortgage loans will tend to
    A. increase during periods of tight money.
    B. increase during periods of loose money.
    C. decrease during periods of tight money.
    D. fluctuate slowly in highly volatile markets.

21. In evaluating applications for FHA mortgage insurance, the FHA considers all of the following EXCEPT
    A. the borrower's capability of repaying the loan.
    B. the value of the property as collateral for the loan.
    C. the borrower's current long-term indebtedness.
    D. the stability of the neighborhood where the property is located.

22. All of the following statements regarding the FHA are correct EXCEPT
    A. The FHA was established in response to the depression of the 1930's.
    B. The FHA offers to insure lenders against losses due to the nonpayment of home loans.
    C. The FHA will insure loans on condominium and cooperatives.
    D. The FHA operates entirely at the taxpayers' expense.

23. The premium for FHA mortgage insurance
    A. is paid by the lender.
    B. is based on loan amount.
    C. does not have to be paid at closing.
    D. is calculated on the sale price or appraisal price, whichever is lower.

24. Regarding the availability to obtain FHA financing,
    A. a nonmilitary borrower desiring an FHA loan must make a down payment.
    B. an FHA-insured borrower can borrow the down payment using a second mortgage against the property.
    C. an investor can obtain an FHA loan with virtually no down payment.
    D. FHA loans are available to owners of very large apartment buildings.

25. Regarding the loan amount that FHA will insure, which of the following statements is true? The maximum . . .
    A. amount the FHA will insure has not changed since its inception.
    B. amount the FHA will insure varies from city to city.
    C. down payment is $5,000 or 3% of the sale price, whichever is lower.
    D. income allowed for an FHA buyer is $35,000 for a family of four.

26. The FHA has been influential in bringing about acceptance of
    A. long-term amortization of loans.
    B. customized construction techniques.
    C. large down payments with lower amounts borrowed.
    D. government assistance in higher priced neighborhoods.

27. FHA mortgage insurance programs are available for
    A. private, single-family residences.
    B. large multi-family residential buildings.
    C. investors purchasing single family homes for rental purchases.
    D. government employees and/or veterans of foreign wars.

28. FHA and VA loans are fully assumable
    A. with an automatic interest rate increase.
    B. with automatic, graduated monthly payments.
    C. without penalty.
    D. without requiring any buyer qualification.

29. FHA and VA loans can be repaid in full ahead of schedule
    A. with a 3-month prepayment penalty.
    B. only when the house is sold to another buyer.
    C. without penalty.
    D. only if the borrower agrees to take out another FHA loan within 24 months.

30. Which of the following loans are referred to as "conventional loans"?
    A. FHA-insured   C. Section 245 loans
    B. VA-guaranteed   D. 80% L/V from a local savings and loan

31. FHA rules that took effect in late 1983 allow all of the following EXCEPT
    A. interest rates to float.
    B. the buyer and seller to negotiate who will pay how many points.
    C. the seller to pay the buyer's mortgage insurance premium.
    D. a junior mortgage on the property at loan origination.

32. The FHA imposed its own minimum construction requirements because
    A. the local building codes did not exist or are weaker than the FHA wanted.
    B. it saves the builder money.
    C. it saves the borrower money.
    D. it keeps the closing cost low.

33. The FHA has played a major role in
    A. formulating loan qualification criteria.
    B. imposing maximum construction standards.
    C. promoting the use of purchase money mortgages.
    D. restricting the availability of housing construction.

34. The Federal Housing Administration
    A. lends money.
    B. insures loans.
    C. sets mortgage rates.
    D. insures borrowers.

35. Under VA loan guarantee programs,
    A. loans are available for the veteran who can make a substantial down payment.
    B. the VA loan guarantee is a substitute for the protection normally provided a lender by a down payment requirement.
    C. the borrower's income must not exceed certain income levels.
    D. borrowers are permitted to borrow the down payment from family members.

36. All of the following are required for a veteran to secure a VA loan EXCEPT
    A. certificate of eligibility.
    B. certificate of reasonable value.
    C. conditional commitment.
    D. income verification.

37. VA loans are available for
    A. single-family and mobile homes.
    B. apartment projects.
    C. strip shopping centers.
    D. houseboats.

38. A home-selling veteran who took out a VA loan can be sure of being relieved of liability to the VA by
    A. selling "subject to" to the loan.
    B. requiring the buyer to obtain new financing.
    C. assisting the buyer by creating a wraparound mortgage.
    D. selling to another veteran who can "freely assume" the loan.

39. Because of loan default losses being suffered by the VA, the VA now charges new VA borrowers a(n)
    A. annual funding fee.
    B. one-time funding fee upon default.
    C. one-time funding fee when the loan is made.
    D. mortgage insurance premium like the FHA does.

40. Regarding mortgage insurance, which of the following statements is true?
    A. PMI insures only the top 20 or 25 percent of the loan.
    B. FHA insures the top 3% of the loan.
    C. Both PMI and MIP may be paid up front with no further monthly fees.
    D. PMI requires a one-time payment, while MIP may be paid in several installments.

41. A buyer purchased a home for $90,000 and secured a 90% L/V loan which was protected by private mortgage insurance, the premium for which was 1/2 of 1% for the first year and 1/4 of 1% annually thereafter. Which of the following statements would be correct?
    A. The premium for the first year would be $405.
    B. The premium would be paid by the lender.
    C. The premium for the first year would be $450.
    D. The first year's premium will be paid monthly.

42. The Rural Housing Service Administration makes loans on farms and rural homes as well as
    A. guaranteeing loans on farms and rural homes.
    B. insuring loans on farms and rural homes.
    C. may be used to finance a small business located in a small, rural town.
    D. financing farming expansions.

43. FHA recognizes that if a building is defective either from a design or construction standpoint
    A. the builder will not get market value for it.
    B. the borrower is more likely to default on the loan and create an insurance claim against the FHA.
    C. the borrower will have to spend more money to correct it.
    D. the building will lower the value of the neighborhood.

44. VA loan discount points may be financed
    A. on any VA loans.
    B. when the seller will not agree to pay them.
    C. if the borrower does not have the cash to pay them.
    D. only on interest-rate-reductions loans (IRRRLs).

45. On VA adjustable-rate mortgages, increases on the interest rate are limited to
    A. 2%   C. 1%
    B. 3%   D. 4%

46. The Rural Housing Service Administration (RHSA) offers programs
    A. for borrowers 65 and older.
    B. for builders of shopping centers in small communities.
    C. for low income families.
    D. to help purchases or operation of farms

SECTION 11.2: Finance Problems and Situations

1. Calculate the total interest charge for borrowing $5,000 for seven years at 10% interest, on a term loan.

   $ _____

   What would be the total amount of principal and interest paid by the borrower?

   $ _____

2. On a long-term loan of $12,000, what will be the interest payment for 3 years, 10 months, and 20 days? The interest rate is 9% per year. Use a 30-day month.

   $ _____

3. Which of the following simple interest loans will produce the greatest number of dollars of interest?

   $60,000 at 10% for 2 months = $ _____

   $ 5,000 at 10% for   2 years = $ _____

   $10,000 at 10% for   1 year = $ _____

4. If an interest payment of $115.50 is made every three months on a $4,200 loan, what is the annual rate of interest?

   _____

5. One month, a principal and interest payment of $900 reduced the principal balance by $80. If the principal balance at the time of payment was $120,000, calculate the annual rate of interest.

   $ _____

6. What will the interest be on $40,000 borrowed at 8% per annum if the principal is borrowed from November 1 through the following June 15?

   $ _____

7. W purchased a home for $100,000 by making a cash down payment of $20,000 and securing a first mortgage loan for the balance of the purchase price. W agreed to pay 10.5% annual interest on the loan, which was to be amortized over a 30-year period in monthly installments. The taxes on the home are $1,320 per year and the annual homeowner's insurance premium is $240. Use the amortization table in Table 11.1 of the text to determine the principal and interest payment.

   $ _____

   Compute the PITI payment on this loan. $ _____

8. R borrowed $50,000 at 11.5% annual interest, to be amortized on a 15-year schedule, but with the entire balance due and payable at the end of 10 years. Use the remaining balance table in Table 11.2 of the text to determine the amount due at the end of ten years.

   $ _____

9. V, who has $27,500 in VA loan benefits available to him, decides to purchase a home using the benefits. He finds a lender who agrees to make a no-down payment loan at a 75% loan-to-value ratio, plus the veteran's benefits. Assuming adequate financial ability on V's part, what would be the maximum price he could pay for the home on these terms?

   $ _____

10. K borrowed $10,000 at 12% annual interest, and agreed to make payments of $120 per month on an amortized loan. Of the first month's payment, how much was applied to interest?

    $ _____

    How much went to reduce the principal balance? $ _____

    How much of the second month's payment went to interest? $ _____

    How much of the second month's payment went to reduce the principal balance?

    $ _____

At the end of these two monthly payments, what is the principal balance of the loan?

$ _____

11. A couple who have reached retirement age decided to sell their home and move to an apartment. They find a buyer who offers to pay them 20% of the agreed purchase price of $78,000 as a down payment and give them a mortgage for the balance, amortized at 9% annual interest for 20 years, in equal monthly installments, including principal and interest. What would be the loan-to-value ratio of this mortgage?

_____

What would be the amount of the down payment? $ _____

What would be the amount of the mortgage debt? $ _____

Using the amortization table in the text (Table 11.1), what monthly payment is required to fully amortize this loan?

$ _____

12. A couple have found a home which they have agreed to purchase at a price of $90,000. Their local savings and loan association agreed to make a loan of 90% of the purchase price or appraisal, whichever is lower. The S&L appraised the home for $86,000. Assuming they decide to purchase the property in spite of the appraisal, what would be their down payment?

What would be the amount of the mortgage loan? $ _____

13. A lender loaned H $120,000 to purchase a new home. The loan was 75% of the purchase price and the interest rate was 9.6% per year. What was the purchase price of the home?

$ _____

What was the down payment? $ _____

14. As a real estate licensee, you are showing homes to a young couple. Through interview, you determine they can afford a monthly payment up to $500, PITI. They have approximately $8,500 cash available for a down payment plus money for anticipated closing costs. You estimate that in your community the combined total of taxes and insurance approximates 20% of total monthly PITI payments. The present market conditions in your community indicate an interest rate of 9.0% for 30-year conventional loans. Use the amortization table in Table 11.1 in the text to determine the maximum loan the couple can afford and the maximum price they could afford to pay for a home.

Maximum loan: $_____   Maximum price $ _____

The Loan and the Consumer

After successful completion of the questions in this chapter, you will be able to:

1. Explain the purpose and features of the Truth-in-Lending Act.
2. Define redlining and annual percentage rate.
3. Explain trigger terms and disclosures.
4. Recognize who must comply and exempt transactions.

5. Describe the loan application and approval process.
6. Explain loan-to-value and its importance.
7. Summarize the purpose and features of the Fair Credit Reporting Act.

1. The federal Truth-in-Lending Act requires that, in certain types of loans, all of the following must be disclosed EXCEPT
   A. the borrower be told how much it is costing to borrow the money.
   B. the borrower be given the right to rescind the transaction within three business days after signing the loan papers.
   C. the amount financed and financing charges.
   D. the appraisal fees and closing costs.

2. All of the following are exempt from the provisions of the federal Truth-in-Lending Act EXCEPT
   A. commercial loans.
   B. personal property loans in excess of $25,000.
   C. financing extended to corporations.
   D. consumer loans to natural persons.

3. The abbreviation APR stands for
   A. average percentage rate.
   B. allotted percentage rate.
   C. approximate percentage rate.
   D. annual percentage rate.

4. The purposes of the federal Truth-in-Lending laws include
   A. a requirement that creditors disclose the full cost of obtaining credit.
   B. provisions allowing consumers to rescind credit transactions within 7 days.
   C. regulations limiting the cost of credit.
   D. disclosing full closing costs at the time of application.

5. Regulations governing the administration of the Truth-in-Lending Simplification and Reform Act are implemented by
   A. the Office of Budget Controls.
   B. the Federal Reserve Board's Regulation Z.
   C. HUD, through the Federal Housing Administration.
   D. the Department of Veteran Affairs under the 1946 Serviceman's Readjustment Act.

6. The annual percentage rate is
   A. usually lower than the interest rate.
   B. made up of the interest rate combined with the other costs of the loan.
   C. generally so low that it is of little concern to the borrower.
   D. an additional charge to the borrower.

7. Which of the following loans would be exempt from the disclosure requirements of the Truth-in-Lending laws?
   A. An unsecured personal loan of $3,000.
   B. An educational loan from a commercial bank.
   C. A second mortgage loan on a residence.
   D. A $30,000 loan for the purchase of a $40,000 automobile.

8. Which of the following advertisements would violate the federal Truth-in-Lending laws?
   A. For sale, $5,000 down, payments of $483.20 per month.
   B. For sale, VA financing available.
   C. For sale, assume large FHA loan.
   D. For sale, seller will carry loan.

9. The Truth-in-Lending laws require that a lender show the borrower all of the following EXCEPT
   A. the number of payments.
   B. computation of early payment credits.
   C. the amount of any balloon payments.
   D. the lender's net yield from loan.

10. All of the following are penalties for violation of the Truth-in-Lending laws EXCEPT
    A. a fine of up to $5,000 and/or imprisonment for up to one year.
    B. civil penalties up to twice the finance charge amount, up to a maximum of $1,000.
    C. court costs, attorney fees, and actual damages.
    D. each violation results in a $1,000 penalty each day the violation continues.

11. A borrower does not have the right, under the Truth-in-Lending laws, to rescind a credit transaction for
    A. a consumer loan of $20,000 on personal property.
    B. the acquisition of the borrower's principal dwelling.
    C. a loan to expand farming activities.
    D. a loan of $30,000 to purchase a mobile home to be used as a vacation home.

12. When evaluating a loan application, a loan officer will NOT consider the
    A. value of the property being offered as security.
    B. condition of the title to the property.
    C. ability of the borrower to repay the loan.
    D. applicant's summer job and periodic overtime earnings.

13. Which of the following pairs of words do not correspond?
    A. Duplex = two units.
    C. Quadraplex = four units.
    B. Triplex = three units.
    D. Hectoplex = eight units.

14. The practice of some lenders of not making loans on properties in certain neighborhoods is known as
    A. blockbusting.
    C. steering.
    B. redlining.
    D. capping.

15. Which of the following is generally true?
    A. As a borrower's equity in his real estate increases, the probability of default on the loan is diminished.
    B. Insured loans are generally made at lower loan-to-value ratios.
    C. Several previous default or repossessions indicated a good credit risk.
    D. As a borrower's equity in his real estate increases, the probability of default on the loan is increased.

16. Generally, before a lender will approve a loan, the borrower must
    A. have insufficient funds for the down payment.
    B. sign a statement if the borrower intends to occupy the property.
    C. sign a statement that the wife (if a couple) will not get pregnant during the first five years of the loan.
    D. produce a male co-signer if the borrower is a woman.

17. Assuming no loan insurance guarantee, a lender would most likely give its lowest interest rate on a loan to buy a(n)
    A. owner-occupied house, 80% L/V.
    B. rental house, 80% L/V.
    C. owner-occupied house, 90% L/V.
    D. apartment building, 80% L/V.

18. Which of the following is given consideration in evaluation of a loan application?
    A. Race.
    C. Sex.
    B. Marital status.
    D. Income adequacy.

19. As a general rule of thumb regarding home loans,
    A. housing expense should not exceed 25% to 30% of gross monthly income.
    B. total fixed monthly expenses should not exceed 25% of gross monthly income.
    C. alimony and child support payments need not be included in the total fixed monthly expenses.
    D. housing expenses include principal and interest payments only, not taxes and insurance.

20. Which of the following would be more favored by a lender in evaluating a loan application?
    A. U.S. Savings Bonds having cash value of $10,000.
    B. Ownership of a recreational lot in another state worth $10,000.
    C. A life estate in a residence valued at $125,000.
    D. $10,000 investment in an oil well yet to be drilled.

21. A lender can legally discriminate in loan terms based on the applicant's
    A. religion.
    B. marital status.
    C. race or skin color.
    D. intention to occupy (or not occupy) the mortgaged property.

22. The right of an individual to inspect his or her file at a credit bureau is found in the
    A. Truth-in-Lending Act.   C. Regulation Z.
    B. Fair Credit Reporting Act.   D. Federal Consumer Credit Protection Act.

23. A buyer has been turned down for a loan to buy a house. He insists that he is credit-worthy. Which of the following is his LEAST useful option?
    A. Request, in writing, a copy of his credit report.
    B. Request a verification of each entry he believes is an error.
    C. Supply an explanation for each entry he believes is an error.
    D. Reapply for the loan through another lender.

24. W once filed for bankruptcy. Generally, how long will this remain a part of W's credit history?
    A. 3 years   C. 10 years
    B. 7 years   D. It will always be on his record.

25. Which of the following would be considered an example of using "trigger terms" as defined in the Truth-in-Lending laws?
    A. "Buy a Single Family Home for only $699 a month!"
    B. "Fantastic opportunity to assume a VA Loan!"
    C. "We have terms to fit any budget!"
    D. "Unique opportunity for low seller financing!"

26. Which of the following would most likely reassure a lender who is concerned about loan repayments in the event that the buyer dies before the loan is repaid?
    A. Insurance policy with a cash value of several thousand dollars.
    B. Insurance policy with a face value equal to or greater than the proposed loan.
    C. No insurance policy because the premiums are too costly.
    D. Proof that the borrower has been named sole beneficiary of $1 million in his parent's will.

27. What loan-to-value ratio is considered the safest for a non-insured owner-occupied residential property?
    A. 70%   C. 95%
    B. 70% through 80%   D. 100%

28. Credit reporting bureaus must comply with guidelines contained in which federal law?
    A. Equal Credit Opportunity Act (ECOA)
    B. Fair Credit Reporting Act (FCRA)
    C. Truth-in-Lending Simplification and Reform Act (TILSRA)
    D. Real Estate Settlement Procedures Act (RESPA)

29. A lender can refuse to make a loan to buy a single-family dwelling located in a(n)
    A. neighborhood primarily occupied by Asians.
    B. area of low income housing.
    C. development of new construction when the subject property is 60 years old.
    D. area primarily used for business and industry.

30. What factor weighs the most in determining credit scores?
    A. Length of credit history.
    B. Payment history.
    C. Credit use.
    D. Amounts owed.

13

Sources of Financing

LEARNING OBJECTIVES

After successful completion of the questions in this chapter, you will be able to:

1. Describe the primary and secondary sources of mortgage money.
2. Explain disintermediation and its effect on home loans.
3. Explain the differences between mortgage brokers and mortgage bankers.
4. Explain the purpose and differences among FHMA, GNMA, and FHLMC.
5. Discuss alternative sources of home loan money.
6. Explain loan servicing.
7. Identify reasons why the cost of home loans varies.

1. The place where a real estate borrower makes a loan application, receives a loan, and makes loan payments describes the
   A. primary mortgage market.
   B. secondary mortgage market.
   C. first loan market.
   D. second loan market.

2. Historically, the foremost single source of funds for residential mortgage loans in this country has been
   A. commercial banks.
   B. insurance companies.
   C. mortgage companies.
   D. savings and loan associations.

3. Certificates of deposit issued by savings and loan associations carry higher rates of interest than passbook accounts in order to
   A. compete with lower yields available from other investments.
   B. prevent disintermediation.
   C. lock in money at a lower interest rate to prevent hasty, unwise investments.
   D. encourage disintermediation.

4. When savings are removed from thrift institutions in large amounts for investment in Treasury securities,
   A. the real estate market enjoys an increase in activity.
   B. disintermediation occurs.
   C. lenders receive commissions from the sales activities.
   D. disintermediation is prevented.

5. Savings and loan associations combat the problems of rising interest rates by
   A. discouraging due-on-sale clauses in mortgages.
   B. encouraging borrowers to accept adjustable rate loans.
   C. encouraging savers to make deposits in short-term accounts.
   D. permitting mortgage assumptions when original interest rates are lower than those on the current market.

6. Reasons for the decline in residential loans made by the S&Ls include all of the following EXCEPT
   A. deregulation of the lending industry.
   B. proliferation of savings and loan organizations.
   C. new laws which allowed higher risk loans.
   D. placing the FSLIC under the FDIC.

7. If the nation's commercial banks are considered as a whole, all of the following statements are correct EXCEPT
   A. Total deposits exceed those in the nation's savings and loan associations.
   B. They are more active in long-term real estate loans than the S&Ls.
   C. The bulk of their deposits are in demand accounts.
   D. They are active in construction loans.

8. Mutual savings banks are
   A. located primarily in the northeastern United States.
   B. owned by outside investors.
   C. quite dissimilar to savings and loan associations.
   D. likely to invest their deposits in high-risk ventures.

9. Life insurance companies are ideally suited to make long-term investments because
   A. premiums are received irregularly in unpredictable amounts.
   B. payoffs can be calculated from actuarial tables.
   C. their financial holdings shield them from the downside of risky investments.
   D. they have been making long-term investments for many years.

10. Life insurance companies invest premium dollars in all the following types of investments EXCEPT
    A. corporate bonds.   C. real estate loans.
    B. loans secured by personal property.   D. government bonds.

11. Generally, life insurance companies are LEAST LIKELY to be interested in originating which of the following types of real estate loans?
    A. Industrial real estate loans.
    B. Multi-family housing loans.
    C. Commercial real estate loans.
    D. Single-family housing loans.

12. One kind of real estate loan calls for the lender to receive interest plus a percentage of any profits from the rental income from a property. All of the following statements about such loans are correct EXCEPT
    A. They are designed to protect the lender from inflation.
    B. They are known as participation loans.
    C. They are most commonly used by mortgage brokers.
    D. They are likely to be utilized by life insurance companies.

13. Mortgage companies will do all of the following EXCEPT
    A. originate loans.
    B. service loans which they have sold on the secondary mortgage market.
    C. keep the loans "in house."
    D. qualify the borrowers.

14. Mortgage banking activities are regularly carried on by all of the following EXCEPT
    A. insurance companies.   C. mutual savings banks.
    B. commercial banks.   D. savings and loan associations.

15. A lender who does not lend money, but brings borrowers and lenders together is known as a mortgage
    A. agent.   C. banker.
    B. broker.   D. dealer.

16. Servicing of loans which they have originated and sold on the secondary mortgage market is regularly carried on by all of the following EXCEPT
    A. commercial banks.   C. mortgage companies.
    B. savings and loan associations. D. mortgage brokers.

17. Municipal bond issues as a source of funds for real estate loans provide
    A. taxable interest for investors.
    B. a source of below-market-rate funds for low- and middle-income families.
    C. standard market rate funds for high-income families.
    D. high risk and higher interest rates for investors.

18. The secondary mortgage market provides
    A. a means for investors to acquire real estate loans without origination and servicing facilities.
    B. a way for a lender to buy real estate loans.
    C. direct contact between investors and borrowers.
    D. employment opportunities for those who originate and service real estate loans.

19. Much of the success of the secondary mortgage market is attributable to
    A. customized loans and loan procedures.
    B. government and private mortgage loan insurance programs.
    C. the increasing influence of small, private investors.
    D. lack of incentives to make high loan-to-value ratio loans.

20. The Federal National Mortgage Association is
    A. a publicly owned corporation.
    B. managed by the federal government.
    C. active in buying FHA and VA mortgage loans.
    D. known as Freddie Mac.

21. When Fannie Mae issues a commitment to purchase a specified dollar amount of mortgage loans within a fixed period of time,
    A. Fannie Mae must purchase all loans delivered under the terms of the commitment.
    B. participating lenders become obligated to sell their loans to Fannie Mae.
    C. Fannie Mae will purchase only loans that are so risky they have been turned down by other lenders.
    D. participating lenders who do not sell at that time must "sit out" the next buying round before becoming eligible again.

22. Regarding Fannie Mae's loan buying policies,
    A. loans must be made using any lender-approved forms.
    B. loans must meet FNMA loan approval criteria.
    C. FNMA sets no annual limits on the size of individual loans which it will buy.
    D. FNMA buys second and third mortgages for up to 90% loan-to-value.

23. FNMA will purchase all of the following EXCEPT
    A. first and second mortgages.   C. government insured or guaranteed loans.
    B. third and fourth mortgages.   D. conventional loans.

24. S sold his home to W and agreed to carry back a fixed-rate loan on the property. The note and mortgage were prepared by a Fannie Mae-approved lender using FNMA qualification procedures. Could this loan be sold to a lender for later resale to FNMA?
    A. Yes, because it is a fixed rate loan.
    B. Yes, because it meets the criteria for the FNMA Home Seller Program.
    C. No, because it is not an insured loan.
    D. No, because it cannot be packaged with lender originated loans.

25. All of the following are true of the Government National Mortgage Association EXCEPT that it
    A. is a federal agency.
    B. operates a mortgage-backed securities program.
    C. is owned by stockholders.
    D. deals in FHA, VA, and FmHA mortgages.

26. Under Ginnie Mae's mortgage-backed securities program,
    A. principal and interest payments are retained by GNMA.
    B. the pool as a whole is guaranteed by Ginnie Mae.
    C. profits are generated by purchasing defaulted loans.
    D. GNMA is best known for its low-income housing programs.

27. The Federal Home Loan Mortgage Corporation
    A. deals primarily in VA mortgages.
    B. was established to serve as a primary market for members of the Federal Home Loan Bank System.
    C. issues securities against its own mortgage pools.
    D. is an agency of the federal government.

28. Participation certificates issued by Freddie Mac
    A. cannot be sold for cash.
    B. can be used as collateral for loans.
    C. are not often held as investments.
    D. can be purchased for as little as $5,000.

29. A nearby Federal Savings and Loan Association owns a participation certificate issued by Freddie Mac. Should any of the mortgages in the pool represented by the certificate default, the losses
    A. are passed on to the participants.
    B. will be entirely covered by private mortgage insurance.
    C. can cause partial payments at irregular intervals.
    D. are retained by Freddie Mac.

30. Basic problems experienced by investors in mortgage-backed securities include unpredictable
    A. yields.
    B. maturity.
    C. rates.
    D. payments.

31. Private financial institutions serving the secondary mortgage market
    A. compete heavily with Fannie Mae, Ginnie Mae, and Freddie Mac.
    B. specialize in markets not served by the "big three."
    C. are losing business to the Big Three, which are assisted by the government.
    D. offer little potential to investors so will remain small and unimportant.

32. Computerized mortgage networks serve as conduits between
    A. lenders and real estate brokerage offices.
    B. investors and the secondary mortgage markets.
    C. borrowers and investors.
    D. borrowers and the secondary market.

33. In the arena of money and capital, home buyers face strong competition for loan funds from all of the following EXCEPT
    A. business borrowers.
    B. consumer credit borrowers.
    C. governmental borrowers.
    D. municipal pension funds.

34. The interest rate charged to borrowers for home loans is LEAST determined by
    A. the cost of money to the lender.
    B. reserves for default and loan servicing costs.
    C. available investment alternatives.
    D. usury laws.

35. Due-on-sale clauses in mortgages may be used by lenders to
    A. encourage loan assumption of loans with less than market interest rates.
    B. increase the rate of interest when the property is sold.
    C. avoid prepayment privileges.
    D. prevent borrowers from negotiating lower interest rates when refinancing.

36. The provisions of the Garn Act apply to
    A. mortgage loans made after October 15, 1982, in U.S. deposit institutions.
    B. carry back financing by sellers.
    C. mortgage companies.
    D. all mortgage loans made before October 15, 1985.

37. A borrower is protected from enforcement of a due-on-sale clause in which of the following situations?
    A. Installment sale contract.
    B. Lease-option with option to buy.
    C. Lease of one year's duration.
    D. Foreclosure of a junior lien.

38. Loan contracts sometimes contain a prepayment penalty in order to
    A. discourage the borrower from shopping for a new loan at a lower interest rate.
    B. decrease the yield from the loan.
    C. prevent the sale of the property to less desirable owners.
    D. compete with VA and FHA which do allow prepayments.

39. Individuals can invest in real estate mortgages by all of the following EXCEPT
    A. investing in mortgage loan pools through certificates guaranteed by Ginnie Mae and Freddie Mac.
    B. buying junior mortgages at a discount.
    C. investing in life insurance pools.
    D. buying stock in Fannie Mae.

40. It is probably true of real estate financing that
    A. it will always change as economic conditions change.
    B. all possible means of financing have been utilized.
    C. it is unlikely that anything new will appear in the future.
    D. computer usage has peaked and will no longer be useful.

41. Predatory lending is
    A. making loans to minors.
    B. making loans in only certain neighborhoods.
    C. unscrupulous lending by taking advantage of consumers lack of knowledge.
    D. is legal in most states.

42. The office of Federal Housing Enterprise Oversight (OFHEO) ensures the capital adequacy and financial soundness of
    A. Fannie Mae.
    B. Freddie Mac.
    C. both A. & B.
    D. neither A. or B.

Types of Financing

After successful completion of the questions in this chapter, you will be able to:

1. Describe variable rate, adjustable rate, and graduated payment.
2. Explain the differences between shared appreciation and reverse mortgages.
3. Discuss seller financing.
4. Describe other types of mortgages and loans, including blanket and package mortgages, construction loans and takeout loan, and installment contracts.
5. Discuss the use of subordination.
6. Distinguish between creative financing and overly creative financing.
7. Explain a wraparound mortgage.

1. In order to make adjustable rate mortgage loans more attractive to borrowers, lenders offer
   A. lower initial interest rates.
   B. gifts such as appliances, trips, etc.
   C. lower insurance rates.
   D. lower down payments.

2. The purpose of adjustable rate mortgages is to more closely match what the lender receives in interest to
   A. the yield available from other types of investments.
   B. what it must pay to attract funds.
   C. what borrowers can afford to pay.
   D. entice investors to buy the mortgages.

3. To the borrower, as compared to a fixed-rate loan of the same maturity, an ARM mortgage loan offers a borrower the following advantages EXCEPT
   A. the ability to qualify for a larger loan.
   B. decreasing monthly payments if market interest rates fall.
   C. lower settlement costs.
   D. prepayment privileges without penalty.

4. Which of the following indexes is NOT used in connection with ARM mortgages?
   A. one-year U.S. Treasury securities.
   B. cost of funds to thrift institutions.
   C. six-month Treasury bills.
   D. consumer price index.

5. A borrower was considering an ARM mortgage from the first lender at a 2% margin and a comparable loan from a second lender at a 3% margin. The loan from the first lender would result in
   A. lower loan payments.
   B. higher loan payments.
   C. identical loan payments.
   D. higher interest rate charges.

6. An ARM mortgage contains a payment cap in order to limit possible increases in the borrower's monthly amortization payments. This cap can result in all of the following EXCEPT
   A. negative amortization.
   B. an increase in the balance owed on the property.
   C. the loan balance exceeding the property value.
   D. reducing the total number of payments.

7. When considering an ARM mortgage, the lender must explain to the borrower, in writing, the
   A. worst-case scenario.
   B. best-case scenario.
   C. average case scenario.
   D. respective credit report.

8. ARM mortgages with teaser rates are avoided by mortgage insurers because
   A. borrowers quickly refinance at even lower interest rates.
   B. the yield is too low to be profitable.
   C. they can lead to early foreclosure when the rates are increased.
   D. borrowers are less likely to pay off the loan early and the lender is stuck with a low yield.

9. The Office of Thrift Supervision (OTS) authorizes saving institutions to make
   A. low down payment loans.
   B. 40 year loans.
   C. adjustable rate loans.
   D. low interest rate loans.

10. To qualify for a reverse mortgage a borrower must have reached the age of
    A. 18.
    B. 21.
    C. 62.
    D. 55.

11. A purchase agreement for a new condominium unit calls for the refrigerator to be financed along with the purchase of the unit. Which of the following statements is NOT true?
    A. The refrigerator will be itemized and included in the mortgage.
    B. The mortgage will be called a package mortgage.
    C. The buyer may not sell the refrigerator without the lender's permission.
    D. The rate of interest on the value of the refrigerator may be higher than that on the real property.

12. Which of the following statements is NOT correct regarding blanket mortgages?
    A. More than one property serves as security for a single mortgage.
    B. Neither property may be sold until the entire debt is repaid.
    C. The mortgage may contain a partial release clause.
    D. The sale of either property may invoke a due-on-sale clause.

13. A couple, both 65 years old, own their home free and clear. They are retired and need supplementary income for living expenses. They have been offered a reverse mortgage by their local savings and loan association. Which of the following statements is NOT correct?
    A. They will receive monthly checks from the lender.
    B. The loan balance plus interest will be due upon the sale of their home.
    C. They must make monthly payments of interest only on the loan.
    D. Upon the death of the survivor, the property will be sold through the estate and the loan repaid from the proceeds.

14. A woman is building a new home and has secured a construction loan from her local bank. When the house is finished, she plans to pay off the construction loan with a permanent loan from a savings and loan association. Which of the following statements is correct?
    A. She will receive the construction loan in one lump sum during the course of the construction.
    B. The permanent loan will be a take-out loan.
    C. The construction loan is considered less risky and therefore she will pay a lower interest rate.
    D. The permanent loan will probably have a higher interest rate than does the construction loan.

15. When an existing loan at a low interest rate is refinanced by a new loan at an interest rate between the current market rate and the rate on the old loan, the result is a
    A. combined loan.   C. wraparound loan.
    B. blended loan.   D. merged loan.

16. A corporation built a building to its exact specifications. It wants to pull out its capital to use for other purposes. The best financing option is the
    A. lease with option to buy.   C. asset integrated mortgage.
    B. installment contract.   D. sale and leaseback.

17. A couple own their home which is presently worth approximately $150,000. They have an existing fixed-rate first mortgage of $50,000 on the property. To help pay for their child's college expenses, they have arranged for an equity loan on the home. Which of the following statements is correct?
    A. Assuming that they can qualify, they can probably secure approval of a loan up to $112,500 based on their equity.
    B. The equity loan will be in first position because it is now larger than the first mortgage.
    C. They must take out the entire loan at the time of inception.
    D. The interest rate will probably be based on the prime rate plus a lender's margin of 1 to 3 percent.

18. Which of the following statements is true regarding seller financing?
    A. The seller of the property is the mortgagee under the mortgage.
    B. Mortgage terms and interest rates are negotiable between a third party lender and the buyer.
    C. If repayment is spread over two or more years, income taxes cannot be calculated on the installment reporting method.
    D. Carry back mortgages are usually salable to investors without discount.

19. Which of the following would discourage the use of a wraparound mortgage?
    A. It is a junior mortgage, subordinate to an existing first mortgage.
    B. The interest rate on the buyer's note is usually lower than the market rate.
    C. It is useless when the first mortgage carries a due-on-sale clause.
    D. The yield to the seller (mortgagee) is usually greater than the interest rate specified on the note.

20. When the holder of a mortgage agrees to accept a position of lower lien priority, and to allow another mortgage to advance in priority, the process is known as
    A. subrogation.   C. subordination.
    B. substitution.   D. subterfuge.

21. A sale may be made and financed under a contract for deed
    A. only when the seller owns the property free and clear.
    B. by combining wraparound financing with an existing mortgage on the property, provided the existing mortgage does not contain a due-on-sale clause.
    C. only when used to finance the purchase of vacant land.
    D. provided that the buyer be approved according to Fannie Mae criteria.

22. Possession without the need to immediately finance the full purchase price of a property can be achieved by using a
    A. lease with option to buy.   C. budget mortgage.
    B. right to first refusal.   D. reserve account.

23. Real estate agents who participate in creative financing arrangements in order to make sales should be careful to avoid participating in transactions which could result in
    A. unencumbered properties.
    B. the loss of their license.
    C. a prison term for the seller and the buyer.
    D. a fine of up to $10,000 for each offense.

24. The most common adjustment period for an ARM payment is
    A. 6 months.   C. 3 years.
    B. 1 year.   D. 5 years.

25. Lenders must provide consumers with a historical example of how the actual changes in index values have affected payments on a $10,000 ARM as a result of
    A. Fair Credit Reporting Act.
    B. Garn Act.
    C. Regulation Z.
    D. Real Estate Settlement Procedures Act.

26. A graduated payment mortgage is appealing to which group of buyers?
    A. Retired couples   C. Military personnel
    B. Empty nesters   D. Young professionals

27. If a buyer is purchasing a fully furnished condominium, she would most likely obtain a
    A. package mortgage.   C. shared appreciation mortgage.
    B. blanket mortgage.   D. reverse mortgage.

28. A reverse mortgage would most likely be utilized by
    A. first-time buyers with low incomes.
    B. a couple with school-age children.
    C. a single person, buying for the first time.
    D. an elderly couple.

29. One major disadvantage to the borrower of an ARM is
    A. lower interest payments initially.
    B. possible negative amortization.
    C. easier to qualify initially.
    D. when interest rates decline, monthly payments will go down.

Taxes and Assessments

CHAPTER

15

LEARNING OBJECTIVES

After successful completion of the questions in this chapter, you will be able to:

1. Explain the purpose of property taxes and how they are determined.
2. Discuss tax sales, tax deeds, and redemption.
3. Define special assessments and explain the process for confirmation and apportionment.
4. Explain how to calculate income taxes on the sale of a residence.
5. Calculate the amount realized and taxable gain on the sale of a residence.
6. Explain the purpose of the Board of Equalization.
7. Explain what the agent's liability is for tax advice.

---

1. Local government programs and services are financed primarily through
   A. ad valorem property taxes.
   B. federal income taxes.
   C. state income taxes.
   D. state sales taxes.

2. Taxes on real property are levied all of the following ways EXCEPT
   A. on an ad valorem basis.
   B. according to the value of the property.
   C. according to the income level of the neighborhood.
   D. annually.

3. All of the following governmental services are paid for by taxes on real property EXCEPT
   A. fire and police protection.
   B. local parks and recreation.
   C. interstate highways.
   D. public libraries.

4. The dollar amount of taxes to be levied on a property may be increased by which of the following means?
   A. Decreasing the tax rate.
   B. Raising the assessment ratio.
   C. Decreasing the assessed value of the property.
   D. Increasing the number of services offered to the community.

5. The assessment ratio of real property in a community may be
   A. one hundred percent of its appraised value.
   B. more than its fair market value.
   C. more than its appraised value.
   D. proportional to tax-exempt properties.

6. Which of the following properties has the highest assessed value?
   A. Market value $75,000, assessed at 75% of value.
   B. Market value $50,000, assessed at 100% of value.
   C. Market value $90,000, assessed at 50% of value.
   D. Market value $130,000, assessed at 35% of value.

7. Tax rates may be expressed as
   A. a millage rate.
   B. dollars of tax per hundred dollars of valuation.
   C. dollars of tax per thousand dollars of valuation.
   D. all of the above.

8. The budget for a city requires $600,000 from real property taxes for the current year. The assessed value of all taxable real property in the city is 24 million dollars. All of the following tax rates would produce the necessary revenues EXCEPT
   A. .025 per $1.00.   C. $25. per $1,000.
   B. $2.50 per $100.   D. 2.5 mills.

9. If a property owner fails to pay property taxes,
   A. the community may attach other assets such as his bank account.
   B. the property owner will lose the property.
   C. his salary may be attached.
   D. the community must wait until the house is sold to collect the taxes.

10. Property named in a tax certificate following a sale for delinquent taxes may be redeemed by any of the following people EXCEPT
    A. the owner.
    B. a lienor.
    C. anyone who will pay the taxes and interest.
    D. first mortgagee.

11. In a state where the redemption period follows the tax sale, a tax deed is issued to the successful bidder
    A. at the conclusion of the sale.
    B. upon the expiration of the redemption period.
    C. at the beginning of the tax delinquency.
    D. upon waiver of redemption rights by lien holders.

12. In a state in which the sale of property for delinquent taxes occurs only after the expiration of a redemption period, the purchaser at a tax sale will receive a
    A. tax certificate.   C. tax deed.
    B. tax lien.   D. tax receipt.

13. An investor plans to bid on real estate being offered at a tax auction. Before bidding on a parcel, he would be wise to
    A. conduct a title search.   C. sign a contract.
    B. purchase title insurance.   D. obtain a tax receipt.

14. G has a deed from local tax authorities granting him all of the rights, title and interest a delinquent owner had in a particular real property. To enhance the marketability of his title, G could
    A. purchase homeowners insurance.
    B. conduct a quiet title suit.
    C. advertise that he is the new owner.
    D. record this deed.

15. Which of the following liens holds the highest degree of lien priority?
    A. Federal income tax liens
    B. Mechanic's liens
    C. Ad valorem tax liens
    D. First mortgage liens

16. The assessed value of land and buildings in a community is
    A. a matter of public record.
    B. available only to the owner of the property.
    C. available only to those who have a financial interest in the property.
    D. known only to the officials who need to know this information.

17. Records of the assessed valuations of all properties within a jurisdiction are known as
    A. appraisal rolls.
    B. allocation rolls.
    C. appropriation rolls.
    D. assessment rolls.

18. A property owner feels that the taxes on his real property are too high. Through the appeal process, he can demand a review of the
    A. amount of tax on the property.
    B. assessed value of the property.
    C. rate of taxation.
    D. assessment ratio.

19. One of the functions of the Board of Equalization is to
    A. equalize assessments between states.
    B. equalize assessments between individual property owners.
    C. settle disputes between the tax assessor and the property owner.
    D. determine the annual tax rate.

20. A city wants to attract a new manufacturing plant to locate within the city. As an inducement, may the city officials offer an exemption from real property taxes?
    A. Yes, on the basis that the economic benefits outweigh the cost to the public.
    B. Yes, because the government's power of eminent domain permits exemptions to private owners.
    C. No, because this would increase the tax burden to other property owners.
    D. No, because only publicly owned land can be exempt from taxation.

21. Which of the following types of property are usually subject to taxation?
    A. Government-owned utilities
    B. Residences owned by elderly homeowners
    C. Property owned by charitable organizations
    D. Hospitals

22. Homes of the same value may bear different tax burdens because of all of the following reasons EXCEPT
    A. delays in reassessment.
    B. different government services being provided in different neighborhoods.
    C. varying sources of revenue from city to city.
    D. the political influence of a small group of property owners.

23. The property tax burden of an individual owner is NOT influenced by
    A. the efficiency of the government.   C. local debt service.
    B. the owner's ability to pay.   D. services furnished by the government.

24. Special assessments of property tax are made for improvements which benefit
    A. a limited number of property owners.
    B. all property owners for a limited time.
    C. the public.
    D. the real estate industry.

25. The cost of which of the following could be met by means of a special assessment?
    A. Improvements to a municipal golf course.
    B. Extension of sewer lines to a privately owned industrial park
    C. Construction of a new station located in a new residential area of the city
    D. Construction of a new school to serve a growing residential area

26. When an improvement district is created, the costs of the improvements are paid from
    A. general revenues.
    B. assessments on properties within the district.
    C. assessments on all city property.
    D. assessments only on commercial property.

27. Special assessments are apportioned according to the
    A. value of the land being assessed.
    B. value of the buildings being assessed.
    C. value of benefits received.
    D. value of the land and buildings being assessed.

28. The city is going to install curbs and gutters in one of its neighborhoods that does not presently have them. The special assessment for these curbs and gutters will be levied against individual properties according to the
    A. benefits received.   C. market value of the property.
    B. assessed value of the properties.   D. appraised values.

29. A family purchased their home for $65,000. The only improvements added were land-scaping and fencing which cost $2,500. They later sold the home for $90,000 and paid a 6 percent sales commission. In order to make the sale, they took back a purchase money mortgage of $10,000 which they sold to an investor for $7,500. For income tax purposes, the gain realized by the family would be
    A. $4,600.   C. $14,600.
    B. $7,100.   D. $17,100.

30. When a person sells land for more than he paid for it,
    A. there is a federal tax applicable to the gain.
    B. the gain is taxed by all state governments.
    C. the gain is taxed at the corporate rate.
    D. no tax is due if the money is reinvested in land within twelve months.

31. All of the following may be included in determining the cost basis of a home in deter-mining income tax liability EXCEPT
    A. cost of legal services in acquiring the home.
    B. fees or commissions paid to help find the property.
    C. repairs done as part of an extensive remodeling project.
    D. replacing broken windowpanes.

32. In order to qualify for inclusion in a home's adjusted sales price, fix-up expenses
    A. must be done within 90 days prior to the time a contract to sell is signed.
    B. must be paid for within 30 days after closing.
    C. must be done within 30 days of putting the house on the market.
    D. may be included only if the buyer requested the repairs in the sale contract.

33. The Taxpayers Relief Act of 1997 has to do with
    A. capital gain tax.
    B. depreciation of real estate.
    C. interest deduction of loans on second homes.
    D. deferring income taxes by using the installment method of reporting gain.

34. The conveyance tax on deeds is $.55 per $100 on the "new money." A property sells for $100,000 subject to an existing $30,000 loan. What is the amount of tax?
    A. $165   C. $550
    B. $385   D. $715

35. W realized a capital gain of $40,000 on the sale of an investment property which he sold for $100,000. He received a $35,000 cash down payment and carried back a $65,000 mortgage. Which of the following statements is NOT correct?
    A. Taxes on the entire gain must be paid in the year of the sale.
    B. Taxes on the gain are due on the portion of gain received in any given year.
    C. Interest earned on the mortgage is taxed as ordinary income.
    D. W may choose to pay all the taxes in the year of the sale.

36. Which of the following may NOT be claimed as a personal tax deduction when a homeowner itemizes on his or her tax return.
    A. Property tax on personal residence
    B. Mortgage interest on a personal residence
    C. Loan points paid by the seller to help a buyer obtain VA or FHA financing
    D. Interest paid on improvement district bonds

37. Under income tax laws passed in 1984 and 1985, a seller who takes a carry back mortgage
    A. must charge 10% interest or be penalized 9% by the IRS.
    B. is subject to penalties if the rate charged is at least equal to the rate on federal securities of similar maturity.
    C. is discouraged from charging a below-market rate.
    D. is subject to state usury laws.

38. Because of the complexity to income tax laws and their impact on real estate, a real estate licensee should
    A. have knowledge of tax laws at the level of an accountant.
    B. avoid knowledge of tax laws so as to avoid responsibility for providing tax information.
    C. know when to warn clients that a tax problem may exist or result.
    D. accompany the client to the accountant to make sure that the information given is relevant and correct.

39. A real estate agent has a responsibility
    A. to discourage clients from seeking tax counsel.
    B. for the quality and accuracy of tax information given by the agent to clients.
    C. to make referrals to the office accountant and/or attorney.
    D. for the accuracy of information given by the tax person.

40. Conveyance taxes on the transfer of title to real property are levied by
    A. the federal government.
    B. some state governments.
    C. counties only.
    D. the Federal Housing Administration.

SECTION 15.2: Property Tax Problems

Q. In determining the amount of taxes to be levied on a parcel of real estate, the following necessary steps will be completed by the local government official in what order?
    ___ Determine the budget requirements of the community
    ___ Assessment of all the taxable real property in the community
    ___ Determine the revenue to be derived from sources other than real property taxes
    ___ Set the tax rate on all taxable real property

1. The city has a total assessed value of all real estate of $240 million. The share of the city budget to be paid by ad valorem taxes is $6 million. Your property in that city is assessed at $40,000.
    A. What will be the tax rate, expressed in mills? _____
    B. What will be the annual taxes on your property? _____

2. If a property has a market value of $240,000 and is assessed at $100,800, what is the assessment ratio? _____

3. In a nearby city, the millage rate is 20 mills for the school budget, 10 mills for city services, and 5 mills for county services. If a property having a market value of $70,000 is assessed at a 50% ratio, what would the annual property taxes be?

    $ _____

4. You own property in a city where the tax rate is $3.50 per $100 of assessed valuation. Your taxes are $1,365 annually on a property which has a market value of $60,000. What is the assessment ratio?

    _____

5. Your property is assessed at $65,000 in a community where the assessment ratio is 52% of value. Based on this, what is the market value of the property?

    $ _____

6. A woman buys a lot by paying the back taxes for the past 4 years. The tax rate is $21.00 per $1,000 of the assessed value. What did she pay for the lot if the assessed value of the lot was $12,000?

    $ _____

7. A couple bought a property ten years ago to use as a second home on weekends. This second home is taxed on the basis of 60% of assessed value, at the rate of $2.50 per hundred. This has been the case for the last five years. However, since the year they bought, their yearly taxes have increased by $450. In the eyes of the tax assessor, how much has the property increased in value?

    $ _____

8. A 100' x 100' lot was assessed at $150 per front foot and the house was assessed at $32,000. What was the total yearly tax if the rate was $4.00 per $100?

    $ _____

9. A house assessed at $102,000 was taxed at 2.2%. Taxes were just increased by 30%. What is the amount of the tax increase?

    $ _____

10. The assessed value of all property in a certain city is $120 million. The city budget is $5,040,000. Your property is assessed at $350,000. What are your taxes?

    $ _____

11. A lender requires that the monthly mortgage payment include 1/12 of the annual taxes. Property value is $100,000. The assessment ratio is 30%. School tax rate is 12 mills; county tax rate is 25 mills. What is the tax payment per month?

    $ _____

12. A property is assessed at $80,000. The tax rate is $26 per $1,000 with a 2% discount for promptness and an 18% per annum charge for delinquency.

    A. Determine the amount owed if taxes are paid before the due date.

       $ _____

    B. What amount is owed if the taxes are paid 2 months after the due date?

       $ _____

    C. What is the difference to the property owner between paying on time and paying 2 months late?

       $ _____

SECTION 15.3: Gain on Sale Problems

This problem follows a couple through their ownership of a home, the sale of the home, and the purchase of another home. Use the data given to calculate their gain and tax liability following the purchase of the second home.

April 1, 1965	Purchase home for $18,500 Closing costs: $500	Basis: $ _____
May 1, 1967	Fence rear yard, cost: $350	Basis: $ _____
July 1, 1970	Paint interior and exterior, cost: $600	Basis: $ _____
June 1, 1972	Add screen porch, cost: $1,500	Basis: $ _____
Sept. 1, 1975	Connect to public sewer, cost: $800	Basis: $ _____
April 1, 1976	Add to central air conditioning, cost: $1,000	Basis: $ _____
June 1, 1986	Remodel bathroom, cost: $5,000	Basis: $ _____
July 10, 1995	Sell home for $149,500	
Aug. 10, 1995	Closing Date; sales commission and closing costs: $10,500	Amount Realized: $ _____

Calculation of gain:

Amount Realized	$ _____
Less Basis	$ _____
Equals Gain	$ _____

Assume that the couple owned their home free and clear of any debts at the time of the sale. Use the data given below to determine their tax liability in each of the following situations.

First Situation:

Aug. 1, 1995   Settlement date on the purchase of a new home
                 at a price of $150,000. Closing costs: $1,000

                                                    Cost of
                                                    New Home: $ _____

Aug. 1, 1995   Settlement date on previous home   Subtract
                                                    Postponed
                                                    Gain: $ _____

                                                    Basis for
                                                    New Home: $ _____

Title Closing and Escrow

LEARNING OBJECTIVES

After successful completion of the questions in this chapter, you will be able to:

1. Describe the buyers' walk-through.
2. Explain the differences between a settlement closing and an escrow closing.
3. Explain "time is of the essence" and dry closing.
4. Calculate tax, interest, and other prorations at closing.
5. Explain what happens when there are delays or a failure to close.
6. Explain the restrictions and benefits of the Real Estate Settlement Procedures Act.

1. The moment in time when a seller conveys title to a purchaser, and when the purchaser fulfills all his obligations pertinent to the sale may be referred to by any of the following terms EXCEPT
   A. close of escrow.
   B. settlement date.
   C. closing date.
   D. completion date.

2. Details that must be handled between the time a purchase contract is signed and the closing typically do NOT include
   A. title search.
   B. deed preparation.
   C. loan arrangements.
   D. preparing a list of items for the seller to repair.

3. A buyer's walkthrough is conducted for the purpose of
   A. appraising the property in order to get a loan on it.
   B. inspecting the property for major structural defects.
   C. meeting the seller and obtaining the keys to the property.
   D. making a final inspection just prior to closing.

4. During the walkthrough, the buyer should
   A. test heating and air conditioning systems.
   B. test appliances that will be removed by the seller.
   C. examine the title to the property for defects.
   D. look for additional items to have repaired by the seller.

5. At which of the following are the buyer and seller more likely to shake hands upon completing the real estate transaction?
   A. Escrow closing
   B. Settlement meeting
   C. Presentation of the offer
   D. Notification that the offer has been accepted

6. A settlement meeting may take place in the offices of
   A. the real estate agent.   C. a title company.
   B. an attorney or lender.   D. any of the above.

7. When a real estate settlement is held in escrow,
   A. there is no closing meeting.
   B. the closing process may not be conducted by mail.
   C. representatives of both parties must be present.
   D. lenders require an attorney to witness the loan documents.

8. At a closing meeting, the seller would sign which of the following instruments?
   A. Deed to the property   C. Promissory note
   B. Mortgage on the property   D. Satisfaction piece

9. Is the following statement correct? "In the course of a settlement meeting, the seller should deliver the deed to the purchaser before the purchaser signs the note and mortgage."
   A. Yes, because the buyer should not pay for the property until receipt of a deed.
   B. Yes, because the buyer cannot mortgage property which he does not own.
   C. No, because the seller should not convey title until he receives payment.
   D. No, because delivery of the deed should be the last step in the transaction.

10. Which of the following is NOT a purpose of a settlement statement?
   A. Provide an accounting of all funds involved in the transaction
   B. Identify all parties who receive funds from the transaction
   C. Set limits to fees charged at closing
   D. Meet the RESPA requirements

11. The final action to be taken to complete a real estate transaction is to
   A. hold a settlement meeting.
   B. sign all instruments.
   C. acknowledge appropriate instruments.
   D. record appropriate instruments.

12. Which of the following are disbursed at a "dry closing"?
   A. Deed to the buyer   C. Real estate agent's commission
   B. Money due the seller   D. Nothing is disbursed

13. When a real estate sale is closed through escrow, all of the following statements are correct EXCEPT
    A. seller delivers the deed to the escrow agent.
    B. buyer and seller meet for the closing.
    C. escrow agent is a neutral third party.
    D. funds due from the buyer are paid to the escrow agent.

14. A seller sold his home to a buyer through a real estate broker. The sale is to be settled through escrow. The escrow agent would be selected by
    A. the seller.
    B. the buyer.
    C. the real estate agent.
    D. mutual agreement between the seller and the buyer.

15. While a buyer's funds are held by the escrow agent, they are kept
    A. in a trust account.
    B. in a safe deposit vault in cash.
    C. uncashed in a safe deposit vault.
    D. uncashed under lock and key in the escrow office.

16. Settlement of the sale of R's home to H is being handled by the XYZ Escrow Company. The escrow agent will be responsible for all of the following EXCEPT
    A. preparation of escrow instructions.
    B. ordering of a title search.
    C. preparation of the purchase agreement.
    D. obtaining title insurance.

17. When a real estate transaction is handled in escrow, the need for which of the following is eliminated?
    A. Buyer and/or seller to employ an attorney
    B. Either party to engage a real estate broker
    C. Title insurance to be ordered
    D. Presence of the buyer and seller to complete the transaction

18. In an escrow closing, funds are disbursed
    A. when all escrow papers have been signed.
    B. as soon as the buyer brings his money in.
    C. after necessary recordings take place.
    D. as soon as the seller signs the deed.

19. At an escrow closing, the closing, delivery of title, and recordation take place
    A. at separate times.
    B. at the same time.
    C. as each document is signed.
    D. as each document is received into escrow.

20. In an escrow closing, the escrow agent serves as agent for the
    A. buyer.   C. buyer and the seller.
    B. seller.   D. buyer, seller, and real estate agent.

21. One advantage of the escrow closing method is that it can eliminate
    A. personal confrontation between buyer and seller.
    B. the need for an attorney.
    C. the requirement for title insurance.
    D. the necessity of recording the deed, mortgage, and note.

22. In addition to the closing of real property sales using standard purchase agreements, an escrow can be used in all of the following situations EXCEPT when
    A. property is being refinanced.
    B. a mortgage loan is being paid off.
    C. property is being sold under an installment contract.
    D. a lease with option to buy is negotiated.

23. When a home is sold and a new loan by an institutional lender is required to complete the transaction, the typical time between purchase contract signing and settlement will most likely be
    A. 0 to 29 days.
    B. 30 to 60 days.
    C. 61 to 120 days.
    D. over 120 days.

24. By itself and without supporting language, the inclusion of the phrase "time is of the essence" in a real estate purchase contract most nearly means the
    A. sale must settle on time or it is automatically void.
    B. buyer can rescind the deal if the closing does not take place on time.
    C. seller can rescind the deal if the closing does not take place on time.
    D. parties are expected to close on time but that reasonable delays for reasonable reasons will probably be tolerated.

25. If the parties to a real estate purchase contract find that it cannot be completed and agree orally to simply drop it with no further liability to either party, should they also sign mutual release papers?
    A. Yes, because the contract must be rescinded in writing.
    B. Yes, but only one party need sign.
    C. No, because it can be rescinded orally.
    D. No, because inaction is enough to rescind it.

26. The seller and buyer sign a real estate purchase contract with the closing to take place in 45 days. Before the closing, the seller gets a better offer on the property. Can the seller accept the better offer?
    A. Yes, because property can always be sold to the highest bidder.
    B. Yes, if the seller and the buyer rescind their contract.
    C. No, because the closing has not yet taken place.
    D. Yes, but the seller has to pay damages to the buyer.

27. Which of the following items would NOT be prorated at a settlement or closing?
    A. Taxes
    B. Rents from income-producing properties
    C. Title insurance policy
    D. Assumed homeowners insurance policy

28. Prorations of items in a real estate closing are made usually as of the date of
    A. signing of the sales contract.
    B. title transfer.
    C. buyers' walkthrough.
    D. the mortgage payment.

29. On June 13, a buyer agreed to assume the seller's 8% loan, which had a balance of $36,720 as of June 1. The day of closing belongs to the seller. Interest on this loan would be prorated as follows:
    A. debit the buyer $138.72.
    B. debit the buyer $106.08.
    C. debit the seller $138.72.
    D. debit the seller $106.08.

30. A seller agreed to sell his home to a buyer, and the closing took place on June 18. The buyer agreed to assume the seller's hazard insurance policy, which was effective as of November 13 of the previous year. The premium was paid in advance for one year from the effective date of the policy. Prorations are made on the basis of 30 days per month, with the buyer responsible for the day of closing. Which of the following statements is true? The annual policy premium was $194.40.
    A. Buyer would be charged $78.30.
    B. Seller would be credited $116.10.
    C. Buyer would be credited $78.30.
    D. Buyer would be charged $194.40.

31. A property on which the annual taxes are $662.40 was sold and settlement will take place on April 14. The taxes in this community are on a calendar year basis and are not yet paid. Based on 30-day months and charging the buyer with the day of closing, the proration will be as follows:
    A. charge the buyer $472.88.
    B. charge the seller $189.52.
    C. credit the buyer $472.88.
    D. credit the seller $189.52.

32. Taxes of $1,320 were paid in advance for the full calendar year. The property was sold and closing took place on August 16. Purchaser was responsible for the day of closing. Taxes would be prorated as follows:
    A. Debit purchaser $495, credit seller $825.
    B. Debit seller $825, credit purchaser $495.
    C. Debit seller $495, credit purchaser $825.
    D. Debit purchaser $495, credit seller $495.

33. A buyer obtained a new loan to buy a home. Closing will take place on December 5, and loan payments are to fall on the first of each month. To accomplish this, the interest proration on this loan will be a
    A. charge to the lender and a credit to the buyer, prorated forward.
    B. charge to the buyer and a credit to the lender, prorated forward.
    C. charge to the lender and a credit to the buyer, prorated backward.
    D. charge to the buyer and a credit to the lender, prorated backward.

34. There is a street improvement assessment currently against the seller's house. If the seller is to sell the property,
    A. by law the seller must pay the assessment in full as part of the settlement.
    B. by law the buyer must pay the assessment in full at settlement.
    C. by law the buyer must assume the assessment.
    D. the seller and the buyer can negotiate which of them will pay the assessment.

35. All of the following must comply with the provisions of the Real Estate Settlement Procedures Act EXCEPT
    A. sales financed by means of an FHA-insured loan.
    B. sales financed by an installment contract.
    C. a sale financed by means of a VA-guaranteed loan.
    D. all home financing through a lender who invests more than a million dollars a year in residential loans.

36. A couple sold the home they owned free and clear. They accepted a down payment of 25% of the purchase price, and carried back a note and mortgage for the remainder. Would the provisions of RESPA apply to this couple?
    A. Yes, because they carried back a mortgage.
    B. Yes, because they took less than 30% down.
    C. No, because no federally related lender was involved.
    D. No, because this was the sale of a home by its owners.

37. Among other things, RESPA prohibits
    A. kickbacks and/or fees for services not actually performed during the closing.
    B. the buyer from selecting his own title insurance company.
    C. lenders from collecting advance payments for taxes and insurance.
    D. HUD from regulating real estate settlement practices.

38. The amount of advance tax and insurance payments collected at closing by a lender for deposit in an impound or escrow account
    A. is not regulated by RESPA.
    B. is limited to the owner's share of accrued taxes prior to closing, plus one-sixth of the next year's estimated tax and insurance payments.
    C. must earn market rate interest, payable to the owner of the funds.
    D. need not be returned to the owner if there is a drop in the amount paid out by the lender.

39. Under provisions of RESPA,
    A. the buyer must be given an estimate of closing costs in advance of closing.
    B. payments outside of escrow are prohibited.
    C. the buyer cannot see the settlement statements until the time of closing.
    D. the lender can use its own closing statement form.

SECTION 16.2: Settlement Problems

1. The seller pays 70% of closing costs and the buyer pays the balance. If closing costs are $540, how much more does the seller pay than the buyer?

   $ _____

2. A two-family flat rented for $300 for one unit and $450 for the other. Both rentals were due on the first of each month. Property was to be closed on November 15 with the seller responsible for the day of closing. Both rents were paid on time. How much would the seller be debited or credited?

   $ _____

3. Taxes of $500 per year are on a calendar basis and are paid for the current year. A vacation cabin is sold for $35,000. Settlement will be on May 1. Your commission is 6%. The mortgage balance is $22,790 and interest has been paid to May 1. Disregarding miscellaneous charges, how much will the owner receive at the settlement?

   $ _____

4. There is a principal balance of $9,000 on a mortgage. The interest rate is 7 1/2% per annum. The taxes and insurance total $540 per year. The monthly payment is $130, which covers interest, taxes, and insurance and the balance is applied to reduce the principal. What is the principal balance after the monthly payment is made?

   $ _____

5. At closing, on November 18, a buyer assumes the existing second mortgage of $12,000. Interest at 10% per annum has been paid up to and including October 31. Prorate the amount of interest that will be credited to the buyer. (Use a 30-day month and charge the buyer with the day of closing.)

   $ _____

6. County taxes of $300 have been paid through the end of the year, and annual school taxes of $540 have been paid through next June 30. Settlement is held on November 1 and belongs to the buyer. How much proration credit is due the seller?

   $ _____

7. June 11 is the settlement day on a 10-unit apartment building. Each unit rents for $600 per month, and all but one tenant has paid for June. If the buyer is responsible for the day of settlement, who would be debited and who would be credited, and how much?

   Buyer $ _____ $ _____

   Seller $ _____ $ _____

SECTION 16.3: Settlement Worksheet

Use the data below to prepare the settlement statement worksheet on the following page. Follow the instructions given in the problem, regardless of the law or custom in your state. You are to determine the dollar amounts of prorated items, and certain other items where the dollar amount is not stated in the problem. Calculate all prorations on the basis of 30-day months, and 360-day years, with the day of settlement accruing to and/or being the responsibility of the purchaser.

DATA: Date of settlement: July 16, 20XX

1.	Purchase price	$62,500
2.	New first mortgage loan	80% of purchase price
3.	Hazard insurance, new policy	$148
4.	Earnest money deposit with contract of sale	$3,000
5.	Mortgage loan payoff, seller's existing loan	$31,211
6.	Taxes, Jan. 1 to Dec. 31, not yet paid	$775, to be prorated
7.	Agent's commission	6% of purchase price
8.	Preparation of deed	$25, charge seller
9.	Title examination (charge seller)	1/2 of 1% of purchase price
10.	Title insurance, owner's and mortgagee's policy (charge buyer)	$2.00 per $1,000 of purchase price
11.	Preparation of carry back mortgage	$25, charge buyer
12.	Loan origination fee on first mortgage	1 1/4% of loan amount
13.	Survey, required by lender	$150, charge buyer
14.	Carry back mortgage given to seller	10% of purchase price
15.	Mortgage insurance premium	$156.25, charge buyer
16.	State transfer tax (buyer pays)	$.20 per $100 of purchase price
17.	Recording fees: deed and first mortgage paid by buyer; carry back mortgage and mortgage release paid by seller	$6 each item

Settlement Worksheet

ITEM	BUYER'S STATEMENT		SELLER'S STATEMENT	
	DEBIT	CREDIT	DEBIT	CREDIT
1.				
2.				
3.				
4.				
5.				
6.				
7.				
8.				
9.				
10.				
11.				
12.				
13.				
14.				
15.				
16.				
17.				
Debit / Credit Totals				
Balance Due from Buyer				
Balance Due to Seller				
TOTALS:				

Calculations

....

....

....

....

Settlement Worksheet

	ITEM	BUYER'S STATEMENT		SELLER'S STATEMENT	
		DEBIT	CREDIT	DEBIT	CREDIT
1.	Purchase Price	62,500.00			62,500.00
2.	1st Mortgage		50,000.00		
3.	Hazard Insurance	148.00			
4.	Earnest Money		3,000.00		
5.	Mortgage Loan Pay-off			31,211.00	
6.	Real Estate Taxes		419.79	419.79	
7.	Agent's Commission			3,750.00	
8.	Deed Preparation			25.00	
9.	Title Examination			312.50	
10.	Title Insurance	126.00			
11.	Prep. of 2nd Mortgage	25.00			
12.	Loan Origination Fee	625.00			
13.	Survey	150.00			
14.	Carryback Mortgage		6,250.00	6,250.00	
15.	Mortgage Ins. Premium	156.25			
16.	State Transfer Fee	125.00			
17.	Recording Fees	12.00		12.00	
	Debit / Credit Totals	63,867.25	59,669.79	41,980.29	62,500.00
	Balance Due from Buyer		4,197.46		
	Balance Due to Seller			20,519.71	
	TOTALS	**$63,867.25**	**$63,867.25**	**$62,500.00**	**$62,500.00**

Calculations

1. No calculation required
2. $62,500 x 80% = $50,000
3. No calculation required
4. No calculation required
5. No calculation required
6. $775 ÷ 12 = $64.58 x 6.5 mo.= $419.79
   (months seller owned property)
7. $62,500 x .06 = $3,750
8. No calculation required
9. $62,500 x .005 = $312.50

10. $62,500 ÷ 1,000 = 62.5
    (round up to 63) x 2 = $126
11. No calculation required
12. $50,000 x .0125 = $625
13. No calculation required
14. $62,500 x .10 = $6,250
15. No calculation required
16. $62,500 ÷ 100 x $.20 = $125
17. 2 x $6 = $12 for buyer, same for seller

CHAPTER

17

Real Estate Leases

LEARNING OBJECTIVES

After successful completion of the questions in this chapter, you will be able to:

1. Explain leasehold estate and explain how to create a valid lease.
2. Explain landlord-tenant laws, Statute of Frauds, rent control, and constructive eviction.
3. Define assignment, option clause, ground lease, economic rent, and contract rent.
4. Distinguish between subletting and assignment.
5. Explain the processes of setting rents and terminating leases.
6. Discuss the functions of on-site management including collection of rents and property maintenance.
7. List professional organizations and designations.

1. Which of the following statements regarding a leasehold estate is NOT true?
   A. The tenant is known as the lessee.
   B. The landlord holds a reversion during the term of the lease.
   C. The landlord is known as the lessor.
   D. The tenant holds a freehold estate.

2. A lease for a definite period of time, which terminates when that time has expired, is called a(n)
   A. estate for years.   C. estate at will.
   B. periodic estate.   D. estate at sufferance.

3. A lease of fixed length that continually renews itself for like period of time until the lessor or lessee acts to terminate it is a(n)
   A. holdover estate.   C. estate at will.
   B. periodic estate.   D. estate at sufferance.

4. Which of the following leases would be unenforceable in court, unless it were in writing?
   A. Two-week lease of a vacation cottage   C. Three-year commercial lease
   B. Month-to-month lease   D. One-year lease on an apartment

5. An owner leased a building to a tenant under an agreement which gave the tenant the right to occupy the premises for two years, with an option to renew for an additional one-year period. In order to be enforceable, must this lease be in writing and signed by the owner and the tenant?
   A. Yes, because all contracts dealing with real property must be in writing in order to be enforceable.
   B. Yes, because the lease is for a period of time in excess of one year.
   C. No, because oral leases for five years or less are enforceable.
   D. No, because a two-year oral lease is enforceable.

6. To be valid, which of the following must be in writing and signed?
   A. Month-to-month lease
   B. Fourteen-month lease
   C. Three-month lease
   D. One-week vacation rental

7. The right of the lessee to uninterrupted use of the leased premises is called
   A. quiet possession.
   B. quiet enjoyment.
   C. quiet rights.
   D. tenant rights.

8. Under the terms of a one-year lease, the
   A. tenant commits to pay a full year's rent, even if he vacates the premises before the year expires.
   B. landlord commits the property to the tenant for six months, renewable if the rent is current.
   C. tenant can terminate the lease early, if he so chooses.
   D. landlord can terminate the lease early if he sells the building.

9. A written lease agreement is still legal even though it fails to include
   A. the terms of the lease.
   B. a property description.
   C. a stated amount of rent.
   D. an assignment clause.

10. A written lease agreement for a periodic tenancy is still legal even though it fails to include
    A. the amount of rent to be paid.
    B. a security deposit.
    C. starting date and duration of the lease.
    D. signatures of both the tenant and the landlord.

11. A tenant leased an apartment from the landlord under a lease which calls for a total rent of six thousand dollars for the year, but is silent as to when or in what installments the rent is to be paid. Under common law the rent will be due
    A. when the tenant takes possession of the premises.
    B. in equal installments on the first day of each month.
    C. when the lease is signed.
    D. at the end of the year.

12. A landlord can charge and a tenant can expect to pay for
    A. damages to the premises by the tenant.
    B. normal wear and tear to the premises by the tenant.
    C. old and worn drapes.
    D. finders fee.

13. The word "waive" means to
    A. say "good-bye."
    B. demand.
    C. relinquish.
    D. die naturally.

14. Consumer protection laws and courts place the burden of upkeep and repairs of rented premises on the tenant in
    A. commercial leases.
    B. residential leases.
    C. apartment leases.
    D. condo leases.

15. W installed built-in bookcases in his rented apartment without the landlord's permission. All of the following statements are correct EXCEPT
    A. The bookcases became fixtures when installed by W.
    B. W can be held responsible for expenses incurred by the landlord in removing the bookcases upon expiration of the lease.
    C. W forfeited his security deposit by installing the bookcases without the landlord's permission.
    D. The bookcases become the property of the landlord upon expiration of the lease.

16. State-enacted landlord-tenant laws tend to
    A. favor the tenant.
    B. strike a reasonable balance between the rights and responsibilities of both parties.
    C. favor the lessor.
    D. favor the landlord.

17. A lease under which the tenant pays a fixed rent and the landlord pays all the operating expenses is a
    A. net lease.
    B. fixed lease.
    C. term lease.
    D. gross lease.

18. A lease which calls for specified rental increases at predetermined intervals is known as a graduated or
    A. step-up lease.
    B. accelerating lease.
    C. escalating lease.
    D. step-down lease.

19. The clause in a lease which allows a landlord to pass along to the tenant certain increases in operating expenses is called a(n)
    A. escalator clause.
    B. non-participation clause.
    C. graduated lease.
    D. accelerating clause.

20. When the tenant pays a base rent plus some or all of the operating expenses of a property, the result is a
    A. gross lease.
    B. net lease.
    C. percentage lease.
    D. graduated lease.

21. A lease in which the tenant pays a rent based upon the gross sales made from the rented premises is known as a
    A. percentage lease.
    B. participation lease.
    C. net lease.
    D. gross lease.

22. All of the following are specifically designed to protect against rising operating costs EXCEPT
    A. a net lease.
    B. an escalator clause.
    C. an index clause.
    D. a gross lease.

23. In Z's one-year apartment lease, she has a clause that allows her to renew the lease for an additional year at a predetermined rent. This is called a(n)
    A. refusal clause.
    B. option clause.
    C. assignment clause.
    D. sublease clause.

24. J's lease of her apartment is silent as to her right to sublet. May J sublet without the landlord's permission?
    A. Yes, because executory contracts may be assigned unless they contain a non-assignment clause.
    B. Yes, because J would remain responsible to the landlord under the terms of the lease.
    C. No, because the landlord would have the right to veto any assignment.
    D. No, because landlord-tenants laws prohibit the assignment of a lease without the landlord's permission.

25. K signed a one-year lease on an apartment with a rental agency. K sublet the apartment to Z who defaulted on the sublease. Any action entered by the landlord would be against
    A. K.   C. both K and Z.
    B. Z.   D. the rental agent.

26. Under the terms of the typical ground lease, the
    A. lessor is the fee simple owner of the land.
    B. lessor pays for and owns the improvements.
    C. the duration of the lease is usually less than five years.
    D. the lessee rarely records a ground lease.

27. The only way for a tenant to terminate a lease for five years is by
    A. constructive eviction.   C. mutual agreement.
    B. eminent domain.   D. actual eviction.

28. A tenant's business has prospered and she needs an additional warehouse. She wants a five-year lease with an escape available at the end of two years, and she wants to be able to stay in the building for an additional five years if her business continues to need the space. Additionally, she wants protection against unexpected rent increases. Her real estate agent would look for warehouses whose owners would offer a
    A. net lease for the next five years.
    B. two-year lease with an option to renew for three years and an option for five more years.
    C. three-year lease with an option to renew for two years followed by an option to buy.
    D. gross lease for two years followed by a three-year net lease with option to buy.

29. Which of the following statements is NOT correct with regard to the contract rent and economic rent of a property?
    A. The rent that a tenant must pay the landlord is its contract rent.
    B. At the beginning of the lease, the contract rent is usually the same as the economic rent.
    C. The rent which a property can command in the open market is its economic rent.
    D. The contract rent and the economic rent may remain the same throughout the term of the lease.

30. G had a five-year lease on a store building which called for the landlord to provide maintenance on the property. Although he notified the landlord on several occasions of a badly leaking roof, the landlord failed to make the necessary repairs, and G had to cease his operations. At this option, G could
    A. stop paying rent until the roof was repaired.
    B. terminate the lease by claiming constructive eviction.
    C. petition the city to acquire the property through eminent domain.
    D. hire a roofer to do the necessary repairs.

31. A tenant complained to the housing authority regarding lack of maintenance for his apartment. The landlord served the tenant with an eviction notice because of his complaints. This eviction was
    A. a retaliatory eviction.
    B. legal.
    C. good business practice.
    D. dictated by law.

32. A tenant has a lease on a service station which is being taken by the state highway department under eminent domain in order to widen the highway. The state must pay compensation to
    A. the tenant.
    B. the landlord.
    C. both of them.
    D. a neutral third party, in trust.

33. W has a five-year lease on space in an office building. After this lease was recorded in the public records, the landlord secured a new mortgage on the property, on which he later defaulted. When the lender foreclosed on the property, could W's lease be terminated by the purchaser at foreclosure?
    A. Yes, because the foreclosure of a mortgage terminates any leases on the property.
    B. Yes, because the purchaser at foreclosure would have the option of honoring the lease or not doing so.
    C. No, because mortgage foreclosure has no effect on a valid lease.
    D. No, because the lease was recorded prior to the mortgage.

34. Experience with rent controls generally indicates that rent control
    A. solves more problems than it creates.
    B. creates more problems than it solves.
    C. assists landlords with larger rent rolls so that they can properly maintain the buildings.
    D. slows down the conversion of rental units to condominium units.

35. An investor who is contemplating building or buying rental housing will
    A. not compare market rents with operating costs.
    B. capitalize the net income to determine how much to pay for the building.
    C. have to plan on raising the rents to cover debt financing.
    D. not plan on positive cash flow for the first several years.

36. The LEAST effective use of advertising money for rental housing is
    A. newspaper classified advertising.
    B. signs and arrows on and near the property.
    C. radio and television advertising.
    D. referral fees or bonuses to tenants who refer friends to the manager.

37. A lengthy tenant application form
    A. tends to encourage marginally qualified applicants.
    B. provides a basis for checking the applicant's reference.
    C. is necessary to provide documentation for HUD.
    D. is required for low-income housing.

38. Property owners can attract tenants in a soft rental market by
    A. increases in rent.
    B. rent concessions.
    C. lowering maintenance standards.
    D. insisting on longer leases.

39. To retain tenants, a property manager should think of them as
    A. permanent residents, even though turnover is expected.
    B. temporary residents who will leave at the expiration of their leases.
    C. ungrateful people who will lower the living standards of the neighborhood.
    D. unstable people since they cannot afford to buy their own home.

40. A property manager can do much to establish and maintain good relations with tenants through
    A. indifferent attention to repairs and maintenance.
    B. good communications with the tenants.
    C. early morning phone calls before the tenant leaves for work.
    D. oral communication discouraging the use of written memorandums or letters.

41. The best defense against losses from uncollected rent is
    A. a threat of legal action against the delinquent tenant.
    B. careful tenant selection, good service, and a firm policy on rent collections.
    C. actual eviction when the rent is late.
    D. personally visiting the tenant to collect the rent.

42. An on-site resident manager serves as
    A. a maintenance person of the property.
    B. the eyes and ears of the property management company.
    C. a deterrent to crime.
    D. a playground supervisor.

43. Which of the following would be classified as off-site management?
    A. Accounting
    B. Handling tenant complaints
    C. Showing vacant space to prospective tenants
    D. Maintenance work

44. A successful apartment manager needs to be all of the following EXCEPT
    A. experienced in managing people.
    B. handy with tools.
    C. fiscally responsible.
    D. advisor to help tenants manage their finances.

45. The Institute of Real Estate Management is a
    A. government agency.
    B. professional property management organization.
    C. university.
    D. proprietary school.

46. The Institute of Real Estate Management awards the designation
    A. CAM (Certified Apartment Manager).
    B. CPM (Certified Property Manager).
    C. MAI (Member of the Appraisal Institute).
    D. RAM (Resident Apartment Manager).

47. A person who holds the designation Systems Maintenance Administrator has completed required courses offered by the
    A. Building Owners and Managers Institute.
    B. Institute of Real Estate Management.
    C. National Apartment Association.
    D. National Association of Home Builders.

SECTION 17.2: Property Management Problems

1. P leased a retail store to M on a percentage basis. The lease calls for a minimum monthly rental of $5,000 plus 4% of the gross yearly business over $600,000. How much rent would P receive yearly from M, if M did a gross yearly business of $1,100,000?

   $ _____

2. A broker and a condominium unit owner enter into a property management agreement under which the broker is to receive as commission 1/3 of the first month's rent of $600 to find a tenant plus 4% of the monthly gross rent in subsequent months. How much has the broker earned in total commissions after a period of 14 months, if he rents the unit and it remains occupied?

   $ _____

3. A city has a rent control law that says that rents may be increased monthly only by 2 1/4% of the cost of improvements. One landlord made improvements of $2,000 and raised the rent from $405 to $455. How much over the rent control did he go?

   $ _____

4. You have the management contract on a three-unit apartment house building and are to receive 6% of the gross rentals as commission. You collect for one month as follows: $500 for each of two units; $400 for one unit; with $140 paid out in repairs. How much was the net amount paid to the owner's account that month?

   $ _____

5. A broker has just negotiated a lease with options on a warehouse. The lease rent is $8,000 per month for the first two years; followed by an option to renew at $9,000 per month for three years; followed by an option to buy the property for $1,200,000. The broker charges 3% of the gross rent for negotiating leases and 3% on sales. If the tenant rents for five years and then buys, what is the total commission earned by the broker?

   $ _____

Real Estate Appraisal

CHAPTER

18

LEARNING OBJECTIVES

After successful completion of the questions in this chapter, you will be able to:

1. Estimate value based on the market comparison approach.
2. Describe a competitive property analysis and identify when to use a CMA.
3. Apply the cost and income approaches to the determination of value.
4. Explain how the three approaches are used to come up with the appraiser's best estimate.
5. Explain the characteristics and principles of value.
6. Discuss recent appraisal regulation.
7. Identify professional appraisal societies and describe their roles.

1. In order to determine the market value of a parcel of real property, the appraiser assumes that
   A. payment will be made in cash or its equivalent.
   B. time for market exposure will be relatively brief.
   C. either buyer or seller will be fairly inexperienced.
   D. either buyer or seller are being pressured into buying or selling.

2. Generally, in the application of the market comparison approach to value determination, a real estate appraiser looks for data on sales of comparable properties which have occurred within the last
   A. six months.
   B. ten days.
   C. one year.
   D. thirty days.

3. Should an appraiser personally inspect each property used as a comparable sale in making an appraisal by the market comparison approach?
   A. Yes, because physical changes may have occurred since the time of the sale of the comparable.
   B. Yes, to avoid errors in making his appraisal.
   C. No, because the present physical condition of the comparable property is relevant to the appraisal.
   D. No, because a physical inspection of the property is not relevant to the appraisal of the subject property.

4. In making an appraisal using the market approach, an appraiser would choose a similar home with equal amenities
   A. listed by a real estate broker but not yet sold.
   B. sold last week at mortgage foreclosure.
   C. sold under market conditions six months ago.
   D. donated last week to a charitable organization with a life estate held by the donor.

5. When there are more comparable properties than an appraiser needs, he should
   A. choose those that require the most adjustments.
   B. choose those that require the fewest adjustments.
   C. utilize all comparables he can find.
   D. choose the one best comparable and discard all the others.

6. A seller listed his home for sale at $100,000 and received a $95,000 offer to purchase from a qualified prospect. All of the following statements are true EXCEPT
   A. The probable upper limit of value on this property is approximately $100,000.
   B. The lower limit of value for this property is probably about $95,000.
   C. The market value of the property is probably between $95,000 and $100,000.
   D. The market value cannot be established unless there are two or more offers.

7. Adjustments for differences between the subject property and comparable property are made to
   A. the subject property.
   B. the comparable property.
   C. either property as indicated by the appraiser's findings.
   D. the appraiser's final estimate of the value of the subject property.

8. In making a market comparison approach appraisal of a residence, the appraiser would NOT make any adjustments for
   A. date of sale of the comparable.
   B. terms of sale of the comparable.
   C. improvements made to a comparable after it was sold.
   D. amenities.

9. In making an appraisal of a single family residence in a neighborhood where values have risen at an average rate of 6% per year over the past two years, what amount would be added to the value of a comparable which was sold six months ago for $80,000?
   A. $240   C. $2,400
   B. $480   D. $4,800

10. In the process of appraising an office building, an appraiser has located a comparable office building which is 240 square feet larger than the subject property. The appraiser estimates construction costs to be $80/sq. ft. and depreciation to be 10%. When the adjustments are made, the value of the
   A. comparable would be reduced by $17,280.
   B. subject property would be increased by $19,200.
   C. comparable would be reduced by $19,200.
   D. subject property would be increased by $17,280.

11. In the market comparison approach to appraisal, adjustments must be made for differences in all the items below EXCEPT
    A. building age, condition, and quality.
    B. landscaping, lot features, and location.
    C. terms and conditions of sale.
    D. acquisition costs to the present owner.

12. In a temperate climate not subject to extreme weather conditions, is any adjustment necessary in appraising a house which has a two-car garage as compared to a similar house with a two-car carport?
    A. No, as long as they both accommodate two cars.
    B. No, because both provide adequate shelter for cars.
    C. Yes, if buyers will pay more for a garage.
    D. Yes, because a garage costs more to build than a carport.

13. Adjustments for advantageous financing would be made in the
    A. market comparison approach to appraisal.
    B. cost approach to appraisal.
    C. income approach to appraisal.
    D. capitalization approach to appraisal.

14. After all adjustments are made to a comparable property, its comparative value for appraisal purposes is known as its
    A. adjusted market price.   C. amended market price.
    B. indicated market price.   D. revised market price.

15. In completing an appraisal by the market comparison approach, the process by which comparables are weighted according to similarity to the subject property is known as the
    A. adjustment process.   C. reconciliation process.
    B. correlation process.   D. weighing process.

16. The value of vacant land is commonly stated in any of the following terms EXCEPT value per
    A. square foot.   C. front foot.
    B. acre.   D. square yard.

17. Two vacant, adjacent lots are being appraised. They each have the same street frontage, but one is twice the depth of the other. The lot with the greater depth will be appraised at
    A. twice the value of the other.
    B. the same value as the other.
    C. half the value of the other.
    D. more than the value of the smaller lot but less than twice the value of the other.

18. In making a market comparison appraisal of vacant lots,
    A. only lots of similar zoning should be employed.
    B. zoning is not important, since zoning laws allow for changes in zoning.
    C. lots with different zoning may be used in a pinch.
    D. lots with different zoning should be used.

19. A competitive market analysis provides a listing agent with all of the following EXCEPT a(n)
    A. guide to the probable sale price of a property.
    B. effective tool for listing a property at a price that will bring about a sale.
    C. basis for determining whether to accept a listing.
    D. appraisal acceptable to a lender.

20. Seller motivation is considered most in the
    A. income approach.
    B. cost approach.
    C. gross rent multiplier method.
    D. competitive market analysis method.

21. Which of the following approaches is most likely to provide only a rough estimate of the value of a rental property?
    A. Cost approach   C. Market comparison approach
    B. Income approach   D. Gross rent multiplier

22. You are appraising a ten-unit apartment building where each unit rents for $450 per month. Three similar apartment buildings have recently sold at the following prices and with the monthly total building rents as shown. Using the gross rent multiplier method, what gross rent multiplier would you apply to the ten-unit building you are appraising?

Sale Price:	$450,000	$382,500	$427,500
Total Monthly Rent:	$5,000	$4,250	$4,750

    A. .0111   C. 9.0
    B. 7.5   D. 90.0

23. Same facts as in question 22 above. Using the gross rent multiplier method, what is the estimated value of the ten-unit building you are appraising?
    A. $33,750   C. $405,000
    B. $337,500   D. $486,000

24. An appraisal by the cost approach will include all of the following EXCEPT
    A. an estimate of the value of the land as if it were vacant.
    B. reproduction or replacement cost of the buildings.
    C. depreciation on the land.
    D. depreciation on the improvements.

25. In appraising a historically significant residence built in the Victorian era using the cost approach, an appraiser will probably appraise it on the basis of its
    A. reproduction cost.   C. replacement cost.
    B. restoration cost.   D. reconstruction cost.

26. What would be the indicated value of a new residence, rectangular in shape measuring 40' by 45', with an attached garage which measured 20' by 20', if construction costs for the dwelling were $60 per square foot and for the garage $30 per square foot?
    A. $108,000   C. $118,000
    B. $112,000   D. $120,000

27. An appraiser is valuing a residence located in an industrial neighborhood. The residence contains four bedrooms, one bath, and is presently in need of a new roof. The property exhibits all the following EXCEPT
    A. physical deterioration.
    B. economic obsolescence on the building.
    C. functional obsolescence on the building.
    D. economic obsolescence on the land.

28. A home in a residential neighborhood is in excellent condition, but which has a poorly designed floor plan, is suffering from
    A. curable depreciation.   C. physical deterioration.
    B. incurable depreciation.   D. economic obsolescence.

29. Which of the following results from factors outside the property?
    A. Functional obsolescence
    B. Physical deterioration
    C. Economic obsolescence
    D. Curable depreciation

30. In applying the income approach to real property, the appraiser is NOT likely to consider
    A. the amount of income produced by the property.
    B. the rate of return demanded by investors.
    C. how long the investment will produce income.
    D. the original cost of the building.

31. The conversion of future income into present value is known as
    A. capitalization.
    B. amortization.
    C. hypothecation.
    D. appreciation.

32. Four students are in an appraisal course. In completing a problem using the income approach, each student used a different cap rate: 8.5%, 9%, 9.5%, and 10%. Which cap rate will produce the highest indicated value for the property?
    A. 8.5%
    B. 9%
    C. 9.5%
    D. 10%

33. What would be the indicated value of a property having an income of $1,200 per month, using a capitalization rate of 11%, rounded to the nearest $100 increment?
    A. $10,900
    B. $15,400
    C. $130,900
    D. $109,900

34. The rents that a property can be expected to produce on an annual basis may be referred to as the scheduled gross or
    A. projected gross income.
    B. effective gross income.
    C. net operating income.
    D. capitalized income.

35. To project the gross income and expenses of a building, the best starting point is
    A. its projected income and expenses for the current year.
    B. the actual record of income and expenses for the past three to five years.
    C. the projected income for the next three to five years.
    D. the projected income for the remaining economic life of the building.

36. In income and expense forecasts, a small error in income projections results in
    A. a larger error in the market value of the property.
    B. an equal error in the market value of the property.
    C. a smaller error in the market value of the property.
    D. no error in the market value of the property.

37. A projected annual operating statement for a rented building would NOT include
    A. property taxes.
    B. insurance premiums.
    C. capital improvements.
    D. utilities.

38. Replacement reserves are set up for items in a building that must be replaced
    A. annually.
    B. more than once in the building's life, but not annually.
    C. only once during the life of a building.
    D. at unpredictable intervals during the building's life.

39. The operating expense ratio of a building is determined by dividing the total operating expenses by the
    A. effective net income.
    B. net operating income.
    C. effective gross income.
    D. actual gross income.

40. Regarding the choice of appraisal approaches, which of the following is a correct statement?
    A. All appraisal approaches are suitable for any type of real property.
    B. The market comparison approach is usually the best method of appraising an apartment building.
    C. Special-purpose buildings are usually best appraised by the cost approach.
    D. The income approach is usually the best method for residential properties.

41. The actual selling price of a property is determined by the
    A. buyer and seller.
    B. seller and appraiser.
    C. appraiser only.
    D. buyer and appraiser.

42. The Appraisal Foundation is a
    A. government agency.
    B. quasi-government agency.
    C. private organization.
    D. affiliate of the National Association of Realtors.

43. The new FIRREA legislation requires that appraisal reports
    A. identify and describe the real estate being appraised.
    B. state the purpose of the appraisal.
    C. define the value to be estimated.
    D. the amount of the fee paid for the appraisal.

44. Standards for review appraisals and reporting were developed by
    A. the Appraisal Foundation.
    B. FIRREA.
    C. the Appraisal Institute.
    D. the National Association of Realtors.

45. A real estate analysis is
    A. the same as an appraisal.
    B. the process of estimating value.
    C. a step-by-step presentation of the facts used by the appraiser to set a value.
    D. a process of providing information on diversified problems in real estate.

46 The use of a property which will give it its greatest current value is its
    A. highest use.
    B. best use.
    C. highest and best use.
    D. substitution.

47. The principle stating that the maximum value of a property tends to be set by the cost of acquiring another equally desirable property is known as the principle of
    A. anticipation.
    B. subrogation.
    C. highest and best use.
    D. substitution.

48. A real estate salesperson gave an owner an off-hand estimate of the value of his home. Relying on this information, the owner listed with the salesperson's broker and contracted to sell the home at the salesperson's estimated value. The property was later appraised by a qualified appraiser for a substantially larger amount. The broker would
    A. not be subject to disciplinary action by the real estate department since the broker hadn't actually made the error.
    B. be liable for civil damages to the property owner.
    C. be complimented for shrewd business dealings (list low, sell quickly).
    D. be eligible to collect a commission for the sale.

49. The principle which refers to the ability of people to pay for land coupled with the relative scarcity of land is known as the principle of
    A. substitution.   C. competition.
    B. supply and demand.   D. diminishing returns.

50. The principle which holds that maximum value is realized when a reasonable degree of homogeneity is present in a neighborhood is known as the principle of
    A. harmony.   C. similarity.
    B. homogeneity.   D. conformity.

51. May a property have different values if the purposes of the appraisal from two or more appraisals are not the same?
    A. Yes, because value is affected by the purpose of the appraisal.
    B. Yes, because not all appraisers see the property in the same light.
    C. No, because a property has only one value at any given time.
    D. No, because the purpose of the appraisal does not affect its value.

52. The process of combining two or more parcels of land into one larger parcel is called
    A. assemblage.   C. salvage.
    B. plottage.   D. reproduction.

53. If two parcels are combined into one larger parcel that is worth more than the total value of the individual parcels, that added value is called
    A. adage.   C. rentage.
    B. estatage.   D. plottage.

54. A market where there is an excess of supply over demand is known as
    A. buyer's market.   C. seller's market.
    B. broad market.   D. thin market.

55. A city with a population of 100,000 has one small lake on which there are twelve houses. Turnover of these houses averages less than one house per year. Can the market for these lake front houses be described as thin?
    A. Yes, because there will be much demand for so few houses.
    B. Yes, because there are few houses and little turnover each year.
    C. No, because this situation describes a broad market.
    D. No, because this situation describes a buyer's market.

56. The appraisal designation MAI stands for
    A. Master Appraisal Instructor.   C. Member of the Appraisal Institute.
    B. Master Appraisal Institute.   D. Mentor, Appraiser Institute.

SECTION 18.2: Appraisal Problems

1. It cost a builder $80,000 to build a house several years ago. Since then, building costs have risen 45% and then decreased 12% below this high point. How much would it cost him to build this same house today?

   $ _____

2. An appraiser determines the replacement cost of a house to be $76,000 at today's prices. He has estimated its present value to be $63,080. What was the percent of depreciation determined by the appraiser?

   _____

3. A man has 117 acres of soybeans that net him $29,250 per year. If land like this is capitalized at 10%, what is his land worth per acre?

   $ _____

4. A builder buys land for $90,000, spends $150,000 for a street, $1,935,000 for a 25-unit condominium structure, and $135,000 for miscellaneous items. He borrowed all the money for 12% per annum for ten months. If he wants to make a 15% profit, for how much must he sell each unit?

   $ _____

5. A home is presently valued at $112,000. What was its previous sales price if it has appreciated 12% since then?

   $ _____

6. On a 110' × 200' lot, a two-story building will be built. Each floor will be 80' × 95' and will cost $38 per square foot. Landscaping will cost $5.00 per square foot exclusive of the building. The land costs $430 per front foot. What will be the total cost of the project?

   $ _____

7. An investor wants to purchase a 10-unit apartment building where 5 units rent for $350 per month and 5 units rent for $400 per month. How much should he pay for the building if monthly operating expenses amount to $1,250, and he wants to earn 8% on his investment?

   $ _____

8. A property earns $900,000 per year and has expenses of 45% of that amount. If the property is capitalized at 12%, what is its value?

   $ _____

Licensing Laws and Professional Affiliation

LEARNING OBJECTIVES

After successful completion of the questions in this chapter, you will be able to:

1. Distinguish among broker and salesperson licensees, and the affiliation one may have with a broker.
2. Explain the role of a state real estate commission or department.
3. Describe nonresident licensing and business firm licensing.
4. List and explain those violations which could lead to license suspension or revocation.
5. Recognize the purpose of a recovery fund, bonds, and a securities license.
6. Discuss the independent contractor issue.
7. Describe the role of the various professional real estate associations.

1. Real estate licensing laws represent a government's effort to ascertain that real estate brokers and salespersons are all of the following EXCEPT
   A. persons of good reputation as to honesty and truthfulness.
   B. competent in real estate knowledge.
   C. knowledgeable about home heating and air conditioning systems.
   D. aware of basic financing.

2. Which one of the following people is required to have a real estate license in order to sell real estate?
   A. Attorney at law
   B. Executor of an estate
   C. Trustee under a deed of trust
   D. Real estate appraiser

3. A real estate broker differs from a real estate salesperson under the law in that
   A. the broker may act independently in conducting a brokerage business.
   B. a salesperson may operate in the brokerage business independently from the supervision of a real estate broker.
   C. higher educational standards are required for a real estate agent.
   D. a salesperson will not be disciplined for wrongdoing, only the broker will.

4. A person who holds a real estate license is a
   A. licensor.
   B. licensee.
   C. vestee.
   D. vestor.

5. A woman owns no real property other than her home and does not hold a real estate license. She told her friends that she was planning to sell her home herself, and they gave her the following advice. Which of these statements is true?
   A. The law does not permit her to sell her home unless she first passes a state administrated real estate exam.
   B. She can sell her home without a real estate license only if she first appoints herself as a trustee for her property.
   C. Only after taking a consumer education course on selling real estate may she market and sell her home without a real estate license.
   D. She can sell her home without holding a real estate license.

6. A real estate listing is a contract between the
   A. owner and the listing broker.
   B. owner, the broker, and the listing salesperson.
   C. owner and the listing salesperson.
   D. broker and the listing salesperson.

7. The ultimate responsibility for a mistake in a document prepared by a real estate salesperson rests
   A. equally upon the salesperson and the employing broker.
   B. upon the employing broker.
   C. only on the salesperson.
   D. the salesperson and his client.

8. Before being granted a salesperson's license, an applicant must do all of the following EXCEPT
   A. pass the examination for salesperson licensure.
   B. name the broker with whom the applicant will be associated or be inactive.
   C. demonstrate competency by obtaining a real estate listing.
   D. complete any state-mandated education requirements.

9. A person who has met all pre-license requirements for licensure may operate as a real estate salesperson upon
   A. notification of having passed the examination.
   B. affiliation with a licensed real estate broker.
   C. filing an application for licensure.
   D. receipt of the license by the employing broker.

10. After licensure as a real estate broker or salesperson, a licensee must, in order to maintain the license, do all of the following EXCEPT
    A. meet any continuing education requirements.
    B. retake the original license examination and pass it.
    C. pay license renewal fees.
    D. renew the license prior to the expiration of any allowable grace period.

11. License examinations which are prepared and administered by a national testing service will NOT include questions based on
    A. general principles of real estate practice.
    B. real estate laws, regulations, and practices of the jurisdiction where the exam is being given.
    C. specific accounting practices relating to all aspects of tax laws.
    D. federal laws pertaining to fair housing, financing, and consumer protection.

12. In most states, it would be illegal for a broker to share a commission with
    A. a salesperson licensed in his employ.
    B. a broker licensed in another state.
    C. another broker licensed in his state of licensure.
    D. a salesperson licensed with another broker in his state of licensure.

13. A broker who wishes to operate outside his home state will usually be required to file a notice of consent with the Secretary of State in
    A. his home state.
    B. each state in which he wishes to operate.
    C. Washington, D.C.
    D. any state.

14. All of the following would be classified as doing business under a fictitious name EXCEPT
    A. John Smith, Real Estate Broker
    B. The John Smith Real Estate Company
    C. Smith Realty
    D. Smith's Real Estate Professionals

15. For a corporation to be granted a license as a real estate broker,
    A. all officers must be licensed as real estate brokers.
    B. all stockholders must be licensees.
    C. the chief executive officer must be a licensed broker.
    D. salespersons may NOT hold office in the corporation.

16. In most states, a licensed brokerage firm
    A. may not operate a branch office license in the firm's name.
    B. may operate a branch office if it is managed by a licensed real estate broker.
    C. can manage a branch office "from a distance."
    D. can open a branch office but all client funds must be deposited in the home office trust account.

17. The requirement that a real estate agent hold a real estate license is set by the
    A. real estate commission.   C. real estate director or commissioner.
    B. legislature.   D. governor.

18. In most states, members of the real estate commission are
    A. full-time employees appointed by the governor.
    B. all licensed real estate agents.
    C. state civil service employees.
    D. appointed volunteers who may or may not hold a real estate license.

19. The staff of the real estate department or real estate division of most states do all of the following EXCEPT
    A. establish regulations governing license applicants.
    B. are full-time civil servants.
    C. investigate complaints regarding licensees.
    D. perform administrative functions of the department or division.

20. A licensee was found guilty of violating real estate license law at a formal hearing before the real estate commission. The LEAST that the licensee can expect is
    A. the revocation of his license.
    B. making an appeal by the licensee before a court of competent jurisdiction.
    C. receiving a public reprimand.
    D. receiving a commission fee for the subject transaction.

21. Protection against financial losses suffered by a party who was the victim of a licensee's wrongful acts may be provided by
    A. bonding requirements for sellers and buyers.
    B. state-sponsored recovery funds.
    C. the local association of REALTORS®.
    D. suing the licensor for damages.

22. Real estate agents who deal in real estate partnerships, timeshare units, rental pools, etc., may find that they will also be required to obtain
    A. an investment counselor's license.   C. a money manager's license.
    B. a securities license.   D. a social security license.

23. Among the considerations to be resolved before deciding to become a real estate agent are
    A. uncertain earnings from commission-only compensation plans.
    B. regular working hours.
    C. close supervision by the employing broker.
    D. limited opportunities to make money.

24. A new real estate salesperson will most effectively use his/her time looking for
    A. a broker that pays a salary or guarantee.
    B. a 100% commission office.
    C. the best possible commission split.
    D. an office that provides sales training.

25. For a real estate salesperson to be considered an independent contractor, all of the following conditions must be met EXCEPT
    A. the associate must be a licensed real estate agent.
    B. compensation must be based on sales production.
    C. there must be a written agreement setting forth the associate's independent contractor status.
    D. the broker must withhold federal income taxes and social security contributions from the associate's earnings.

26. Affiliation with a national network of franchised real estate brokerage most appeals to
    A. firms having from 10 to 50 salespeople.
    B. large national real estate firms.
    C. firms of over 200 salespeople.
    D. small firms of less than 10 salespeople.

27. The term "REALTOR®" applies to any
    A. licensed real estate salesperson.
    B. licensed real estate broker.
    C. member of a state real estate commission.
    D. member of the National Association of REALTORS®.

28. The REALTORS®' Code of Ethics covers a REALTOR®'s relations with
    A. his clients.
    B. the general public.
    C. fellow REALTORS®.
    D. each of the above.

29. Membership in institutes such as the REALTORS®' National Marketing Institute and the Farm and Land Institute
    A. is open to any licensed real estate broker or salesperson.
    B. requires membership in the National Association of REALTORS®.
    C. is open to any person.
    D. is automatically granted to a member of the National Association of REALTORS®.

30. A real estate broker violating a provision of the license law
    A. is entitled to a commission if one is involved.
    B. could have his license revoked.
    C. will not have to pay a fine.
    D. will not be concerned about a public reprimand.

31. The state's real estate department, division or board is empowered to take legal action against all of the following EXCEPT
    A. licensed real estate brokers.
    B. licensed real estate salespersons.
    C. an unlicensed person who violates the fair housing laws.
    D. a person who acts as a licensee without a license.

32. W, who is not licensed to sell real estate, rented his neighbor's house to a friend. The neighbor took W to dinner as promised. Did W violate real estate licensing law?
    A. Yes, because there was compensation involved.
    B. No, because the compensation was minor.
    C. No, because the compensation was not money.
    D. No, because they were friends.

33. Which of the following could legally receive compensation for selling real estate on behalf of another person without a license as a broker or salesperson?
    A. Licensed real estate appraiser
    B. Executor of an estate
    C. Resident manager of an apartment house
    D. Licensed auctioneer

34. A telephone answering service for a broker's office may do which of the following?
    A. Give information to a caller about listings available
    B. Take a listing by telephone
    C. Ask qualifying questions of the prospective buyer
    D. Take down the caller's name and phone number

35. Real estate regulations set the minimum commission to be charged as
    A. 3%.
    B. 4%.
    C. 6%.
    D. there is no minimum set.

36. A real estate listing may be advertised only in the name of the
    A. cooperating broker.
    B. salesperson who obtains the listing.
    C. principal licensed broker.
    D. real estate salesperson on the premise.

37. A broker's license is revoked for one year. His two salespersons, who are not the cause of the revocation,
    A. must be placed on inactive status during that time.
    B. may, upon proper application, transfer to another broker.
    C. would lose their licenses for one year.
    D. may continue to operate the broker's business.

38. A builder desires to employ a licensed salesperson on commission to sell houses built by him. The builder must
    A. obtain a salesperson's license.
    B. notify the state of the contract between himself and the salesperson.
    C. obtain a broker's license.
    D. pay the salesperson less than the usual commission.

39. When a broker discharges a salesperson, he should
    A. give the salesperson his license.
    B. return the license to the real estate department, division or board.
    C. remove the license from the wall and keep it on file until all of the salesperson's deals have been closed out.
    D. instruct the salesperson to return his license to the real estate commission.

40. A license may be revoked upon proof of
    A. dispute between broker and salesperson as to a commission.
    B. continued misrepresentations.
    C. refusal to accept an overpriced listing.
    D. not selling enough real estate.

41. A woman who is studying for her real estate license has taken a job as a receptionist at a real estate office. One afternoon, while all the sales personnel are out, a man comes into the office and asks for the price of a property on which her company has a "For Sale" sign. She recognizes the value of a new client and wants to be as helpful as possible. By law, she can
    A. tell the man the price and terms as listed, but not show the property or write up an offer.
    B. tell the man the price only and ask him to come back.
    C. hand him a copy of the listing.
    D. say nothing about the price and terms and ask how he can be contacted by a sales-person.

42. Members of a national trade association representing minority real estate professionals use the trade name
    A. Appraiser.   C. NARES.
    B. GRI.   D. Realtist.

The Principal–Broker Relationship: Employment

20

LEARNING OBJECTIVES

After successful completion of the questions in this chapter, you will be able to:

1. Identify the various kinds of listings.
2. Explain the purpose behind the exclusive authority to purchase.
3. Describe the multiple listing service, the listing period, and agent's authority.
4. Define procuring cause and explain the principle of earning commission.
5. Explain how to terminate a listing contract.
6. Discuss alternative listing brokers.
7. Calculate commissions.

1. A real estate listing
   A. is an employment contract between a property owner and real estate broker.
   B. authorizes a real estate broker to sell and convey title to an owner's real estate.
   C. is an employment contract between the salesperson and owner of the property.
   D. permits a real estate broker to authorize repairs and remodeling if he determines that such work will make the property more marketable.

2. All of the following statements are true EXCEPT
   A. a listing is a contract between an owner and the listing salesperson.
   B. the broker is legally liable for the proper execution of a listing contract.
   C. sales associates may advertise the listings in the name of their broker.
   D. sales associates operate under the authority of an employing broker's license.

3. A sales associate secured a written listing on a property for sale, signed by the owner and the employing broker. Is this an enforceable listing contract?
   A. Yes, because the broker is a licensed agent.
   B. Yes, if all essential elements of a listing contract are present.
   C. No, because no contract exists until the property is sold.
   D. No, because no consideration will be paid until the property is sold.

4. A typical exclusive right to sell listing binds the owner to all of the following EXCEPT
   A. exclude other brokers from advertising or placing a sign on the property.
   B. pay a commission if a purchaser is found who agrees to buy at the price and terms stipulated in the listing.
   C. pay a commission to the broker even if the owner finds the buyer.
   D. relieves the owner from paying a commission if the owner finds the buyer.

5. Under the terms of an advance fee listing, the listing broker receives
   A. an hourly fee for time spent in selling the property.
   B. no compensation for out-of-pocket expenses.
   C. any amount received over the seller's net price.
   D. nothing when the house actually sells.

6. The amount of commission to be paid the broker for selling a property is
   A. set by state law.
   B. negotiated at the time a buyer is found.
   C. set forth in the rules of the state real estate commission.
   D. stated in the listing contract.

7. Which of the following is NOT true of an exclusive right to sell listing?
   A. Brokers will usually exert maximum sales effort under this type of listing.
   B. The broker receives a commission regardless of whether the property is sold.
   C. The broker is due a commission even if the owner sells the property himself.
   D. The property may not be listed with another broker during the listing period.

8. An exclusive agency listing
   A. permits the owner to sell by his own efforts without liability to pay a commission to the listing broker.
   B. allows the owner to list concurrently with other brokers.
   C. requires the owner to pay a commission to the broker even if the owner found the buyer.
   D. is the most advantageous to the real estate broker.

9. An owner gave an open listing to brokers S, J, and M. S advertised the property for sale. J showed it to several prospects. M secured an acceptable offer from the only person to whom he showed the property. Which of the following statements is correct?
   A. The commission would be divided among S, J, and M.
   B. The owner is liable to broker S for the advertising expense.
   C. If the owner had found a buyer through his own efforts, he would be liable for a commission to each broker.
   D. M is due a commission if the owner accepts the offer to purchase.

10. All of the following are true of net listings EXCEPT
    A. many states prohibit a broker from accepting a net listing.
    B. most brokers are reluctant to accept them, even when permitted to do so.
    C. all net listings are open listings.
    D. the commission is the excess above the seller's net price.

11. An owner wants to list his home for $100,000 with a broker at 6% commission and at the same time advertise it himself for $96,000. He feels that if he can sell it on his own he will be money ahead even though the price is lower. Legally, the owner can do this if he signs a(n)
    A. exclusive right to sell listing.   C. any listing agreement.
    B. exclusive agency listing.   D. net listing.

12. A broker secured a written listing agreement on a property. He later found a buyer who was ready, willing, and able to buy at the price and terms stated in the listing contract, but the owner refused to sign a sales agreement because of animosity toward the buyer. Is the broker entitled to a commission even though no sale was consummated?
    A. Yes, because a commission was earned when the listing was signed.
    B. Yes, because the broker produced a ready, willing, and able buyer at the price and terms requested in the listing.
    C. No, because no sales contract was signed by the owner.
    D. No, because there was not an offer and acceptance.

13. An advance cost listing differs from an advance fee listing in that
    A. the broker is due compensation for out-of-pocket expenses, but no hourly fee.
    B. the commission will not be based on the sales price.
    C. the seller sets a minimum net price and the broker gets anything over that.
    D. the broker is unlikely to cooperate with other brokers.

14. Under the terms of a multiple listing agreement, if a broker other than the listing broker sells the property, the owner
    A. may be liable for two commissions on the sale.
    B. may sell of his own efforts without any obligation to pay a commission.
    C. need not pay a commission to the listing agent.
    D. pays one commission which is divided between the listing and selling brokers.

15. The advantages of a multiple listing arrangement include
    A. greater market exposure of the property.
    B. the possibility of a lower sales price.
    C. a slower sale.
    D. less market exposure of the property.

16. A broker secured a "no sale, no commission" listing on a property, signed by the owner and the broker. A buyer was found who was ready, willing, and able to buy, and a sales agreement was signed by both buyer and seller. The sales agreement was later canceled arbitrarily by the seller. Is the seller liable for a commission to the broker?
    A. Yes, but only for half the commission.
    B. Yes, because the cancellation was arbitrary on his part.
    C. No, because the sale was not closed.
    D. No, because this type of contract is not enforceable.

17. Under the terms of an exclusive agency listing, the broker showed a property to a prospect and notified the seller of the showing. The prospect then approached the seller directly and bought the property at a lower price using a "straw-man" to hide the buyer's identity from the broker. Can the broker recover a commission on this sale?
    A. Yes, because he was the procuring cause of the sale.
    B. Yes, because the property was sold during the listing period.
    C. No, because the owner has the right to sell by his own efforts without payment of a commission.
    D. No, because he did not introduce the straw-man to the property.

18. When a property under an open listing is shown to a prospect by two different brokers and a sale results, the commission is
    A. payable to the broker who first showed the property to the buyer.
    B. divided between the two brokers.
    C. payable to the broker who actually made the sale.
    D. payable in full to each broker.

19. An exclusive listing contract with a definite termination date may be terminated by all of the following EXCEPT
    A. distribution of the property.
    B. death of the listing agent.
    C. expiration.
    D. mutual agreement.

20. If a purchaser arbitrarily defaults on a purchase contract, any earnest money previously paid, in the absence of an agreement to the contrary, will be
    A. paid to the broker as compensation for his efforts.
    B. divided between the broker and the owner/seller.
    C. returned to the purchaser.
    D. paid to the owner/seller.

21. Which of the following is most likely to accept only listings that he thinks will sell quickly?
    A. Flat-fee brokers
    B. Full-service brokers
    C. Discount brokers
    D. Self-help brokers

22. Sometimes homeowners attempt to sell their property themselves without the aid of a broker because the
    A. broker would expose the property to too many prospective buyers.
    B. sales commission would consume too much of their equity in the property.
    C. homeowner doesn't want to have the broker's sign in his yard.
    D. broker would screen out unqualified buyers.

23. In the case of an exclusive authority to purchase, the
    A. broker has a responsibility to the purchaser rather than to the seller.
    B. buyer must be cautious when discussing personal finances with his agent.
    C. principal needs to be assured as to the scope of employment of the broker.
    D. purchaser should distrust the broker's expertise and competence.

24. An agent received a 3% commission on one-fourth of her total sales. On the remainder she received a 6% commission. What was her average commission for all of her sales?
    A. 4.25%
    B. 4.5%
    C. 5.25%
    D. 5.75%

25. Three properties sold for a total of $120,000. The gross commission is 8%. Office policy is to give 10% of all commissions to the office manager. The balance is then divided, giving 45% to the office and the remainder to the salesperson who listed and sold the property. How much did the salesperson earn?
    A. $960
    B. $4,752
    C. $5,400
    D. $9,600

26. A rental agency receives one-third of the first month's rent and 3.5% of each month's rent after that. If the agency leases the apartment for one year at $360 per month, how much does the rental agent get?
    A. $12.60
    B. $138.60
    C. $258.60
    D. $271.20

27. A vacant lot was purchased three years ago for $35,000. It was recently listed for sale at a price 20% greater than that. If the seller accepts an offer that is $3,000 below list price, what would she receive after paying the 6% commission?
    A. $36,480
    B. $36,660
    C. $36,900
    D. $439,480

28. A broker charges 6% on the first $100,000, 5% on the next $100,000, 4% on the next $200,000 and 3% above that. On a $1,000,000 sale, what will be the commission?
    A. $30,000
    B. $37,000
    C. $60,000
    D. $463,000

29. In order for the seller to net $100,000 after paying a real estate commission of 7%, how much does the property have to sell for?
    A. $107,000
    B. $107,527
    C. $110,000
    D. $112,000

30. A broker listed a house for $120,000 with the seller agreeing to pay a 7% commission. The seller agreed to accept $112,500 and then asked the broker to cut his commission. The broker replied that the seller was already cutting the broker's commission by accepting the lower sale price. How much less did the broker receive with the lower sale price.
    A. $262.50
    B. $525
    C. $7,875
    D. $8,400

SECTION 20.2: Commission Calculations

Answer the following questions assuming a list price of $94,500, a sales commission rate of 6%, and existing first mortgage of $57,150.

1. If the property sells for the listed price and the buyer assumes the existing first mortgage, how much commission is due the listing broker?

    $ _____

2. If a prospect is found who offers $93,000 and the owners accept, how much commission will the listing broker receive?

    $ _____

3. If the sellers say they will take a net of $88,000 after paying a 6% commission, for how much must the property sell?

    $ _____

4. On properties that are listed and sold by this company, it deducts a $100 multiple listing fee from the commission received and then splits the balance 25% to the listing sales associate, 45% to the selling associate, and 30% to the company. If the property sells for $94,000, how much does each of the following receive?

    Listing sales associate $ _____

    Selling sales associate $ _____

    The company $ _____

5. On properties that are listed by this real estate company and sold by another broker, a $100 MLS fee is deducted from the commission and the balance is split 25% to the listing sales associate, 25% to the company, and 50% to the selling broker. If the property sells for $94,200, how much do the following receive?

    Listing sales associate $ _____

    Selling broker $ _____

    The company $ _____

6. Continuing question #5, at the selling broker's office, commissions from the sale of properties listed with other brokers result in a 50–50 split between the broker's office and the sales associate. How much does each receive?

Cooperating broker $ _____

Selling sales associate $ _____

7. If the salesperson who listed and sold this property at the first company received $3,927 and that represented 70% of the 6% commission collected from the seller, how much did the property sell for?

$ _____

The Principal-Broker Relationship: Agency

LEARNING OBJECTIVES

After successful completion of the questions in this chapter, you will be able to:

1. Define the different types of agency authority.
2. List the duties of a licensee to his principal as well as to third parties.
3. Discuss the obligations of the principal to the agent.
4. Explain the duties of the agent to third parties.
5. Discuss the pitfalls of dual agency.
6. Explain the concept of buyer agency.
7. Discuss Interstate Land Sales Disclosure Statements, federal anti-trust laws, and the need for errors and omissions insurance.

---

1. In a listing situation, a broker owes certain duties to his principal. In return, the principal is responsible for
   A. loyalty to the broker.
   B. obeying the broker's instructions.
   C. maintaining the property.
   D. accounting of money and property.

2. When an agent is given the right to transact all types of matters on behalf of the principal, he serves as a
   A. notary public.
   B. third party.
   C. universal agent.
   D. special agent.

3. An agent who is authorized to bind his employer in a trade or business is a(n)
   A. special agent.
   B. general agent.
   C. exclusive agent.
   D. principal agent.

4. The real estate broker's relationship to the owner of property listed for sale with the broker is that of a(n)
   A. general agent.
   B. universal agent.
   C. limited agent.
   D. special agent.

5. Which of the following is true about listing contracts?
   A. A corporation may be an agent.
   B. A natural person may be an agent.
   C. A sales associate may be an agent.
   D. A broker is agent for the principal.

6. When an agent's authority arises from custom in the industry, it is identified as
   A. implied authority.
   B. ostensible authority.
   C. customary authority.
   D. conventional authority.

7. A broker owes fiduciary responsibilities to
   A. the owner of the property listed by him.
   B. third parties with whom he deals.
   C. his sales associates.
   D. his attorney.

8. A broker was part owner of an apartment building along with two co-owners. When they decided to sell the building, the broker was named as the agent in the listing agreement. The broker thus held an agency
   A. by ratification.
   B. coupled with an interest.
   C. by estoppal.
   D. by implication.

9. Fiduciary responsibilities of an agent to his principal include all of the following EXCEPT
   A. faithful performance.
   B. loyalty.
   C. accounting for funds or property received.
   D. provision of legal advice.

10. When a broker acts as an agent for both purchaser and seller in a single transaction, it is known as a(n)
    A. agency by estoppal.
    B. dual agency.
    C. agency coupled with an interest.
    D. agency by ratification.

11. A broker may act as an agent for both parties in a single transaction only with the permission of
    A. the property owner.
    B. the real estate commission.
    C. both parties.
    D. the purchaser.

12. K introduced an owner to a prospective buyer. The owner and prospect conducted negotiations between themselves without the assistance from K. The role of K was that of a
    A. dual agent.
    B. middleman.
    C. single agent.
    D. cooperating broker.

13. What should the broker do with earnest money if the seller defaults?
    A. Keep it; he earned the commission
    B. Return it to the buyer
    C. Place it into an attorney's trust account
    D. Turn it over to the seller

14. The placing of funds belonging to others in a broker's personal bank account is
    A. known as commingling.
    B. not grounds for revocation of the broker's license.
    C. called check kiting.
    D. a form of embezzlement.

15. A broker who misrepresents a property to a prospect may be subject to all of the following EXCEPT
    A. loss of his rights to a commission.
    B. revocation of his broker's license.
    C. criminal prosecution.
    D. civil action for damages.

16. An owner who gives false information regarding the listed property
    A. may avoid paying a commission to the broker.
    B. can sue for specific performance.
    C. may have to pay damages to the broker.
    D. may rescind the contract.

17. An agent who fails to investigate the cause of an apparent underlying defect in a property which he is selling may be found
    A. criminally liable.
    B. liable for civil damages.
    C. guilty of a felony.
    D. not guilty of puffing.

18. When an agent engages someone to look into a question raised by a purchaser, he
    A. does not have to be certain of the competency of the person so engaged.
    B. may be liable for civil damages if the person is not professionally competent.
    C. is not acting as agent, so has no responsibility for the outcome.
    D. can privately receive referral fees.

19. Can an agent be protected from liability to disclose defects in a property by stating in writing that the property is being sold "as is"?
    A. Yes, because the statement makes it clear that the purchaser is aware of all problems that might arise.
    B. Yes, because of the rule of caveat emptor.
    C. No, because he may still be liable for having withheld material facts about the property.
    D. No, because the purchaser waives any right to future claims by accepting the property "as is."

20. If a principal asks an agent to participate in an illegal or unethical act in selling a property, the agent should
    A. advise against it, but if the principal insists, quietly participate.
    B. have no part of it.
    C. encourage the principal in doing it.
    D. report the principal to the real estate department.

21. A broker can be indemnified against legal actions by those with whom he deals by purchasing
    A. errors and omissions insurance.
    B. middleman insurance.
    C. property insurance.
    D. employee insurance.

22. Puffing or puffery
    A. can be useful in persuading a buyer to buy.
    B. can be used without caution.
    C. is a non-factual statement which should be recognized by a reasonable person as exaggeration.
    D. is frequently misunderstood as "gospel truth."

23. Should a broker breach his fiduciary responsibility to his principal, he may find himself subject to all of the following EXCEPT
    A. disciplinary action by the real estate department.
    B. civil action by the principal.
    C. criminal prosecution.
    D. the possible loss of his license.

24. The obligation of an agent to a principal includes
    A. compensation.
    B. reimbursement.
    C. indemnification.
    D. obedience of lawful instructions.

25. In dealing with third parties in a real estate transaction, a broker should be careful to avoid all the following EXCEPT
    A. giving misleading or incorrect information.
    B. disclosing his loyalty to his principal.
    C. giving or accepting undisclosed fees.
    D. concealing his identity as an agent of the principal.

26. The relationship of a sales associate to the employing broker is
    A. that of a special agent.
    B. subject to all laws and rules of agency.
    C. an employer–employee relationship.
    D. that of a universal agent.

27. When acting as a cooperating broker, an agent should make it clear to all parties in the transaction
    A. that his legal responsibilities must be to the purchaser.
    B. whether he is acting in the interest of the purchaser or seller.
    C. that he is merely a middleman.
    D. that he is not bound by the agency relationship.

28. When a buyer employs a broker to represent him in negotiations for a property,
    A. the commission to the listing broker is eliminated.
    B. offers to purchase can be based on the gross amount the seller will receive.
    C. the problem of divided broker loyalty is eliminated.
    D. the broker will often reduce his commission to assist the buyer.

29. The requirement that prospective buyers be given a HUD property report applies to
    A. all interstate land sales.
    B. resales of subdivision lots being sold to residents of another state.
    C. all subdivision lots located in one state and sold to residents of another state.
    D. new subdivision lots being offered to residents of another state.

30. The property report required by federal or state law to be given to prospective purchasers
    A. indicates government approval of the property.
    B. must be given to the purchaser before a purchase agreement is signed.
    C. may be eliminated if the property value is less than $100,000.
    D. will not protect purchasers from misrepresentation, fraud, and deceit.

31. Benefits of buyer representation to the buyer include all of the following EXCEPT
    A. the buyer's broker is loyal to the buyer.
    B. buyers are shown only listed properties.
    C. the buyer's broker can investigate properties offered for sale by owners.
    D. the buyer's broker can either be paid by the seller or the buyer.

32. Violation of federal anti-trust laws on price fixing can result in all EXCEPT
    A. criminal penalties.
    B. civil penalties.
    C. time in a federal penitentiary.
    D. a nominal fine.

33. If brokers in a given region were to agree to charge the same commission rate, with no variation between real estate offices, this would be an illegal activity known as
    A. boycotting.
    B. allocation of markets.
    C. price fixing.
    D. steering.

34. When a flat fee broker attempted to show other brokers' listings, they all decline to co-operate with the flat fee broker. This might appear to be
    A. a legal activity of not associating with one's competitors.
    B. an illegal activity known as boycotting.
    C. a wise business practice since the flat fee brokers charge less.
    D. a quick method to force the competition out of business.

Fair Housing, ADA, Equal Credit, and Community Reinvestment

LEARNING OBJECTIVES

After successful completion of the questions in this chapter, you will be able to:

1. Explain the historical constitutional impact of fair housing legislation on ownership of real property.
2. Describe the 1968 fair housing legislation and the amendments.
3. Define terms such as steering, block busting, community reinvestment, and the CRA statement.
4. Delineate those acts not prohibited by the 1968 Fair Housing Law.
5. Summarize the ADA as it relates to real estate agents.
6. Explain the purpose and application of the Equal Credit Opportunity Act.
7. Explain the purpose of the Community Reinvestment Act.

1. The Civil Rights Act of 1866 prohibits
   A. racial discrimination.
   B. steering.
   C. block busting.
   D. discrimination for any reason.

2. A common misconception is that one of the following is prohibited by the Fair Housing Act of 1968, as amended. Which is NOT protected under the Act?
   A. Discrimination in advertising
   B. Denial of availability of housing on the basis of religion
   C. Discrimination in terms or conditions for sale or rent
   D. Discrimination on the basis of age

3. An amendment to the Fair Housing Act of 1968, signed by the president in 1988, prohibits
   A. discrimination on the basis of physical disability.
   B. the offering of different loan terms by commercial lenders based on race or religion of the loan applicant.
   C. refusing to sell, rent, or negotiate with any person.
   D. steering and block busting.

4. The practice of directing home seekers to particular neighborhoods on the basis of race, color, religion, sex, or national origin
   A. is known as steering.
   B. is prohibited by the Civil Rights Act of 1866.
   C. constitutes block busting.
   D. amounts to redlining.

5. Which of the following is true regarding the inducement of panic selling in a neighborhood for financial gain?
   A. It is encouraged by the Fair Housing Act of 1968.
   B. It is limited to fear of loss of value because of the changing of the racial composition of a neighborhood.
   C. It is known as block busting.
   D. The prohibition applies only to licensed real estate agents.

6. The Fair Housing Act of 1968 applies to
   A. special purpose buildings such as schools and churches.
   B. commercial offices.
   C. industrial parks.
   D. single and multi-family housing.

7. The owner of a single-family house in which he lives wants to sell. If he does not use discriminatory language in advertising, has not sold any other house within the past two years, and does not employ an agent, may he discriminate on the basis of race in selecting a purchaser?
   A. Yes, because fair housing laws permit discrimination in this situation.
   B. Yes, because the law applies only to sales made by licensed agents.
   C. No, because this would be prohibited by the Civil Rights Act of 1866.
   D. No, because this would be prohibited by the Fair Housing Act of 1968.

8. An unmarried couple wants to purchase a condominium unit but have been refused because they are not married but are living together. Can the developer be prosecuted in federal courts for refusing to sell to them?
   A. Yes, because this violates the federal fair housing laws.
   B. Yes, because this constitutes discrimination in housing as determined in the Jones v. Mayer case.
   C. No, because discrimination on this basis is not prohibited by federal fair housing laws.
   D. No, because this violates the provisions of the Fair Housing Act of 1968.

9. A church which operates housing for the elderly may restrict occupancy to members of the church if
   A. membership in the church is open to all persons.
   B. the units are to be rented, but not if they are being offered for sale.
   C. membership in the church is closed to minorities.
   D. the church does not accept any governmental financial assistance.

10. A local country club has several guest bedrooms which are made available to members and guests for a nominal charge, but are not available to the general public. Does this constitute a violation of the federal fair housing laws?
    A. Yes, because rental housing of this nature must be open to the public.
    B. Yes, because the charging of a fee constitutes a commercial purpose.
    C. No, because the club is exempt under sections of the 1968 Fair Housing Act.
    D. No, because this does not constitute steering or block busting.

11. A victim of discrimination in housing has several options when seeking enforcement of the 1968 Fair Housing Act. However, he may NOT file a(n)
    A. complaint with the Department of Housing and Urban Development.
    B. action in federal court.
    C. complaint with the U.S. Attorney General.
    D. complaint with the state real estate department.

12. A person seeking enforcement of the Civil Rights Act of 1866 may do so by filing
    A. an action in federal court.
    B. a complaint with the U.S. Attorney General.
    C. an action in county court.
    D. a complaint with HUD.

13. A licensed real estate agent is offered a listing by an owner who stipulates that he will not sell to any person of a certain national origin. The agent should
    A. take the listing and leave it up to the owner to reject offers from these people.
    B. refuse to accept the listing.
    C. report the owner to the real estate department.
    D. file a complaint against the owner with HUD.

14. The U.S. Constitutional Amendment which prohibits any state from depriving a person of life, liberty, or property without due process is the
    A. Fourteenth Amendment.   C. Thirteenth Amendment.
    B. Fifth Amendment.   D. First Amendment.

15. Housing covered by the 1968 Fair Housing Law includes
    A. single-family homes owned by private individuals when represented by a broker.
    B. for sale by owner of his own home.
    C. lodging provided by a private club for use by members of the club.
    D. owner-occupied dwellings of four or fewer units.

16. Acts EXEMPT from coverage by the 1968 Fair Housing Law include
    A. the occupancy of dwellings owned by a religious organization operated for commercial purposes to persons of other religions.
    B. management of a twenty-floor office building.
    C. the sale of single-family houses by a private individual who owns three or fewer such houses if no broker or discriminatory advertising is used.
    D. a non-occupant owner renting an apartment in his triplex.

17. Under which law is a lender prohibited from taking age into account in determining ability to repay?
    A. Equal Credit Opportunity Act   C. Fair Credit Reporting Act
    B. Community Reinvestment Act   D. Civil Rights Act of 1866

18. A resident manager had two empty apartments. However, when a single parent with a five-year-old child applied, she was told that the building was "Adults Only." Is this a violation of the Fair Housing Law?
    A. Yes, because it was discriminating in the terms for renting housing.
    B. Yes, because it was applying different terms for home renting.
    C. No, since it was neither steering nor block busting.
    D. Yes, because it was denying that housing was available for rent when it really was available.

19. A rental agent requires a credit report from each prospective tenant. The Federal Equal Credit Opportunity Act allows the rental agent to do which of the following?
    A. Turn down the applicant because of age.
    B. Disapprove the application because the applicant is divorced.
    C. Charge the prospective tenant a fee to cover the cost of the report.
    D. Show the credit report to another tenant.

20. Some lenders and insurance companies refused to make loans or provide insurance for homes located in certain integrated neighborhoods. This illegal practice is called
    A. underwriting.   C. block busting.
    B. redlining.   D. steering.

21. The Americans with Disabilities Act (ADA) deals primarily with
    A. multi-family housing.   C. historical buildings.
    B. commercial property.   D. single family homes.

22. The ADA provides
    A. standards by which to measure a person's severity of disability.
    B. broad exemptions for many business establishments.
    C. access requirements.
    D. individuals to test for compliance.

23. The ADA specifically affects the real estate industry by requiring
    A. licensees to be responsible for monitoring racial quotas.
    B. licensees to verify that a buyer is a citizen or permanent U.S. resident.
    C. licensees to supervise the removal of barriers.
    D. the real estate licensee to determine whether or not the building he is managing is in compliance.

24. A creditor who fails to comply with the Equal Credit Opportunity Act would be subject to
    A. civil liability for damages up to $100,000 in individual actions.
    B. civil liability for damages of the lesser of $500,000 or 1% of the creditor's net worth in class actions.
    C. criminal punishment of up to three years imprisonment.
    D. unlimited punitive damages.

25. The Community Reinvestment Act expands the expectation that financial institutions
    A. must serve the financial needs of their communities.
    B. must lower credit standards in order to make more loans in poorer areas.
    C. provide maps detailing their redlining activities.
    D. may keep secret the types of credit it offers to the public.

26. Financial institutions seeking to expand must meet guidelines addressed in the Community Reinvestment Act. What government entity considers these applications?
    A. FSLIC (Federal Savings and Loan Insurance Corporation)
    B. FHLMC (Federal Home Loan Mortgage Corporation)
    C. HUD (Housing and Urban Development)
    D. FHLBB (Federal Home Loan Bank Board)

27. A better term to use instead of minorities is
    A. physically challenged.   C. a person of color.
    B. protected class.   D. familial status.

28. One or more individuals under the age of eighteen who are living with a parent or legal guardian fits the Fair Housing definition of
    A. merged or blended households.
    B. extended families.
    C. nuclear families.
    D. familial status.

29. Penalties for violation of the Federal Fair Housing Law include
    A. punitive damages limited to $1,000.
    B. unlimited punitive damages.
    C. an injunction to permit the sale or rental to proceed prior to the hearing.
    D. nothing for actual damages caused by the discrimination.

30. In a discrimination case concerning the Federal Fair Housing Act, the burden of proof is on the
    A. respondent.
    B. complainant.
    C. HUD secretary.
    D. broker involved.

Condominiums, Cooperatives, PUDs, and Timeshares

LEARNING OBJECTIVES

After successful completion of the questions in this chapter, you will be able to:

1. Deliver an overview of condominiums, their organization, operation, benefits, and drawbacks.
2. Describe condominium conversions and condominium financing.
3. List what to inspect before buying.
4. Explain the advantages and disadvantages of cooperative apartments and the unique character of cooperative financing.
5. Define the PUD and explain its purpose.
6. Describe the key features of resort time-sharing.

1. The popularity of condominium ownership may be attributed in part to
   A. abundance of land in desirable areas.
   B. lower construction costs.
   C. the desire to rent rather than own.
   D. enactment of Section 234 of the National Housing Act.

2. Section 234 of the National Housing Act
   A. provides a legal model for condominium ownership.
   B. prohibits FHA insurance on mortgage loans on condominium units.
   C. effectively shut down condominium conversions.
   D. set unreasonably high standards for developers of condominiums.

3. State laws which provide the legal framework for condominium ownership may be identified by any of the following terms EXCEPT
   A. strata titles act.   C. condominium act.
   B. cooperative housing act.   D. horizontal property act.

4. Condominium developments are distinguished by the existence of
   A. separate and common elements.   C. resident superintendent.
   B. a system of city government.   D. proprietary leases.

5. Individual units in a condominium development are classed as
   A. separate property.
   B. common elements.
   C. cooperative elements.
   D. limited common elements.

6. Within a condominium development, common elements are owned by
   A. the owners' association.
   B. all unit owners, who hold undivided interests in the elements.
   C. the condominium developer.
   D. individual unit owners as community property.

7. Which of the following would be classified as limited common elements in a condominium development?
   A. Elevators
   B. Hallways
   C. Assigned parking spaces
   D. Manager's apartment

8. The plan for a condominium development which converts a single parcel of land into individual separate property estates and an estate composed of all common elements may be referred to as
   A. an enabling declaration.
   B. a master lease.
   C. bylaws.
   D. lot and block description.

9. The rules by which an owners' association operates are known as
   A. bylaws.
   B. covenants, conditions, and restrictions.
   C. house rules.
   D. ordinances.

10. Enabling declarations for condominium developments are usually filed by the
    A. property tax assessor.
    B. lender for the project.
    C. owners' association.
    D. condominium developer.

11. The purchaser of a condominium unit receives a
    A. deed from the seller.
    B. separate deed to the common elements.
    C. deed from the owners' association.
    D. shares of stock in the condominium.

12. Once the units in a condominium development have been sold and the association turned over to the unit owners, the association can change any of the following EXCEPT the
    A. bylaws.
    B. enabling declaration.
    C. CC&Rs.
    D. house rules.

13. As compared to a local (city) government, the role of the board of directors of a condominium development approximates that of the
    A. mayor's office.
    B. city manager's office.
    C. police department.
    D. city council.

14. Day-to-day management of a condominium development may be provided by
    A. an on-site manager.
    B. the board of directors.
    C. rotation among the owners.
    D. a management committee.

15. The funds for maintaining the annual budget of a condominium are obtained by
    A. association dues assessed upon each unit owner.
    B. taxes on the value of the units.
    C. liens on individual units.
    D. a mortgage on the common elements.

16. In a condominium, the authority to raise homeowner fees (association dues) rests with the
    A. board of directors.
    C. condominium act.
    B. management company.
    D. city and county.

17. An owners' association should set aside reserves. For which of the following is the unit owner responsible?
    A. Painting of the building's exterior
    C. Driveway resurfacing
    B. Roof replacement
    D. Replacing a non-working dishwasher

18. The owners' association of a condominium is typically responsible for the payment of
    A. hazard insurance premiums on the common elements.
    B. maintenance within individual units.
    C. property taxes.
    D. internal furnishing.

19. The guest of a unit owner was injured by stepping on broken glass in the swimming pool at the Sunset Hills condominium. Liability for this injury would probably initially fall upon
    A. the unit owner.
    C. management company.
    B. the condominium association.
    D. developers.

20. Owner K defaulted on the mortgage loan on his condominium unit. At foreclosure, the high bid was not sufficient to satisfy the obligation, and the lender secured a deficiency judgment of the remainder of the amount due. This judgment would be entered against
    A. K's unit in the condominium.
    B. the condominium corporation.
    C. the condominium owners' association.
    D. any other property, real or personal, owned by K.

21. Failure to pay condominium association dues will result in a lien against the
    A. owners' association.
    B. delinquent owner's unit.
    C. city in which the condominium is located.
    D. enabling declaration.

22. In a condominium, property taxes are assessed against
    A. the owners' association for proration among unit owners.
    B. the master deed for proration by the association's board of directors.
    C. each individual unit with a bill sent to each unit's owner.
    D. the property management company which in turn collects from unit owners.

23. The purchase of a condominium unit may be financed by means of
    A. no government-related loan.
    B. a choice of any loans available for residential properties.
    C. a proprietary lease.
    D. special "condo" loans.

24. The purchaser of a condominium unit
    A. surrenders personal freedoms to community rule.
    B. gains freedom of choice.
    C. gains a great deal of responsibility.
    D. can maintain a great deal of anonymity.

25. A couple have owned a condominium unit at Sea View Condos for two years. In order to enhance the view from their unit, they want to enlarge one of its windows. Can they do this?
    A. They can do this as long as they don't injure adjoining units.
    B. To do this would not violate the CC&Rs.
    C. Since the windows do not belong to them, they cannot ever enlarge them.
    D. They can do this if given permission by the owners' association.

26. Ownership of the interior space of your home and garage and an undivided interest in the building structures, common areas, and land area of the entire project describes a
    A. condominium.   C. PUD.
    B. cooperative.   D. corporate form of ownership.

27. Which of the following are characteristics of a cooperative housing development?
    A. Tenants hold fee title to their units.
    B. Cooperatives are regulated by horizontal property acts.
    C. Cooperatives occupy their units under a proprietary lease.
    D. Tenants are members of an association that holds title to the common areas.

28. A cooperator defaulted on his share of the monthly mortgage payments on the cooperative where he lived. The cooperative corporation has several options to consider. However, one thing it may NOT do is
    A. foreclose on his unit.
    B. terminate him as a shareholder.
    C. resell his shares to someone else.
    D. bring civil action in court to recover the delinquent amount.

29. Traditionally, the resale of cooperative shares has been financed by means of
    A. installments sales agreements.   C. conventional loans.
    B. second mortgages on the seller's unit.   D. FHA loans.

30. Regarding the difference between condominiums and cooperative ownership, which of the following statements is correct?
    A. The government of a cooperative is very similar to that of a condominium.
    B. A condominium owner is liable for the mortgage debt on his neighbor's unit.
    C. Cooperators own fee simple while condo owners have a proprietary lease.
    D. Coop apartments may be financed separately from the rest of the building.

31. The governing body of a cooperative is called a
    A. cooperation.   C. CC&R.
    B. corporation.   D. board of directors.

32. Which is the oldest form of owner-occupied community housing in the U.S.?
    A. Condominium ownership   C. Timeshared ownership
    B. Planned unit development   D. Cooperative ownership

33. A unit owner in a planned unit development holds title to all of the following EXCEPT
    A. the air above his unit.   C. a share of the common areas.
    B. the land beneath his unit.   D. fee simple title to his unit.

34. Which of the following is true of ownership in a planned unit development?
    A. Title to the common areas is held by the owners' association.
    B. There are no CC&Rs governing individual owners as with condominiums and cooperatives.
    C. Density is lower in PUDs than in a typical suburban development.
    D. Ownership in a PUD is burdensome and not popular.

35. In a planned unit development, the owners' association may have control over
    A. interior paint colors.
    B. the number of persons who occupy a dwelling unit.
    C. the type of financing available to the purchaser.
    D. approving the buyer in a resale transaction.

36. In a condominium, cooperative, and planned unit development, rules governing the use of recreation facilities will be found in the
    A. deed to the property.
    B. enabling declaration.
    C. bylaws.
    D. CC&Rs and house rules.

37. The concept of dividing up and selling living units at a vacation facility for specified lengths of time each year is
    A. known as resort timesharing.
    B. a recent development in individual ownership of real estate.
    C. an old concept used by large corporations as benefits for employees.
    D. a stable investment for younger people.

38. Of the two principal forms of timeshare formats, which comprises the larger percentage of the market?
    A. Right-to-use
    B. Fee simple
    C. Each holds an approximately equal market share
    D. Statistics are not available

39. Under the right-to-use plan of timesharing, the purchaser
    A. holds title to real property.
    B. is a tenant in common with other users of the unit.
    C. is given a contractual right to occupy a living unit at a resort property for one week a year for a certain number of years.
    D. makes regular payments over the years he utilizes the property.

40. The purchaser of a timeshare unit under the fee simple format
    A. holds title for a limited time.
    B. receives a deed to his share of ownership.
    C. uses a special timeshare lease.
    D. may not use a note and mortgage to finance his purchase.

41. A person is considering the purchase of a timeshare unit in a ski resort located in the Rocky Mountains. In terms of original cost, the least expensive purchase would be one week in a
    A. right-to-use development during the month of May.
    B. fee simple development during January.
    C. fee simple development during the month of June.
    D. right-to-use development during the month of December.

42. An attractive feature of timeshare ownership to a prospective purchaser is
    A. the purchase of future vacations at a stated, regularly graduated price.
    B. the ability to exchange one's timeshare among units at other resorts.
    C. returning to the same location every year for one's vacation.
    D. the rising appreciation demonstrated by timeshare resales.

43. In terms of investment possibilities, timeshares are generally regarded as
    A. low risk, high appreciation probability.
    B. high risk, low appreciation probability.
    C. high risk, high appreciation probability.
    D. about equal to other forms of real estate investment.

44. The sale of timeshares is regulated in about twenty-five states by
    A. the National Association of License Law Officials.
    B. the National Timesharing Council.
    C. the National Association of Realtors.
    D. state legislation.

Property Insurance

1. The concept of insurance is to
   A. reimburse the insured for financial losses.
   B. insure that a loss-causing event will not occur.
   C. cover expenses for accidents on other people's property.
   D. protect against loss of value during a buyer's market.

2. The New York fire form does NOT provide coverage for losses
   A. by fire.
   B. by lightning.
   C. sustained while removing property from damaged premises.
   D. by flood.

3. The money paid for insurance is called the insurance
   A. rider.
   B. endorsement.
   C. peril.
   D. premium.

4. The insurance endorsement is also known as an attachment or a(n)
   A. rider.
   B. binder.
   C. assignment.
   D. certificate.

5. Coverage for additional perils can be obtained by
   A. purchasing a separate policy.
   B. removing an endorsement to a regular fire insurance policy.
   C. purchasing an annuity.
   D. removing hazards from the property.

6. The financial responsibility which one has to others as a result of one's actions or negligence is known as
   A. personal libel.
   B. public liability.
   C. community responsibility.
   D. individual awareness.

7. A homeowner's insurance policy will NOT protect against which of the following?
   A. Public liability directly connected with the insured property.
   B. Damage to household goods contained in the insured premises.
   C. Flood damage to the insured premises.
   D. Theft of personal property.

8. A typical homeowner insurance policy does NOT cover
   A. the dwelling house.
   B. living expenses while damage to the residence is being repaired.
   C. personal property within the dwelling.
   D. automobiles in a garage on the premises.

9. Which of the following homeowner policy formats covers the most perils?
   A. HO–1
   B. HO–2
   C. HO–3
   D. HO–5

10. Coverage for the damage due to the weight of ice, snow and sleet would NOT be found in which of the following policies?
    A. HO–1
    B. HO–2
    C. HO–3
    D. HO–5

11. Which of the following homeowner's policies is best suited for older homes?
    A. HO–3
    B. HO–5
    C. HO–6
    D. HO–8

12. A typical HO–2 homeowner's policy does NOT cover damage caused by
    A. windstorm.
    B. vandalism.
    C. freezing water pipes.
    D. earthquake.

13. An "all-risk" homeowner policy (HO–5) includes coverage for damage resulting from all of the following EXCEPT
    A. smoke.
    B. nuclear accident.
    C. explosion.
    D. falling objects.

14. A tenant in a rented dwelling who wants to insure against perils other than the dwelling itself should purchase which of the following policies?
    A. HO–2
    B. HO–3
    C. HO–4
    D. HO–5

15. A tenant is renting a dwelling unit in a condominium. To insure his home furnishings and personal liability arising from the rental, he should ask for a(n)
    A. condominium policy.
    B. landlord's policy.
    C. tenant's policy.
    D. owner's policy.

16. An HO–6 policy provides a condominium unit owner with protection which covers
    A. personal property within the unit.   C. the swimming pool.
    B. the common elements.   D. the buildings.

17. Medical payments provided under a homeowner policy can be paid to
    A. the named insured.
    B. guests of the insured on the premises.
    C. claims arising from business pursuits.
    D. family members of the insured.

18. When a property is mortgaged to a lending institution, the lender will require the owner to provide
    A. fire and extended coverage on structures.
    B. personal property coverage.
    C. medical payments coverage.
    D. liability coverage.

19. The lender on a condominium unit will require proof that the
    A. unit owner carries liability insurance.
    B. condominium association carries insurance on the common elements.
    C. every unit owner carries liability insurance.
    D. board of directors carries errors and omissions insurance.

20. Mr. G has a home that would cost $60,000 to replace. He carries $45,000 in insurance. A fire causes damage that will cost $20,000 to repair. Applying the 80% coinsurance calculation, how much would he receive to repair the damage?
    A. $15,000   C. $18,750
    B. $16,000   D. $20,000

21. Lenders on real estate mortgages require that the borrower provide
    A. a partial replacement cost policy.
    B. insurance on the full amount of the loan.
    C. insurance in an amount equal to the purchase price of the property.
    D. inflation guard coverage.

22. An insurance policy which fixes the insurance company's liability to the insured to the actual cash value of the insured property is said to provide
    A. "old for new" coverage.   C. "old for old" coverage.
    B. "new for old" coverage.   D. "new for new" coverage.

23. A homeowner's policy in an amount equal to 80% of the replacement cost of the house would, in the event of a loss, pay
    A. actual cash value of the loss.
    B. less than actual cash value of the loss.
    C. replacement cost less depreciation.
    D. full replacement cost up to the face amount of the policy.

24. All of the following mortgages require either flood insurance or a certificate that the mortgaged property is not in a flood zone EXCEPT
    A. VA-guaranteed mortgages.
    B. FHA-insured mortgages.
    C. mortgages carried back by sellers.
    D. mortgages obtained from federally chartered savings and loan associations.

25. If an insurer cancels a policy that contains the New York fire form, the insurer
    A. must give a 10-day notice.
    B. must issue a prorated refund of the unused portion of the policy.
    C. need not give any notice to the insured.
    D. is not required to refund any of the unused portion of the policy.

26. A landlord package policy provides coverage for all EXCEPT
    A. property damage.   C. medical expenses.
    B. liability.   D. personal property of the tenant.

27. If the insured wishes to cancel his New York fire form policy, the insured
    A. must give a 5-day notice.
    B. will receive a prorated refund.
    C. will be penalized with an extra month's premium.
    D. will receive a refund based on short-rate premiums.

28. An insurer may suspend a homeowner's insurance policy if
    A. the insured allows the hazard exposure to the insurer to increase beyond the risks contemplated when the policy was issued.
    B. the property is occupied for long periods of time.
    C. the property is under insured.
    D. the premium is paid too far in advance.

29. The purchaser of a new home may protect himself against loss due to structural defects by having the home inspected before purchase and by
    A. purchasing insurance under the Home Owners Warranty Program.
    B. purchasing title insurance.
    C. purchasing homeowner's insurance.
    D. adding an endorsement to his tenant's policy.

SECTION 24.1: Insurance Problems

1. A homeowner owns a home that would cost $80,000 to replace at present replacement costs. He reasons that any loss sustained would probably be less than this amount, as he is located near a fire department and someone is at home most of the time. In order to save money on his insurance premiums, he purchases a homeowner's policy in the amount of $40,000. Should the property suffer a loss costing $15,000 to repair, what would be the amount of recovery? Actual cash value of the loss is $10,000.

    $ _____

2. The homeowners have HO–2 coverage on their home in the amount of $130,000. Replacement cost is currently estimated at $135,000. The fireplace chimney becomes clogged with soot, resulting in smoke damage amounting to $800 from a fire in the fireplace. What amount will the homeowners recover from the insurance company?

    $ _____

3. A woman works in an office located in a high-rise office building. She parks her car in an assigned space adjacent to the building. High winds blow a sign off the roof of the building. The sign lands on the woman's car, resulting in several hundred dollars in damage. Who is responsible for paying to repair the damage? And why?

    _____

    _____

Land-Use Control

After successful completion of the questions in this chapter, you will be able to:

1. Describe the many aspects and results of land-use controls.
2. Define the concept of zoning, spot zoning, down zoning, variances, and nonconforming use.
3. Explain the application of subdivision regulations and building codes.

4. Explain the use of deed restrictions.
5. Describe the environmental impact statement.
6. Explain the purpose of planning ahead and the need for master plans.
7. Define transferable development rights.

1. All of the following are examples of public land-use controls EXCEPT
   A. zoning laws.
   B. subdivision regulations.
   C. master plans.
   D. deed restrictions.

2. Land-use controls would NOT be imposed by
   A. state governments.
   B. local governments.
   C. subdivision developers.
   D. lenders.

3. Zoning laws may NOT be used to regulate which of the following?
   A. The purpose for which a building may be constructed
   B. The number of persons a building may accommodate.
   C. The placement of interior partitions.
   D. The height and bulk of a building.

4. Through zoning, a community can protect existing land users from all of the following, EXCEPT
   A. encroachment by undesirable uses.
   B. uncontrolled development.
   C. incompatible uses of land.
   D. competitive business establishments.

5. The basic authority for zoning laws is derived from a state's
   A. powers of eminent domain.   C. right of escheat.
   B. right of taxation.   D. police powers.

6. Symbols or code abbreviations used to designate land-use zones such as agricultural, residential, commercial or industrial zones are
   A. uniform throughout the United States.
   B. the same for all counties within each state.
   C. not uniformly used throughout the United States.
   D. designated by state statute.

7. Zoning laws
   A. tell a landowner the use to which he may put his land.
   B. compensate an owner for loss of property value due to zoning.
   C. do not consider the right of the individual to develop his land.
   D. do not consider the economic and social impact of development on the land.

8. Checking the zoning on a parcel of land is a matter of
   A. going to the zoning office of the city or county where the parcel is located and inquiring as to its zoning.
   B. dismissing the zoning ordinance as being important as to the permitted uses for that zone.
   C. looking at the deed in the recording office.
   D. consulting the survey for any visible signs of use.

9. Applied to land use, zoning laws may
   A. encourage diversity in land usage.
   B. set maximum square footage requirements for buildings.
   C. determine the location of a building on a lot.
   D. dictate construction standards for buildings.

10. Should a landowner develop his land without first obtaining a building permit, he could be
    A. sent to jail.   C. charged with a misdemeanor.
    B. forced to tear down the building. D. evicted.

11. A use of property which is not in agreement with present zoning laws is
    A. called a nonconforming use.
    B. not permitted under a so-called "grandfather clause."
    C. a variance.
    D. an exception to the code.

12. A grandfather clause in a zoning ordinance will permit the owner of a building which is in nonconforming use to do which of the following?
    A. Enlarge the building   C. Extend its life
    B. Remodel the exterior   D. Perform all normal maintenance

13. A zoning variance
    A. allows an owner to deviate from existing zoning law.
    B. involves a change in the zoning law.
    C. does not permit a use inconsistent with the zoning classification.
    D. is a reference to the exterior design of a building.

14. A convenience store was given a conditional use permit to operate in a residential subdivision for the sale of food items only. Later, the owners decided that they would like to add a line of hardware items. Could they do so under the provisions of their conditional use permit?
    A. Yes, because the conditional use permit allows them to do so.
    B. Yes, because once the conditional use permit has been granted, the items in their inventory cannot be restricted.
    C. No, because the conditional use permit restricts their inventory to food items.
    D. No, because adding hardware items would constitute a zoning variance.

15. When a small area of land in an existing neighborhood is rezoned, this is called
    A. down zoning.   C. conditional zoning.
    B. spot zoning.   D. a zoning variance.

16. The zoning of a parcel of land was changed from apartment zoning to single-family residential use only. Which of the following statements is true?
    A. The rezoning constituted down zoning.
    B. The owner would be compensated for the loss of land value.
    C. This is an example of the government's right of eminent domain.
    D. The owner has a right to challenge the amount being offered to him.

17. A garden apartment development is situated between an office park and a subdivision of single-family residences. These apartments are in a
    A. buffer zone.   C. spot zone.
    B. down zone.   D. commercial zone.

18. Before a subdivider can sell lots in a new subdivision,
    A. all mapping requirements must be met and the subdivision plat recorded.
    B. the subdivision plat should be made, but not recorded until the first lot is sold.
    C. plats must be filed with the federal office of Environmental Controls.
    D. the lender must approve all zoning requirements.

19. Minimum standards for materials and construction of buildings are set by
    A. zoning laws.   C. deed restrictions.
    B. building codes.   D. subdivision regulations.

20. Building codes are employed to
    A. regulate the architectural style of buildings.
    B. establish acceptable material and construction standards for buildings.
    C. prevent a concentration of the population in a small area.
    D. prevent fires by requiring proper distance between buildings.

21. Before a newly constructed building may be utilized by tenants, the owner must secure a certificate of
    A. inspection.   C. approval.
    B. utilization.   D. occupancy.

22. A deed given by a grantor to the grantee contained a restriction prohibiting occupancy of the property by anyone other than persons of the Caucasian race. This restriction
    A. invalidates the deed.   C. is enforceable.
    B. is unenforceable.   D. requires a zoning change.

23. A subdivider wants to limit the height to which trees can grow so as to preserve views. He would most likely do this with a
    A. zoning amendment.   C. buffer zone.
    B. conditional use permit.   D. deed restriction.

24. Future uses of land within a community may be regulated by all of the following EXCEPT
    A. deed restrictions.   C. subdivision regulations.
    B. zoning laws.   D. building codes.

25. A master plan for land use within a community should
    A. provide a balance between social and economic needs within the community.
    B. be inflexible so that it need not be concerned with future growth.
    C. strike a proper mix of neighborhoods based on racial and religious concerns.
    D. plan declining citizen participation and reduce community services.

26. The effect of a proposed development on a community is determined by the preparation of a(n)
    A. property disclosure report.   C. prospectus.
    B. environmental impact statement. D. community master plan.

27. Environmental impact statements as a tool in land use planning provide
    A. limited impact on better decision making regarding land uses.
    B. a means of estimating the effect of planned development on the environment.
    C. are required and regulated by the EPA.
    D. provide basic information to homeowners for landscaping their homes.

28. An environmental impact statement will NOT reveal the effect of a planned development on
    A. air quality.   C. property values.
    B. automobile traffic.   D. school enrollments.

29. An owner converted a single-family home into two apartments. He now wants to list the property for sale with a broker. The broker
    A. should ascertain whether the conversion conforms to zoning requirements.
    B. does not have to be concerned if proper building permits were obtained since the building is already converted.
    C. should ask his attorney to check the recording office to see if the new conversion has been recorded.
    D. should not ask questions about the conversion since all he is being asked to do is to market the property.

30. A developer is looking for acreage to develop into a residential subdivision. A broker shows the developer an attractive parcel at the edge of town that is currently zoned for agricultural but looks ripe for development. Of the following choices, which would be the most rational for the developer?
    A. Make an extremely low offer so that if the zoning cannot be changed to residential, the developer will not lose too much.
    B. Pay the asking price and hope for the best.
    C. File for a zoning change on the property and, if it is approved, offer to buy it.
    D. Make an offer on the property now with a contingency that zoning be changed to residential before settlement.

31. An owner has lived in a 40-year-old house for the past three years. He calls a broker in to list the property for sale. Upon inspection of the house, the broker notices an extra bathroom that was added since the house was built; also, the bathroom has no means of ventilation to the outside. The broker asks if the bathroom had been built with a permit and the owner replies that he does not know as it was there when he bought the house. The owner goes on to say that all the fixtures work fine and for ventilation he leaves the bathroom door open to the hallway. If you were the broker, would you
    A. refuse the listing on this point alone?
    B. refuse the listing until you talked to the building department?
    C. take the listing and not worry about the bathroom since the seller assures you that it is not a problem?
    D. take the listing, talk to the building department, then advise the owner as to his options?

32. A landowner who is denied a proposed development of his land by the community's planning authorities
    A. can force the community to purchase the land under eminent domain.
    B. will receive payment for the loss in the land's value.
    C. can change the zoning if he gets enough people to sign a petition for change.
    D. can do nothing.

33. Large windfalls and wipeouts in land value which are brought about by land-use controls may sometimes be eliminated by creating
    A. an environmental impact statement.   C. permitting adverse possession.
    B. transferable development rights.   D. a tax shelter.

34. To date, transferable development rights have been used to protect
    A. historical buildings.   C. environmentally sensitive land.
    B. agricultural land.   D. all of the above.

Real Estate and the Economy

LEARNING OBJECTIVES

After successful completion of the questions in this chapter, you will be able to:

1. Explain how an economic base is important to a community.
2. Discuss the effect of the economy on real estate and explain the short-run demand on housing.
3. Explain the aspects of the long-run demand for housing.
4. Describe the applicable tax laws, fiscal and monetary policy as they affect the market.
5. Recognize the effect of inflation and define the types of inflation.
6. Explain how the government impacts the economy.

1. Industries which produce goods and services for export are referred to by all of the following terms EXCEPT
   A. base industries.
   B. export industries.
   C. primary industries.
   D. backbone industries.

2. Which of the following terms would NOT apply to an industry that produces only goods or services which are locally consumed?
   A. Service industry
   B. Accessory industry
   C. Secondary industry
   D. Filler industry

3. The real estate brokerage business is an example of a(n)
   A. base industry.
   B. secondary industry.
   C. export industry.
   D. primary industry.

4. The Hartford Manufacturing Company, which was the largest employer in the city of Westview, recently closed its plant in that city. This will probably result in
   A. increasing real estate values.
   B. a slow-down in construction of new homes.
   C. an increase in the population of Westview.
   D. the opening of some service industries.

5. The existence of a base industry
   A. is essential to the economic health of a community.
   B. leads to unstable local real estate values.
   C. leads to unemployment and unsaleable housing.
   D. may stifle the creation of new jobs.

6. Generally, for every job created by a base industry, there will be created in service industries approximately
   A. an equal number of jobs.   C. one job for every two base jobs.
   B. two jobs.   D. four jobs.

7. When there is a sudden increase in the demand for housing in a community, the price of existing housing will
   A. rise slowly over the next twelve months.
   B. rise rapidly, than fall slightly as supply catches up with demand.
   C. not reflect the increased demand for approximately twelve months.
   D. drop initially, and then rapidly rise.

8. When the supply and demand relationship in a market is unbalanced because of excess supply, it is to the advantage of
   A. buyers.   C. sellers of services only.
   B. sellers.   D. buyers of services only.

9. Generally, a person's peak earning years occur at ages
   A. 25–35 years.   C. 45–55 years.
   B. 35–45 years.   D. over 60 years.

10. Typically, most homeowners acquire their largest and most expensive housing between ages
    A. 25 to 35.   C. 45 to 55.
    B. 35 to 45.   D. over age 60.

11. The post-World War II baby boom includes persons aged
    A. 30 to 40 in 1950.   C. 45 to 50 in 1995.
    B. 35 to 45 in 1960.   D. 50 to 60 in 1980.

12. What is the effect on demand for housing of a dramatic increase in the birth rate?
    A. An immediate effect
    B. A long-range effect
    C. No effect at all
    D. Moderate increase immediately and then a slight drop off

13. Real estate values are NOT affected by the federal government's
    A. tax rules.   C. deficits.
    B. zoning requirements.   D. monetary policies.

14. Under U.S. federal tax laws that allow mortgage interest deductions on federal income taxes, what would be the after-tax cost to a homeowner in the 28% tax bracket of a home mortgage loan made at a 12% rate of interest?
    A. 3.36%   C. 9.5%
    B. 8.64%   D. 10.00%

15. Federal tax laws have traditionally allowed owners of investment properties to deduct all of the following EXCEPT
    A. depreciation on land.   C. operating costs.
    B. maintenance costs.   D. ad valorem taxes.

16. Economists agree that there are three factors that establish criteria for home sales:
    A. job growth, low interest rates and lowering home prices.
    B. job growth, higher interest rates and rising home prices
    C. job growth, low interest rates and rising home prices.
    D. better built homes, more homes on the market and more buyers.

17. Which has the greatest effect upon the interest rate an individual must pay for a real estate mortgage loan?
    A. Federal governmental borrowing
    B. State governmental borrowing
    C. Local governmental borrowing
    D. Competition from commercial and industrial borrowers

18. In order to keep prices from falling in an economy that is growing at 4% per year, which of the following adjustments in the money supply is necessary?
    A. 4% decrease   C. 2% increase
    B. Constant, no change   D. 4% increase

19. When a government prints more money than is needed for economic growth, the result is a
    A. short-term drop in interest rates.   C. long-term drop in interest rates.
    B. long-term decrease in inflation.   D. short-term rise in interest rates.

20. All of the following have made home purchases by persons of modest income easier EXCEPT
    A. FHA loan insurance programs.
    B. creation of extra money by the Federal Reserve.
    C. VA loan guaranty programs.
    D. income tax deductions for mortgage loan interest and taxes.

21. The advent of the secondary mortgage market
    A. increased sources of money for real estate mortgage loans.
    B. contributed to real estate speculation and inflation in the late 1970s.
    C. offers little to financing in today's market.
    D. helped only major borrowers, not the FHA and VA borrowers.

22. Cost-push inflation is the result of
    A. increased manufacturing costs.   C. changes in the money supply.
    B. increased demand for a product.   D. changes in interest rates.

23. Demand-pull inflation has little to do with
    A. manufacturing costs.
    B. the availability of money.
    C. buyers bidding against each other.
    D. too much money chasing too few goods.

24. When too much money chases too few goods, it is known as
    A. cost-push inflation.   C. real-cost inflation.
    B. demand-pull inflation.   D. monetary-base inflation.

25. Inflation brought on by increased effort necessary to produce the same quantity of a good or service is known as
    A. demand-pull inflation.   C. cost-push inflation.
    B. real-cost inflation.   D. monetary inflation.

26. The real cost of interest is the
    A. rate stated on the promissory note.
    B. inflation-adjusted cost.
    C. annual percentage rate.
    D. rate stated on the promissory note plus any discounts.

27. By the year 1980, in order to curb inflation, the monetary growth policy of the Federal Reserve became one of
    A. generous supply.
    B. negative supply.
    C. restrained supply.
    D. constant, no-growth supply.

28. Expectations about inflation tend to
    A. lag actual changes.
    B. parallel actual changes.
    C. precede actual changes.
    D. have little influence on inflation.

29. Which of the following is more likely to be the LEAST demanding of appreciation potential in the ownership of real estate?
    A. Owner of a rental residence.
    B. Owner who occupies a property as a principal residence.
    C. Business which owns apartment buildings.
    D. Corporation which owns office buildings.

30. Ultimately, interest rates for real estate mortgage loans are determined by the
    A. marketplace.
    B. Federal Reserve Board.
    C. nation's banking system.
    D. savings and loan associations.

31. The Federal Reserve Board's objectives for the United States economy include
    A. high unemployment.
    B. unstable prices.
    C. steady growth in productive capacity.
    D. fluctuating foreign exchange rate for the dollar.

32. The Federal Reserve Board influences the national economy by adjusting
    A. interest rates.
    B. the money supply.
    C. mortgage rates.
    D. interest rates on credit cards.

33. An increase in the monetary base at a rate faster than that of the gross national product will lead to
    A. a temporary boost in interest rates.
    B. temporary stimulation of economic growth.
    C. long-term economic growth.
    D. stable interest rates.

34. If the government increases taxes
    A. reduces private income and the consumer cannot spend as much..
    B. the consumer's money can be spread through the economy.
    C. it tends to lead to a more prosperous economy.
    D. it will lower the interest rate.

35. The 1997 Taxpayers Relief Act
    A. will benefit eligible veterans in financing home purchases.
    B. should greatly increase commercial and residential real estate activity.
    C. will help only borrowers who obtain FHA financing.
    D. benefits only married personal home sellers.

Investing in Real Estate 27

1. A positive cash flow occurs when a property generates income in excess of
   A. mortgage payments.
   B. depreciation and operating expenses.
   C. appreciation and mortgage payments.
   D. operating expenses and mortgage payments.

2. ABZ Realty offers you a four-unit residential building where each unit rents for $500 per month. Given a 5% vacancy rate, operating expenses of $700 per month, and mortgage payments of $1,500 per month, you can anticipate a monthly
   A. net spendable of $200.   C. negative cash flow of $200.
   B. net spendable of $300.   D. negative cash flow of $300.

3. Same facts as in question 2, plus these: The monthly mortgage payment consists of $1,400 in interest and $100 in principal reduction and depreciation is $1,000 per month. How much is the monthly taxable income generated by this property?
   A. ($300)   C. ($1,200)
   B. ($1,000)   D. ($1,300)

4. What is the cash-on-cash ratio for a property which generates an annual cash flow of $16,900 and could be purchased with a down payment of $130,000?
   A. .219   C. .12
   B. 7.69%   D. .13

5. Mortgage balance reduction is
   A. an out-of-pocket expense.
   B. a deduction for tax purposes.
   C. tax exempted.
   D. quite large at the beginning of the loan period.

6. Depreciation on rental property
   A. represents an out-of-pocket expense to an investor.
   B. is a deduction against income taxes.
   C. must be paid each year.
   D. can be deferred for several years.

7. The value of depreciation on an investment property is
   A. inversely proportional to the investor's tax bracket.
   B. the same to all investors, regardless of their tax bracket.
   C. directly proportional to the investor's tax bracket.
   D. not a factor in the investment decision.

8. Tax laws allow depreciation on a building to be
   A. started over each time the property is sold.
   B. more than its value.
   C. added to the age of other buildings to extend their depreciation.
   D. depreciated more than once by each owner.

9. For an investment property, all depreciation claimed in excess of actual loss in value comes back to be taxed upon
   A. selling the property.
   B. trading the property.
   C. receipt of additional rental income.
   D. either selling or trading the property.

10. Equity build-up in a property can be the result of
    A. increasing the loan to value.
    B. appreciation.
    C. depreciation.
    D. declining property values.

11. W purchased a home for $100,000, putting up $20,000 cash and taking an $80,000 mortgage loan. Now, several years later, the loan balance is still $75,000, but the home is worth $120,000. W's equity
    A. at time of purchase was $80,000.
    B. now is $45,000.
    C. buildup is $20,000.
    D. and loan reduction is $55,000.

12. Negative leverage occurs when
    A. borrowed funds cost more than they produce in benefits.
    B. an investment property depreciates in value.
    C. the borrower is unable to repay the loan promptly.
    D. the lender insists on an "on-demand" note.

13. A woman is considering the purchase of a $1,000,000 apartment building by paying $250,000 cash down and borrowing the balance with a non-recourse mortgage loan. If the land is worth $150,000 and the building $850,000, under the "at risk" rule to investment real estate, will she be able to depreciate the entire $850,000?
    A. Yes, because ACRS overrides any "at risk" rules.
    B. No, because "at risk" would limit her depreciation to $250,000 plus loan reduction.
    C. No, because she has no basis in the property.
    D. Yes, over 31.5 years.

14. When one holds land as an investment, expenses such as taxes and interest are
    A. not deductible for income tax purposes.
    B. deductible in the year in which the expenses were incurred.
    C. deductible the following year.
    D. deductible only when the property is sold.

15. In relation to the monthly income produced, which of the properties listed below tend to be overpriced?
    A. Houses/condominiums   C. Office buildings
    B. Apartment buildings   D. Warehouses

16. Houses and condominiums are attractive to some investors because
    A. they can generate a negative cash flow.
    B. they often resell at a higher price than would be justified by rents alone.
    C. they often generate attractive positive cash flows.
    D. they decline in value which can be used to off-set a high income.

17. To be considered a good investment, when a property which generates a negative cash flow is sold,
    A. there must be a substantial increase in property value.
    B. there need be little increase in property value.
    C. the investor is best off if the property has decreased in value.
    D. must show a strong loss in order to reduce taxable income.

18. A woman is buying a 15-unit apartment building. The building will require
    A. two full-time managers.
    B. one full-time manager.
    C. a part-time manager who lives on the property.
    D. no on-site manager, just a couple of hours a week of her spare time.

19. An apartment building is usually considered large enough to support a full-time manager who lives on the property if it contains at least
    A. 25 units.   C. 75 units.
    B. 60 units.   D. 100 units.

20. Management costs per unit of an apartment building
    A. do not change as the number of units increases.
    B. rise in proportion to the number of units.
    C. stay the same until the number of units double; then costs double.
    D. drop as the number of units increase.

21. A man is looking for a job as a manager for a 20 to 30 unit apartment building. If hired, he will be expected to do all of the following EXCEPT
    A. file the owner's tax returns.   C. take rental applications.
    B. show vacant units.   D. perform maintenance tasks.

22. A person's investment objective is to produce the highest possible cash flow per invested dollar. Should he choose an investment in an office building in preference to a similar investment in an apartment building?
    A. Yes, because office buildings cost less to build than apartments.
    B. Yes, because office buildings usually return a greater yield on investment.
    C. No, because apartments usually can demand a higher rent per square foot.
    D. No, because operating costs on apartments are less than on office buildings.

23. Which of the following usually nets the highest cash flow per dollar invested?
    A. Single-family residence
    B. Two-to-four unit apartments
    C. Large office building
    D. Vacant land

24. Generally, the cost of providing amenities is greatest in
    A. office buildings.
    B. single-family dwellings.
    C. small apartment buildings.
    D. large apartment complexes.

25. Tenant turnover expense is greatest in which of the following types of property?
    A. Office buildings
    B. Small apartment buildings
    C. Large apartment buildings
    D. Single family residences

26. In giving a tenant a long-term lease, the owner takes the risk that
    A. the lease will make the building easier to sell.
    B. operating costs may increase without an increase in rent.
    C. the tenant may "skip" without finishing the lease.
    D. the proper tenant mix is not maintained over a long period.

27. The risk in locating an office building is
    A. greater than with residential properties.
    B. less than with residential properties.
    C. about the same as with residential properties.
    D. no different than with residential properties.

28. Usually, the earlier an investor enters into a real estate development investment,
    A. the lower the risk he undertakes.
    B. the less the potential reward he expects to receive.
    C. the less safe the investment, so the return on investment will be lower.
    D. the greater the profit he expects.

29. The developer's profit on a new real estate development is taxable
    A. upon completion of the project.
    B. when the property is finally sold.
    C. upon listing of the property.
    D. at phases during development.

30. Upon completion of a new development, tax benefits are
    A. no longer available.
    B. equal to those available during the development stages.
    C. higher than those available during the development stages.
    D. lower than during the development stages.

31. Which of the following would expect to receive a higher return per investment dollar? An investor who purchased during
    A. the first decade of building life.
    B. the second decade of building life.
    C. the third or fourth decade of building life.
    D. any portion would expect the same return.

32. For most people, when is the best time in life to undertake high-risk investments?
    A. Under age 25
    B. Age 25 to 45
    C. Age 55 to 65
    D. Over age 65

33. A couple in their late twenties are thinking about their lifetime investment strategy. In what order should they consider the following strategies?
    I. Emphasis on low-risk investments and liquidation of assets
    II. Emphasis on high return, risk-taking and tax shelter
    III. Emphasis on moderate return, moderate risks and tax shelter
    A. I, II, III   C. II, III, I
    B. II, I, III   D. III, II, I

34. A strategy to minimize taxes calls for sound investments that maximize tax shelter during
    A. peak income years.   C. early income years.
    B. post-retirement years.   D. after age 55.

35. Mrs. R. invested in real estate by investing in a limited partnership which purchased two shopping centers. As a limited partner, she will enjoy
    A. management of the properties by hiring a good property manager.
    B. expanded financial liability.
    C. greater risk because of the two properties.
    D. the same tax benefits as she would enjoy as a sole owner.

36. In a limited partnership, which participants cannot lose more than the amount they have invested?
    A. General partners   C. Organizers
    B. Limited partners   D. Managers

37. From the investor's point of view, the best way to compensate the organizers of a limited partnership is by means of a
    A. fixed fee.
    B. share of the partnership's profits.
    C. brokerage fee on properties purchased
    D. brokerage fee on properties sold.

38. The risk of an investor losing his money is known as
    A. downside risk.   C. upside risk.
    B. backside risk.   D. limited risk.

39. To receive maximum benefits from a limited partnership, a person considering such an investment should
    A. plan to sell very early on before the properties are refinanced or sold.
    B. remember that limited partnerships are difficult to sell for the proportional worth of the investor's interest.
    C. plan to be actively involved in the day-to-day management.
    D. remember that such an investment is not very liquid.

40. Federal laws regulating limited partnerships are administered by the
    A. Federal Trade Commission.
    B. Securities and Exchange Commission.
    C. Real Estate Commission.
    D. Federal Housing Authority.

41. A disclosure statement given to prospective investors in a limited partnership, outlining the plans and proposals for the partnership, is called a
    A. prospectus.   C. cash flow.
    B. forecast statement.   D. binder.

42. Laws that permit a state government to halt the sale of an investment opportunity (such as a limited partnership) are called
    A. disclosure laws.
    B. blue-sky laws.
    C. federal trade laws.
    D. deceptive trade practices laws.

SECTION 27.2: Investment Problems

Study the investment properties described below, then match them up with the investors described in the section that follows the property descriptions. It is possible that more than one property would be suitable for any investor, or vice-versa. After you have made your selections, give a brief summary of your reasons for the selection.

I. **Condominium apartment** in a new high-rise building, just completed. Has all amenities, a good location on major bus routes, shopping and all other service facilities nearby, 80% conventional financing available. After the mortgage amortization, association dues and taxes, you estimate that rental income will generate a small negative cash flow. The prospects for appreciation are good. Present and future indicators signify a strong rental market for this type of unit over the foreseeable future. Professional management is available.

II. **Small apartment building** containing 5 units, ten years old. New refrigerators installed in each unit within past year. Located in a stable middle class neighborhood, convenient to shopping and on a bus route. Tenants pay own utilities, except for heat and air conditioning. Is presently managed by the owners, a married couple who live in one unit. Husband is ill and has been advised to move to another climate. All apartments are now rented on one-year leases which have from six to ten months to run. Present rent schedule indicates a modest positive cash flow.

III. **Garden apartment development** with 48 units, 12 in each of four buildings. The development is 12 years old, well maintained, and is managed by a professional management firm. Operating statements for the past several years show a good cash flow, but this is based on an existing mortgage loan on which the balance is low in relation to present value, and is at a rate of interest which you estimate to be at least 2% per annum below the present rate for similar loans. The existing loan cannot be assumed. Existing market conditions in the area indicate that if refinanced on available terms, the operating statement would reflect a strong negative cash flow. Location, construction, and market condition indicate a probable appreciation of 30% over the next ten years.

IV. A **syndicate** is being formed to construct an office building in a prime downtown location. Syndicators have been in business for 15 years, and all have considerable experience in the field. Several prior enterprises have all been successful. The syndicate will be organized as a limited partnership. The property will be managed by the organizers upon completion. Firm lease commitments from credit tenants have been secured for nearly 50% of the space. Market conditions show a need for modern office space in the community. Syndicators have set a minimum investor participation in the syndicate at $50,000. Projections indicate a strong cash flow upon completion plus excellent investment tax credits.

V. **Single family house,** two years old, in suburban tract development. It has three bedrooms, two baths, central air, and well maintained. Present owner is being transferred. VA loan representing 90% of present appraised value may be assumed. Estimated rent, based upon rents presently being received for similar homes in the development, would produce a small negative cash flow after deductions for mortgage amortization, taxes, insurance, and reasonable allowances for maintenance and vacancy. Market value has appreciated 6% per year since it was built, and projections are for it to continue at about this rate for the foreseeable future. A strong rental market indicates excellent possibilities for immediate rental to responsible tenants.

Match the investors described below to the properties previously described. You may assume that in each case the price is agreeable, and that adequate financing can be obtained. Remember it is possible that more than one property may be suitable for each investor, and vice-versa.

1. **Corporate executive** with income all from salary and bonuses. Earnings place him in a tax bracket above 50%. Employment requires long hours at work and considerable travel out of the city for days at a time. Executive has considerable funds available in the form of savings and investments in securities. Prospects for increased earnings are good, and present scale of living allows for continued savings. Age 42 years.

   Recommended Investment #:   I   II   III   IV   V

   Reasons for recommendation: _____

   _____

   _____

   _____

2. **Married couple,** husband 57 years old, employed as machinist in local manufacturing plant. Wife is 55 years old, does not work. Both in good health. Own present home worth an estimated $55,000, free and clear. Plans are for husband to retire in three years and would like an investment that would supplement their retirement income. Have several thousand dollars in savings in company credit union, plus a few thousand cash value in life insurance. Wife finds present home too large for present needs.

   Recommended Investment #:   I   II   III   IV   V

   Reasons for recommendation: _____

   _____

   _____

   _____

3. **Young married couple,** husband 30 years old, wife 28, no children. Both work, he as a junior executive and she as an airline flight attendant. All income is from salaries and husband's annual bonus. Several thousand dollars equity in home, plus cash in savings and mutual fund investments. Investment objective is to shelter some income from taxes and to build estate. Husband does some traveling in his work.

   Recommended Investment #:   I   II   III   IV   V

   Reasons for recommendation: _____

   _____

   _____

   _____

4. **Group of doctors** organized as a corporation. All of them work very long hours at their practice. The corporation has accumulated over $150,000 in undisbursed profits. Individual investment objectives are to build estates and secure all possible immediate tax shelter against personal income.

Recommended Investment #:   I   II   III   IV   V

Reasons for recommendation: _____

_____

_____

_____

5. **Bachelor,** 38 years old, no plans to marry. Has an above average income from employment as accountant in civil service position. Modest savings. No need for additional income, but desires to shelter some income from taxation, and to provide guard against inflation through investment with potential for greater appreciation than available through savings.

Recommended Investment #:   I   II   III   IV   V

Reasons for recommendation: _____

_____

_____

_____

Answer Key

CHAPTER 2

1. D Land, by definition, includes all natural attachments. Real estate includes anything affixed to the land and can include appurtenant buildings and anything else attached, but not emblements, harvestable annual crops.

2. B The deed conveys ownership of the buildings and improvements as well as the land because they are considered appurtenant the land.

3. A Fixtures were personal property which are now permanently attached to the land or buildings thereon.

4. B Any property not considered to be real estate is classified as personal property.

5. B The cost of the article has no bearing on whether an article has become a fixture; but the manner of attachment, its adaptation to the land, and the existence of an agreement between the parties would be considered.

6. A An oriental throw rug would not be a fixture, but built-in appliances and custom-fitted wall-to-wall carpet installed over plywood sub flooring would be.

7. D Personal property installed in a rented building by a tenant for the operation of a business is a trade fixture, and remains the property of the tenant if removed before expiration of the lease.

8. B Emblements are personal property; but fixtures, shrubbery and air rights are classified as real property.

9. D An appurtenance is a right, privilege, or improvement which belongs to and runs with the land. Easements, rights-of-way and condominium parking stalls meet this test.

10. B Riparian rights allow owners to use water from a stream which abuts their land.

11. B The owner of land which abuts a stream has riparian rights to use water from the stream.

12. B Percolating water is water not confined to a defined underground waterway.

13. A The table at which water will be located is known as the water table.

14. B A street address is sufficiently accurate for use in a residential lease contract, but not in most other real estate contracts.

15. A Any permanent identifiable object may be used as a monument in a metes and bounds description. Only the iron pipe fits these criteria.

16. B The first corner of a parcel of surveyed land is known as the point of beginning.

17. D Determine by adding the distance from north to east (90°), and then add half the distance from east to south (45°) = 135°

18. D The surveyor may travel in either direction, but will always begin at one corner identified as the point of beginning. Angular bearings are measured from north or south toward east or west. He must physically inspect the property.

19. D Principal meridians, guide meridians, and longitude lines all run north-south. Standard parallels run east-west.

20. A Base lines run in an east-west direction. Guide meridians run north-south.

21. B A quadrangle measures 24 by 24 miles and is created by the guide meridians and correction lines.

22. A Sections are numbered as follows:

    6 5 4 3 2 1

    7 8 9 10 11 12

    Section 10 is directly south of section 3.

23. A A township consists of 36 sections, is six miles on a side, and contains 36 square miles.

24. B Ranges run north-south, and are identified by counting them east or west of the principal meridian.

25. A An acre is any parcel of land, in any shape, which contains exactly 43,560 square feet.

26. A A section of land measures 1 mile on a side and has one sq. mile ($1 \times 1 = 1$).

27. A $1/4 \times 1/4 \times 1/4 = 1/64; 640 \times 1/64 = 10$ acres

28. D The terms "recorded survey system," "lot-block-tract system" and "recorded map system" all refer to identification of land by recorded plat. The assessor's parcel system has its own reference system.

29. A Formal land description may be based on a recorded deed or a recorded mortgage, but not an assessor's parcel No., a tax map, or an unrecorded mortgage.

30. A A "grid system" or "coordinate system" based on latitude and longitude is used in several states.

31. B Datum is the point, line, or surface from which vertical height or depth is measured in a vertical land descrip-

tion. A plat is a map showing the boundaries of a parcel of land.

32. B Either a benchmark set by government survey team or the surface of the parcel may be used as the datum to describe subsurface minerals.

33. B The elevation is used to describe an air lot. The other items listed here are not relevant when describing an air lot.

34. A Topographical features such as hills, valleys, etc., are on contour maps.

35. D Scarcity, a man-made characteristic, is an economic characteristic. Immobility, indestructibility, and non homogeneity are all physical characteristics of land (note that fungible means freely substitutable).

36. C Non homogeneity is a physical characteristic of land. Scarcity, modification, and situs are all economic characteristics of land.

37. A One parcel of land cannot be precisely substituted for another, and thus land is nonfungible.

38. B The term **situs** refers to the preference of people for a given location. **Fixity** refers to the fact that land requires a long time to pay for itself.

39. D "Location, location, location" means that people will pay more for certain preferred sites than for other sites.

Tests of a Fixture

1. A	5. A	9. B	13. B
2. A	6. A	10. A	14. A
3. A	7. B	11. A	15. A
4. A	8. A	12. B	16. A

Lot Types

A. Cul de sac lots: 9, 10, 11, 12, 13, 14

B. Flag lot: 5

C. Corner lots: 3, 16

D. Inside lots: 2, 4, 6, 7, 8, 15

E. Key lot: 2, 15

F. T-lot: 6

Subdivision Plats

1. C This describes lot 12. You begin at the northernmost P.R.M., then travel 225.99 feet southeasterly to the northern corner of lot 12 and then around lot 12 in a clockwise direction.

2. A Lot 22 faces north (the facing side of a lot is the street side).

3. C Lot 11 is 80′ × 125′ and lot 12 is 90′ × 125′. All other pairs have equal square footage.

4. D Lot 24 is 100′ × 139.54′ = 13,954 sq. ft., thus is approximately 13,950 sq. ft.

5. C Bonview Drive is 30′ from each side to the center, hence a total width of 60′.

6. D The radius shown for the Bonview circle is R = 50′; hence the diameter is twice that or 100′.

7. C Lot 16 has frontage of 65.92′ plus 18.69′, for a total frontage of 84.61′.

8. A Lot 20 has 76.04′ of street frontage, as does lot 23. The other pairs do not have equal frontage.

9. B The northern corner of lot 12 is formed by the intersection of lines N 53° 29′ 40″ E and S 36° 30′ 20″ E. From S 36° 30′ 20″ E to due south is 36° 30′ 20″. Note that N 53° 29′ 40″ E is the same line as S 53° 29′ 40″ W. From S 53° 29′ 40″ W to due south is 53° 29′40″. Adding 53° 29′ 40″ to 36° 30′ 20″ gives 90° 00′ 00″, the total angle of the northern corner of lot 12.

10. C The fastest way to solve this is to know that from due north to due south is 180° 00′ 00″. S 36° 30′ 20″ E is 36° 30′ 20″ less than 180°, and when subtracted from 180° is 143° 29′ 40″. By the way, the long way around is 180° + 36° 30′ 20″ = 216° 30′ 20″.

11. B The easement shown by the dashed line runs along the backyards of lots 24, 25, and 26.

12. C The depth of a lot is the distance from front to back; in the case of lot 26 that is 139.54 feet.

Rectangular Survey

1. C The easiest way to work rectangular survey problems is to read the description backward. Thus, with the NE 1/4 of the SW 1/4 of the SE 1/4, you first look for the SE 1/4, then within it the SW 1/4, then within that the NE 1/4. This describes parcel U.

2. A Parcel H is a half of a half of a quarter of a quarter of a section. That's 1/2 × 1/2 × 1/4 × 1/4 × 640 = 10 acres.

3. B Work in reverse, starting in the NE 1/4, then within it the SE 1/4 and then within that the N 1/2. This leads you to parcel K.

4. B Parcel X is 1/2 of 1/4 of 1/4 of 1/4 of a section. Lengthwise, it occupies 1/2 of 1/4 of the south side of section 12. That makes it 1/2 × 1/4 × 5,280′ = 660′. The width is 1/4 × 1/4 × 5,280′ = 330′.

5. D Parcel Q is 1/4 × 1/4 × 640 = 40 acres. Parcel Y is the same, so the total is 80 acres.

6. B Again, go in reverse starting in the NW 1/4, then within that the NW 1/4, and within that the E 1/2.

7. A Again, go in reverse starting in the NE 1/4, then within that the SE 1/4, and within that the N 1/2.

8. D Start in the SE 1/4, within that the SW 1/4, within that the SE 1/4 and within that the NW 1/4.

9. D Start at the northeast corner of the section, follow the directions and remember that a section is 5,280 feet on a side.

CHAPTER 3

1. B Under the allodial system, individuals may own land. This is not possible under the feudal system.

2. C The king, or sovereign, owned the land under the feudal system, and was responsible for providing government services.

3. A Governments may acquire ownership of privately owned land under emi-

nent domain, but not through police power, taxation or rent control.

4. A The power of eminent domain may be used to take private land for public use through the process of condemnation.

5. D Severance damages may be paid when a portion of a parcel of land is being taken, or as compensation for damages to the remaining land after a portion was taken through condemnation.

6. B Police power is a government's right to make reasonable rules for the use of privately held land.

7. D Restrictive covenants are a means of private land-use controls. Rent controls, building codes and zoning laws are examples of a government's exercise of its police powers.

8. B Property owners are not compensated for a loss suffered from a government's exercise of its police powers.

9. B An owner who fails to comply with the government's exercise of police powers is subject to civil and/or criminal penalty, but not to confiscation or escheat.

10. C Property escheats to the state or county (in some states), not to the city or federal government.

11. A An owner who is without heirs may avoid having property escheat to the state by leaving a valid will or by giving it away prior to death.

12. A The federal government has the responsibility for protecting property owners from acts of foreign governments.

13. D The holder of fee simple title to land may not violate building, health and safety codes, but may occupy and use it, restrict its use, and devise it by will.

14. C A private owner may disinherit heirs, but may not refuse to sell to the government, reject a claim for taxes or repudiate zoning laws.

15. B The term "estate" refers to one's legal rights in the land, not to its quantity in physical terms, nor to its value.

16. A The holder of a life estate holds whatever rights are conveyed to him by the fee simple title holder.

17. B With reference to land, the term "title" refers to evidence of ownership.

18. A An encumbrance is anything which impedes or impairs the title to real property.

19. A A will is not an encumbrance to the title to real property, but restrictive covenants, mortgages or leases are encumbrances.

20. A An easement is a right of use and enjoyment of another's land for a special purpose.

21. B An easement by prescription arise from constant use rather than a document.

22. D An easement by prescription is acquired by constant use without the existence of a written document.

23. B The easement is an easement appurtenant which runs with the property. The dominant estate is held by the holder of the easement (K) and the servient estate is held by the landowner (M).

24. C A utility easement is a commercial easement in gross, and encumbrance to the servient estate. There is no dominant estate.

25. B A party wall is jointly owned and neither owner may damage or destroy it without the other's consent.

26. A An easement appurtenant may be terminated by combination of the dominant and servient tenements, by abandonment or when its purpose no longer exists. It cannot be terminated unilaterally by the holder of the servient tenement.

27. D An encroachment is the unauthorized intrusion of a building or improvement on another's land.

28. B A deed covenant, also known as a deed restriction, is a private agreement that governs the use of land.

29. B Failure to abide by a restrictive covenant may result in a civil action by the grantor or by adjacent property

owners. It will not result in criminal action by the government or other property owners.

30. C A restrictive covenant in a deed is an encumbrance but not a lien. Mortgages, unpaid taxes and judgments are liens.

31. A A mortgage lien is a voluntary lien which arises from actions of the parties. Tax and judgment liens are statutory liens which arise from operation of law.

32. A The mechanic's lien attaches to the property on which the work was performed or for which materials were supplied.

33. B A mechanic's lien attaches to the land and buildings named in the lien, but not to personal property within the structure.

34. D Ad valorem tax liens are superior to all other liens in priority.

35. A The estate is a fee simple determinable.

36. C The estate is a qualified fee estate and a fee simple estate subject to condition precedent, i.e., a certain condition must precede title passage.

37. B The estate is a life estate held by the parents and R holds a reversion.

38. B The estate is a life estate and as the life tenant she is entitled to any income produced during her tenancy. She is responsible for property taxes during her life tenancy and she, not her son, may sell or convey her life interest.

39. C A life tenant must pay taxes on the property during the life tenancy.

40. D A leasehold estate is an estate less-than-freehold.

41. A An interest acquired by a lease is a leasehold and estate less-than-freehold.

42. A An estate for years is of definite duration and does not automatically renew itself upon termination.

43. B A lessee who assigns his rights to another party becomes the sublessor.

44. B A sublessee may be granted only those rights in the property which are held by the lessee.

45. A Unless a landlord or tenant acts to terminate it, an estate from period-to-period automatically renews itself and continues indefinitely.

46. C An estate at will is terminable by either party at any time with notice.

47. A A tenant retaining possession of a premises after termination of the lease without the landlord's agreement is known as a tenant at sufferance.

48. D A license to use land is not an encumbrance on the land. It is a personal privilege, revocable, and not assignable.

49. C A theater ticket is a license. Since it is a personal privilege it can be canceled.

50. A Chattels are personal property.

51. A Common law derives its authority from custom and usage.

52. B Statutory law is created by enactment of legislation.

53. B Laws governing the licensing of real estate agents are examples of statutory law, enacted by state legislatures.

54. C. Life estate created for the life of another.

Land Area Problems

1 The area of the lot $= 125' \times 160' = 20,000$ sq. ft. Cost per sq. ft. $= \$19,000 \div 20,000$ sf. $= \$.95/\text{sf}$. The gain per sq. foot $= \$1.15 - \$.95 = \$.20/\text{sf}$. $(40' + 10') \div 2 \times 125' \times \$.20/\text{sf}. = \textbf{\$625}$ answer

2. Lot size $= (400' + 420') \div 2 \times 150' = 61,500$ sq. ft. Lot cost $= \$30,750 \div 61,500$ sq. ft. $= \$.50/\text{sq. ft.}$ Encroachment $= (20' \times 150') \div 2 \times \$.50 = \$750$. $\$750 - \$475 = \textbf{\$275}$ (cheaper to move fence)

A note on what to do first: The rule is to perform all calculations inside all parentheses first. Then do the multiplication and division. Then do the addition and subtraction. Thus, in Line 1 of number 2 above, the first step is to add 400' and 420'. The sum is then divided by 2 and multiplied by 150'.

CHAPTER 4

1. C Ownership in severalty is ownership by one person. This may be an individual person or a partnership, corporation or other legal entity owning in its name solely.

2. A An owner of property in severalty has freedom of choice as to use or disposition of the property, but does not necessarily have the ability to defeat a spouse's claim of dower or curtesy.

3. B Tenants in common do not need separate deeds to their respective shares of ownership in the property. One deed with all of their names is sufficient and customary.

4. A Whenever the co-owners have unequal shares of ownership, they are tenants in common, and there cannot be survivorship among tenants in common, so naming each other as heirs in the wills is necessary to convey the interest on death.

5. A Tenants in common hold undivided interests in the entire property. One tenant cannot claim a portion for his own use.

6. C A tenant in common may dispose of all or part of his interest independent of the other tenants and without their permission.

7. B Difficulty of disposing of undivided interest and liability for debts against the property are hazards of co-ownership, both tenancy in common and joint tenancy.

8. C Joint tenants have equal interest in the property, and the right to survivorship, and take title in one document or deed. Joint tenants are fully liable for debts incurred on the property.

9. B Right of survivorship exists among joint tenants, but not tenants in common, limited partnerships, or corporations.

10. B New joint tenants may not be added to an existing joint tenancy without forming a new joint tenancy.

11. A Only by using a will can M retain the flexibility to change her mind later.

12. C Should any unity of joint tenancy be broken, the estate becomes a tenancy in common.

13. A The new co-owner (M) will be a tenant in common with the remaining joint tenants, who remain joint tenants among themselves. M will own one-third undivided interest and Y and Z will continue holding a two-thirds undivided interest.

14. B The concept of tenancy by the entireties is based upon English law, which treats a husband and wife as one legal unit.

15. C At death the survivor owns the property in severalty. They do not have disposable interests, and should a tenancy by the entireties be terminated by divorce, the parting spouses become tenants in common with one another.

16. D A spouse's right of curtesy or dower is defeated by holding title to property as a joint tenant with another person.

17. A In the absence of any other agreement, tenants by the entireties who get divorced become tenants in common with one another.

18. B The premise that husband and wife are equal partners is fundamental to the concept of community property law.

19. C Any property purchased after marriage is treated as community property in states which have community property laws.

20. C This property will be treated as community property since it was purchased with marital funds. Both spouses' signatures will be required on the deed if it is sold.

21. A Following marriage, a person's earnings are considered to be marital funds, and any property purchased from these earnings will be treated as community property. The husband's name need not appear on the deed.

22. B Under community property law, a spouse may devise his or her share to anyone, provided the surviving spouse

does not have survivorship rights such as with joint tenancy ownership.

23. C In community property states, property not held as community property is designated as separate property.

24. D A limited partnership has a general partner or partners, and all other partners are limited partners.

25. B The list of partners must be published in the county and state where the partnership owns property.

26. B In a general partnership, each partner has unlimited financial liability, and pays individual taxes on earnings from the partnership.

27. D Corporate income is taxed to the corporation, and may be taxed as individual income upon disbursement to stockholders.

28. B Limited partnerships permit the pass-through of profits while limiting the financial liability of limited partners to the amount of their investment.

29. B Limited partnerships are managed by a general partner or partners. Limited partners have little or no voice in the management decisions.

30. B Limited liability, minimum management responsibilities, and direct pass-through of profits have all contributed to the popularity of the limited partnership form of ownership.

31. B Before investing in a limited partnership one should determine whether or not it is suitable for one's personal objectives and investigate the past performance of the general partners.

32. A A joint venture is formed to carry out a single project.

33. D Shares of stock are more liquid than sole ownership of real property.

34. C Only in a corporation do owners possess shares of stock as evidence of ownership.

35. A Double taxation on income is possible in the corporation form of ownership.

36. A Protection from personal liability exists within the corporate form of ownership, but not in a general partnership.

37. D The management policies of a corporation are determined by its board of directors and then implemented by its officers. Stockholders have no management role, but do elect the board of directors. Day-to-day operations are the responsibility of the corporate officers.

38. B A testamentary trust takes effect after the death of its creator.

39. B A member or manager of a limited liability company is not liable for its debts, obligations or liabilities. Such a company may be organized by anyone 18 years or older and may not be a corporation or partnership. The name of a limited liability company must include "Limited," "LTD" or "LIC."

Ownership Situations

1. A. A cloud on the title exists due to rights held by Mabel.

   B. None, except that it is customary to file a death certificate and a description of the property in the public records to make the matter clear to anyone searching the title.

   C. Tenants in common.

   D. Sell the unwanted interest, or buy the other's interest, or petition for partition.

   E. The property would be sold and proceeds divided.

   F. The property can be attached and sold only if Mabel dies first. (This is why lenders require both to sign.)

2. **Community Property**

   A. Mabel can keep this as separate property.

   B. This is legal. No dower rights exist under community property.

   C. Separate property. No dower rights exist under community property.

3. A. The surviving joint tenant would acquire full ownership. This cannot be defeated by will.

B. The widow would have no rights under joint tenancy only. The surviving joint tenant would have survivorship rights.

4. A. Tenancy in common is presumed.

B. Brown 20%; Jones 30%; Smith 50%.

C. Ownership would not be split among the apartment units, as each owner holds an undivided interest in the whole property.

D. Smith can sell to Green without the agreement of Jones or Brown. All would be tenants in common.

E. The rules of intestate succession would apply.

F. This would be community property. His spouse or his descendants, depending on state law, would acquire his interest if he dies intestate.

G. Earnings would be apportioned among the owners according to their respective interests.

5. A REIT is composed of trustees and beneficiaries, the latter providing capital by the purchase of beneficial interests. Trustees invest this capital and the results are allocated and paid to the beneficiaries.

A. The investors are called beneficiaries.

B. REIT earnings are taxed only once at the beneficiary level provided certain rules are met.

C. Double taxation results, once to the REIT and once to the beneficiary, if the rules are not met.

CHAPTER 5

1. C The Statute of Frauds requires that transfer of real property ownership be written.

2. A The actual act of transferring ownership of land is known as a grant.

3. A For a deed to be valid, the grantor must be of legal age and of sound mind. The grantor must sign the deed; it need not be recorded to be effective. The grantee can be of any age.

4. B The statement of love constituted a good consideration, sufficient for the validity of the deed.

5. A The words of conveyance are the grantor's statement that he is making a grant of the property to the grantee. They do not warrant that the grantor has the right to convey.

6. D A fee simple estate, life estate or easement may be conveyed by deed, but not a leasehold.

7. C A property description in a deed must be specific enough so as not to be misunderstood. Only the description in response C meets this test.

8. D Even though a deed conveys only air or mineral rights, the deed must contain a legal description of the land and words of conveyance, as well as the grantor's signature.

9. B The grantor must sign a deed for it to convey title. The grantee's signature is not necessary.

10. A A deed does not convey title until it is delivered and accepted.

11. B The covenant of quiet enjoyment assures that the grantee will not be disturbed by someone else claiming an interest in the property.

12. D The covenant against encumbrances, not the covenant of warranty forever or the covenant of further assurance, assures that the title to the property is not encumbered by undisclosed encumbrances.

13. B A covenant of further assurance assures that any additional documents necessary for the perfection of the grantee's title will be executed by the grantor.

14. D The covenant of warranty forever is the absolute guarantee that the title and the rights to possession are as the deed states.

15. D Deeds are usually acknowledged to make them admissible to record. An acknowledgment is not essential to the deed's validity or enforceability.

16. B A special warranty deed warrants only against defects occurring during the

grantor's ownership. It does not contain all five covenants and warranties, as do the other deeds named.

17. A A general warranty deed provides the grantee with the most assurances of title, and is the best deed the grantee can receive.

18. A Rights that pass with the conveyance are identified as appurtenances.

19. A The phrase "the grantee's heirs and assigns forever" indicates the conveyance of a fee simple estate.

20. A The word "assigns" in a deed refers to anyone to whom the grantee may later convey the property.

21. C Rights which are not to be conveyed by deed may be excluded in the deed and will not be conveyed.

22. A The description of the land in a deed automatically conveys any buildings on the land.

23. D The exact form and wording of a deed are flexible as long as all essentials are present and in conformity with state law.

24. B The grantor under a grant deed is responsible for encumbrances during the period of time that he owned the property. The grantor is not responsible for encumbrances of future owners.

25. C Special warranty deeds warrant against defects occurring during the grantor's ownership, but not against defects existing before that time.

26. A A quitclaim deed conveys only the grantor's interest at the time of conveyance.

27. B Quitclaim deeds are often used to remove a cloud from a title or to convey the grantor's interest without imposing upon the grantor any future obligations to defend the title.

28. B Gift deeds usually take the form of bargain and sale deeds to avoid committing the grantor to any warranties of title.

29. D The grantor must state his legal authority to convey the property in a guardian's deed.

30. D The words "remise" and "release" are most likely to be found in a quitclaim deed.

31. A Either a sheriff's deed or a referee's deed in foreclosure may be used to convey title as the result of mortgage foreclosure.

32. A A correction deed, also called a deed of confirmation, may be used to correct an error in a previously executed and delivered deed.

33. D Courts which are empowered to admit and certify wills are called either probate courts or surrogate courts.

34. C Title acquired by inheritance from a person who died intestate is known as title by descent or title by intestate succession.

35. A The term "escheat" refers to the passing of title to the state when no will or heirs can be found for the decedent's estate.

36. B A handwritten will signed by the testator but not witnessed is a holographic will.

37. C Title acquired by occupation of another's land is called title by adverse possession.

38. D To successfully claim title by adverse possession, a claimant must have been in actual possession of the land in an open and notorious manner continuously for the statutory period in the jurisdiction. If the claimant had the owner's permission to occupy the land, there would not be adverse possession.

39. A J has color of title.

40. A Assumption of the rights of a previous adverse possessor, either through adverse possession or assignment, is known as "tacking on."

41. C An easement by prescription is acquired by prolonged adverse use.

42. B A claim of adverse possession can be forestalled by ejecting the trespasser or by giving the trespasser the right to trespass.

43. C Accretion is the process of increasing the size of a parcel of land by the gradual deposit of water-borne soil.

44. B Reliction results from the recession of the waterline, exposing dry land.

45. A Land acquired through accretion or reliction is known as ownership by accession.

46. C Conveyance of land by a government to a private citizen is called a public grant.

47. B Land may be transferred from the public domain to private ownership by means of a land patent.

48. B Dedication is a voluntary gift of privately held land to the public domain.

49. D Common law dedication arises when a landowner, by act or work, shows that he intends land to be dedicated, even though no written dedication has been made.

50. A Forfeiture can result from a grantee's failure to meet a condition or limitation imposed by the grantor.

Deed Situations

1. Executor's deed. This is a legal requirement when probating a will.

2. Quitclaim deed. C conveys whatever rights he might still have to the purchaser.

3. General warranty deed. This offers the most protection to the grantee.

4. Gift deed. This is a special warranty deed with the wording "for natural love and affection" as consideration. With only one covenant, he limits his liability exposure.

5. The buyer would ask for a warranty deed or grant deed depending upon the state. These would provide the most protection available from a deed.

6. Preprinted forms may not be correct for the user's state, they may not fit the user's needs, and they may be filled in improperly.

7. Title insurance may be available. The grantee's purpose may require less than a warranty deed.

8. A will can be changed until the death of the testator. A grant cannot be changed once it has been made.

9. Color of title is some plausible suggestion of an ownership interest; for example, a relative claiming an interest in a deceased's estate, or a trespasser of long standing.

CHAPTER 6

1. A The Statute of Frauds requires that written deeds be used to show ownership.

2. C Recording an instrument in the public records provides both legal notice and constructive notice.

3. D The tenants give constructive notice by their occupancy and the investor should make inquiry as to the rights of each tenant. Apartment rental agreements are rarely recorded.

4. D Actual notice is gained by what one has actually seen, heard, read or observed.

5. A The public recorder's office is a central information station for documents pertaining to interests in land. It is kept up by the local, not the federal, government.

6. B Instruments which affect land transfers are recorded in the jurisdiction in which the land is situated.

7. B Documents are recorded by submitting the original document which is then photocopied and placed on file.

8. A An unrecorded deed is binding upon the parties to the deed, but not to subsequent purchasers, subsequent lenders, or the public generally.

9. A S, the first grantee, did not provide legally required notice by recordation or by taking possession of the property. T does give notice and becomes the publicly recognized owner of the property.

10. D Priority of recorded instruments is established by the date of recordation.

11. B A month-to-month lease is not usually recorded. Deeds, mortgages and options are usually recorded.

12. B Records in the public recorder's office are public records and available for inspection by anyone.

13. B   A prospective purchaser of real estate is presumed to have inspected both the land itself and the public records pertaining to the land.

14. A   Instruments should be recorded immediately after delivery to provide constructive notice and to establish priority of claim.

15. B   Documents are acknowledged to make certain that the person signing the document is the same person as the one named in the document, that the signing was voluntary, and to make the document admissible for recordation.

16. B   An abstracter will usually begin a title search by checking the grantee index, then the grantor index, then tracing the title back to its origin and finally checking the other public records as appropriate.

17. B   Instruments are recorded in chronological order, as received for recordation.

18. C   A chain of title is a historical record of ownership without reference to encumbrances or other documents affecting the title.

19. D   Records of the civil courts, probate courts, mortgage records and judgment rolls all have to be checked to establish an unbroken chain of title.

20. B   The name of the borrower would be filed alphabetically in the mortgagor index.

21. C   Chattel mortgage records are records of mortgages on personal property and would not normally be checked when searching land titles.

22. B   Pending lawsuits are indexed in the lis pendens index.

23. A   One who is engaged in searching land titles as an occupation may be referred to as an abstracter or as a title searcher.

24. B   A summary of all documents affecting title to a given parcel of land is known as an abstract of title.

25. A   An attorney's report as to who holds the fee title to a property and any rights or interest held by others is known as an opinion of title.

26. D   An abstracter is responsible for mistakes due to negligence, but is not held responsible for forged deeds, unextinguished dower rights or unrecorded deeds.

27. B   Title insurance provides the best protection against any incomplete or defective records of the title to land.

28. D   Title insurance is not casualty insurance and does not insure against a loss arising from any form of casualty such as a tornado, fire, etc.

29. D   The original purpose of title insurance was to provide protection for attorneys and abstracters.

30. B   Title insurance companies require a title report showing the apparent condition of the title before issuing a title insurance policy. No physical inspection of the property is required.

31. B   A binder is a commitment to insure the title to the property. A preliminary title report is not an insurance policy and does not commit the title insurance company to insure the title.

32. D   Title insurance does not insure against claims which could have been disclosed by a visual inspection or inquiry of persons in possession of the property.

33. D   A current survey would disclose any encroachments on the property, but these would not be disclosed by an abstract of title, title insurance or an attorney's opinion of title.

34. C   The premium for a title insurance policy is a single premium, paid only upon issuance.

35. D   A lender's policy of title insurance is issued in an amount equal to the original amount of the mortgage loan, not the acquisition cost. The coverage declines as the loan is amortized; the policy does not make exceptions for claims that could have been anticipated by a physical inspection of the property; and the policy is assignable to subsequent holders of the mortgage loan.

36. A   A title insurance policy issued for lender's protection is called a lender's policy.

37. B   The combined cost for both an owner's and a lender's title insurance policy is slightly more than the cost of an owner's policy alone.

38. B   Legal expenses incurred fighting a court claim are assumed by the title insurance company and are not deducted from any later settlement with the insured.

39. B   The $10,000 paid to settle the claim would be deducted from the coverage, leaving $20,000 coverage remaining.

40. B   Marketable title is title which is free of reasonable doubt as to ownership of the property.

41. D   Since title insurance insures only the title to the property, the need for casualty insurance, constructive notice and a survey of the property are not eliminated.

42. B   An owner's policy of title insurance provides greater assurance of marketable title than an attorney's certificate of title, a preliminary title report or a mortgagee's policy of title insurance.

43. B   A quiet title suit does not remove legitimate claims to title such as outstanding mortgages. It is a judicial proceeding which quiets the claims of those without a genuine interest in the property. As such it is used to clear up a disputed title.

44. A   The home owner could file a quiet title suit or negotiate and obtain quitclaim deeds from the minor owners.

45. A   A Torrens certificate of title is founded on a judicial decision; an attorney's certificate of title is founded on an opinion of the condition of the title.

46. A   A quiet title suit is necessary for a Torrens certificate. Marketable title acts do not require a suit.

47. C   Title insurance covers events that happened in the past (not just the last 40 years) but which are discovered after taking title to the property.

Short Answer Questions

1. Notice is given by physical occupation of one's land and by recording it in the public records.

2. Most states require an acknowledgment by the person executing a document before it can be recorded. Persons authorized to take acknowledgments include notaries public, recording office clerks, commissioners of deeds, judges and consular agents.

3. A title search will include a check of mortgage liens; any tax (federal, state and local) liens; mechanics' liens; pending litigation; judgment rolls; birth, marriage and death records; probate records, etc.

4. The owner's policy is good for the face amount of the policy indefinitely while the mortgagee's declines in coverage as the loan is repaid. The mortgagee's policy does not make exceptions for property inspection, while the owner's policy does.

5. A casualty policy protects against losses occurring from an event that has not yet happened. A title policy protects against past events that have not been discovered.

6. Title insurance is desirable because (a) the grantor can purchase insurance on the covenants he makes, (b) the grantor feels better protected, and (c) mortgage lending is more attractive.

7. Marketable title is title that is free from reasonable doubt as to who the owner is. Cures for less than marketable title include quiet title suit, title insurance, and quitclaim deeds from those claiming an interest in the property.

8. The mortgage electronic registration system, commonly known as MERS, is a computerized book registration system of tracking the beneficial interest of "bundle of rights" connected with both residential and commercial real estate loans.

CHAPTER 7

1. A   The agreement to buy and sell the car resulted from the stated intent of the parties. It was not necessary for the contract to be in writing, nor was an earnest money deposit required. The inclusion of a contingency did not affect its status as an express contract.

2. C   An implied contract arises from the actions of the parties, and not their stated intent, as would occur with a written or oral agreement.

3. D A bilateral contract is based upon a promise from one party in exchange for a promise from the other party.

4. C The contract was based upon a valuable consideration in the form of the exchange of promises.

5. D A unilateral contract is based upon a promise from one party in exchange for an act from the other party.

6. B A unilateral contract is enforceable against the offeror, but not against the offeree.

7. B A contract for forbearance is an agreement not to do a certain thing.

8. C The lender's agreement not to foreclose constituted an agreement not to do a certain thing, thus a contract for forbearance and an expressed contract.

9. C When one party to a contract is not bound by the contract, the contract is voidable by the party who is not bound by it.

10. B Any contract which does not meet the requirements of law would be classified as void.

11. A A power of attorney is a legal instrument which appoints a person as the attorney-in-fact for another person.

12. B The powers of an attorney-in-fact are derived from a power of attorney.

13. D A power of attorney may not be granted orally. It must be written, acknowledged and recorded.

14. C The authority to execute a contract in the name of a corporation must be granted by the corporation's board of directors.

15. A Built-in appliances become fixtures and a part of the realty unless excluded from the sale or removed prior to the offer to sell.

16. D A contract existed as soon as S, the seller, signed the purchase agreement. The purchaser, P, had previously signed the offer but no contract existed until it was signed by the seller.

17. B The statements of the seller, P, Jr., constituted innocent misrepresentation and made the contract voidable by the buyer. P, Jr., did not commit fraud, and the contract could not be voided by him.

18. C There cannot be mutual agreement when a contract is made under menace, undue influence, or duress.

19. A A contract signed under duress may be disavowed by the injured party only.

20. A Undue influence is the taking of an unfair advantage. Duress is the use or threat of force to complete the signing of a contract against one's will.

21. D Fraud occurs when one party deliberately deceives the other party to a contract.

22. B Only the injured party may disavow a contract based on fraud.

23. D A licensee who commits fraud may be subject to criminal prosecution, civil action for damages, and license revocation.

24. B The broker's statement to the purchaser constituted innocent misrepresentation, and the contract would be voidable by the purchaser only. Fraud was not present, and the broker would not be subject to license revocation.

25. A A contract made in jest is not based on mutual agreement and does not reflect contractual intent.

26. C Contracts with an unlawful objective are treated as void.

27. B A contract which requires a violation of the law is not enforceable, even though partial performance has taken place.

28. B The total amount to be paid for the property is the consideration. Earnest money is evidence of good faith and available as liquidated damages.

29. B A gift of property to a friend is based on a good consideration. Barter, trade, or sale constitute a valuable consideration.

30. D A mistake in a contract results from ambiguity in negotiations. It is not the result of ignorance, innocent misrepresentation, or poor judgment.

31. C An executory contract is one in which something still remains to be done. An executed contract is one which has been fulfilled.

32. C The Statute of Frauds requires that all contracts for the sale or mortgage of real estate be in writing. This requirement does not apply to month-to-month rentals or leases for one year or less.

33. C The parol evidence rule permits oral evidence to fulfill an otherwise incomplete contract.

34. C An assignment is a contract that transfers a right or interest. It does not release the parties from further liability under that contract. It is not a special form of power of attorney.

35. A A lessee who assigns his lease becomes both the assignor and the sublessor.

36. D Novation is the substitution of a new contract for an earlier contract, or the substitution of new parties to an old contract.

37. D R's objectives could be met by novation or by mutual rescission, but not by assignment or unilateral rescission.

38. A If a contractual objective should become legally impossible to accomplish, the law will consider the contract to be discharged. Lawsuits for specific performance, monetary damages, and liquidated damages would be inappropriate because a court would not enforce them.

39. B Under the Uniform Vendor and Purchaser Risk Act, the risk of loss to the property from casualty remains with the seller until title passes to the purchaser or possession is given to the purchaser, whichever occurs first.

40. B Failure to live up to one's contractual obligations constitutes a breach of contract.

41. B Legal action to compel a breaching party to carry out the remainder of a contract is known as an action for specific performance.

42. B The statute of limitations limits the time in which a wronged party may bring legal action for obtaining justice.

43. A An illiterate person may enter into a contract and it is valid.

44. D A seller may revoke his offer of employment, while a broker could renounce the listing.

Contract Situations

1. Taxicab ride, restaurant meals, barber shop. In each case, the proprietor makes an offer by way of his actions and facilities. When a customer accepts these services, he implies that he will pay, even though no verbal or written contract exists.

2. A marriage is a bilateral contract wherein both parties make promises to each other. A reward poster constitutes a unilateral contract for it is a promise by the offeror, but the offeree does not have to act. However, if he does, the offeror is committed to carry out his promises.

3A. S's defense would be that she was a minor and that contracts with minors for nonessential items are voidable by the minor.

3B. The contract is void since there was not mutual agreement as to the parcel of land involved.

3C. The contract is still valid and the buyers can sue the seller for specific performance.

3D. The contract is still valid and the buyers can sue the seller for specific performance.

4. Pauline could disavow the contract on the grounds of duress and menace.

5. The consideration would be stated as "love and affection" and be classified as good consideration.

6A. The deed is valid if it meets the requirements of a deed.

6B. A verbal agreement to sell real estate is not enforceable at law. Therefore, P cannot hold O to the price of $100,000 if O changes his mind before delivering the deed.

6C. Statute of Frauds

CHAPTER 8

1. C The buyer should have reached a firm decision to buy the property before signing a contract, but the contract gives him time to arrange financing, have the title examined, and determine the marketability of the title.

2. A A valid sales contract commits each of its parties to its terms and is enforceable in a court of law. It neither insures title nor guarantees loan approval.

3. B A formal real estate sales contract may be identified as a purchase contract, an offer to purchase, or a purchase offer, but not as an option contract.

4. D Provision for the purchaser's offer, an earnest money deposit, and the seller's acceptance are typically found in a real estate sales contract. What the buyer intends to change is not relevant.

5. C This agreement may be referred to as a land contract, contract for deed, or an installment contract.

6. A The amount of earnest money deposit is determined by negotiation.

7. D An escrow agent, the real estate broker, or an attorney may handle the paperwork and details of title transfer. A recorder of deeds would not be involved at this time.

8. C The process of apportioning taxes, interest, insurance, etc., is called proration.

9. B The buyer and the seller must allow the tenant to continue to lease since he has a one-year lease with time remaining. The seller cannot terminate the lease on one month's notice, give 30-day notice, or change the terms, i.e., raise the rent.

10. D The inclusion of a termite and dry rot clause in a sales contract is required by mortgage lenders.

11. C The buyer is typically given physical possession of the property on the day of close of escrow or settlement.

12. B The allocation of settlement expenses is negotiable between buyer and seller.

13. B The contract was voidable by the purchaser because it was subject to his ability to secure necessary financing. The seller does not have this option.

14. D The buyer may sue for specific performance, rescind the contract, or sue for monetary damages, but cannot demand liquidated damages, unless the contract provides for them (which is rare).

15. C An offer may be withdrawn at any time before it is accepted.

16. A If the term "time is of the essence" is included in a contract, the time limits set by the contract must be faithfully observed or the contract is voidable.

17. B An attorney should be consulted if the buyer has any doubts or questions as to the legal effects of the offer.

18. D The entire offer is considered to be rejected if the seller accepts part but not all of its conditions.

19. D Most real estate sales contracts are prepared by having the agent fill in blank spaces on a form which was approved by an attorney.

20. D Should a party to a sales contract die after its execution but before performance is completed, the contract remains binding on the other party and upon the estate of the decedent.

21. B In some states real estate agents use a binder to hold a deal together until a more formal contract can be prepared by an attorney.

22. A A letter of intent is not an agreement to enter into a contract and is not binding on either party.

23. A Both the seller and the buyer should be represented by an attorney, but there is generally no need for the agent to have legal representation.

24. B An installment calls for a deed to be delivered upon fulfillment of the contract terms, but gives the purchaser the right of occupancy during the contract period. It is not an option, nor are any monies paid to be considered "returnable" earnest money.

25. A Traditionally, the language of install-ment contracts for the purchase of real estate has tended to favor the vendor, i.e., the seller.

26. A The increasing use of installment con-tracts in real estate sales has led to some state laws designed to protect the buyer's interests.

27. A The purchaser's interests may be pro-tected by requiring the seller to place a deed in escrow and having the con-tract recorded in the land records.

28. D Details spelling out responsibilities for maintenance, payment of taxes and in-surance, and for casualty loss are all part of a well-written installment con-tract.

29. B Equitable title is a purchaser's right to acquire legal title to real property un-der the terms of a valid purchase agreement.

30. A Equitable title can be transferred by sale, inherited, mortgaged, or trans-ferred by deed.

31. A The seller retains legal title, but the buyer now holds an equitable interest in the property. The seller may not void the contract.

32. C Equitable title can be transferred by an assignment of a purchase contract or by novation with the seller's agree-ment.

33. B A lease with option to buy gives the tenant the right to purchase the prop-erty at any time during the option pe-riod at a preset price, not after the op-tion period.

34. B A lease-option tends to favor the op-tionee because the option may or may not be exercised by the optionee and the optionor has no choice but to ac-cept the optionee's decision.

35. A The lease-option and purchase contract should be negotiated at the same time to avoid future disagreements.

36. B Evidence of the tenant's option to buy should be recorded to establish the ten-ant's rights and the fact that these rights date back to the date of recorda-

tion. With an option, the owner is re-quired to see if the tenant decides to exercise the option. The tenant is under no obligation to do so.

37. C An option to buy is an executory con-tract because it is unfulfilled, and a unilateral contract because it is based on a promise in exchange for an act.

38. D The agreement was not a lease-option because it did not contain the elements of an option to buy.

39. B Property exchanges are popular among investors because of low cash requirements and possible deferral of income taxes on otherwise taxable gain from the first property.

40. B Taxes on the gain from the sale of an owner-occupied dwelling are not due if it was owned for 24 months.

41. D Properties that are being exchanged need not be of equal value, and more than two properties may be ex-changed. Cash, also known as boot, may be involved in the transaction.

42. C The 1984 Tax Reform Act requires that the designated property to be ex-changed be identified within 45 days of the original closing, that title be ac-quired within 180 days of closing, and that the property be received before the designating party's tax return is due.

43. D This trade can be successfully done by using either approach A or answer C. It won't work for W if he accepts the money offered by J in response B.

Math Problems

1. $(200' \times \$96.50 + 2 \times \$1,000) \times 1.30 = $ **\$27,690**
   Note that $200' \times 435.6' = 2$ acres

2. $150' \times 180' \times .75 = 20,250$ sf., without buildings
   $150' \times 180' \times .15 = 4,050$ sf., sold to state
   $20,250$ sq. ft. $- 4,050$ sq. ft. $=$ **16,200** sq. ft.

3. A. $75' \times 120' \times \$1.50/sf. \times 8$ lots $= \$108,000$

B. $13,600 per lot $\times$ 8 lots = $108,000

C. 75' frontage $\times$ $185 $\times$ 8 lots = **$111,000**

D. Sale price for entire parcel = $110,000

4. $3,000 + ($72.50 $\times$ 130 mos) − $11,000 = **$1,425**

5. (60 acres $\times$ $1,500) − $77,000 = **$13,000** paid to T

CHAPTER 9

1. B A promissory note is evidence of the borrower's debt to the lender. The mortgage provides collateral for the debt.

2. D It is not necessary for a note to be recorded in the public records in order to be valid evidence of a borrower's debt.

3. A Only the borrower need sign a note for it to be enforceable.

4. A A promissory note which does not specify that it is to be secured by a mortgage or deed of trust is both a personal obligation and an unsecured obligation of the borrower.

5. A The location of the execution of a note is stated on the note in order to establish which state's laws govern the note.

6. B The words "or order" in a promissory note make it a negotiable instrument, thus giving the lender the right to transfer collection rights to another party.

7. B The borrower is the obligor under a note secured by a mortgage. The note is the borrower's obligation.

8. C The acceleration clause in a note permits the lender to demand immediate payment of the entire balance due.

9. B Customarily, a mortgage is recorded but a promissory note is not.

10. B A promissory note is evidence of the borrower's debt, and a mortgage hypothecates property as collateral for a loan.

11. B Hypothecation is the process by which a borrower's property serves as collateral for a debt without the borrower giving up possession of the property.

12. B The lender is both the mortgagee under the terms of the mortgage and the obligee under the terms of the promissory note. The obligor is the maker of the note and the borrower.

13. A Under the title theory of mortgages, the mortgage deeds title to the property to the lender but allows the borrower the use of the property.

14. A The defeasance clause states that a mortgage becomes null and void when the note is paid in full.

15. C The covenant against encumbrances appears in a general warranty deed, not in a mortgage.

16. A The mortgage will hypothecate the house and lot on which it is located, but not other real estate holdings of the mortgagor.

17. B An alienation clause permits the lender to demand immediate repayment of the note if the mortgaged property is sold or otherwise conveyed. It is also known as a due-on-sale clause.

18. A The condemnation clause in a mortgage requires that any money received from a sale under eminent domain be used to reduce the balance owed on the note.

19. B The satisfaction of mortgage should be recorded in the public records in order to give public notice that the debt has been satisfied.

20. B A partial release is used to release one or more properties from the obligations of a blanket mortgage.

21. C A person who takes property "subject to" is not personally liable to the lender or the seller. The seller, however, is still liable to the lender under the original terms of the note and mortgage.

22. C The purchaser is responsible to the seller, and the seller to the lender when a loan is assumed.

23. A A seller can be relieved of liability for an assumed loan by novation, the substitution of the purchaser for the seller

as the mortgagor under the original note and mortgage. The balance on a loan which is being assumed should be verified with the lender. A seller is still liable selling "subject to."

24. B   An estoppal certificate is used to secure verification from the borrower of the outstanding balance on a loan when the loan is being sold by a mortgagee or note holder.

25. D   Under the so-called "race statutes," the priority of a mortgage lien is determined by the order of recordation.

26. B   A junior mortgage is any mortgage that is lower in priority than the first or senior mortgage on a property.

27. D   By means of a subordination agreement, the holder of a mortgage agrees to accept a position of lower lien priority than a subsequent mortgage on the same property.

28. B   Most mortgage foreclosures are the result of a borrower's failure to make loan payments on time.

29. D   A borrower who is behind in mortgage payments should first meet with the lender as soon as possible.

30. B   Nonjudicial foreclosure is normally less expensive and faster than judicial foreclosure, so will usually be the lender's preference when a choice is permitted.

31. D   The purpose of a foreclosure action is to terminate the mortgagor's rights in the mortgaged property, cause the property to be sold at public auction, and satisfy the lender's claims from the proceeds of the sale.

32. B   A notice of lis pendens is a public notice of pending legal action, filed in the public records of the jurisdiction of the mortgage property.

33. B   Equitable redemption begins when the loan is in default, and ends when the property is sold at a foreclosure sale.

34. C   Foreclosure of a mortgage does not eliminate real estate tax liens. They remain in force against the property.

35. A   Should the amount received from a foreclosure sale be insufficient to satisfy the indebtedness, when permitted by law, a lender may request a deficiency judgment against any other property of the mortgagor as a means of recovering the amount due on a loan.

36. C   The purchaser at foreclosure will usually receive a special warranty deed signed by the officer of the court who handled the foreclosure sale.

37. D   The statutory redemption period begins at the time of the foreclosure sale, and terminates upon expiration of the statutory period in the jurisdiction.

38. D   A successful bidder who receives title and possession immediately following the foreclosure sale will tend to be willing to pay more for the property than in circumstances where title and possession will be delayed because of the mortgagor's rights of statutory redemption.

39. B   The borrower whose loan has been foreclosed by power of sale can appeal the issue to the courts, but not to obtain a judicial foreclosure.

40. C   Judicial foreclosure may sometimes be avoided by power of sale or by entry and possession.

41. A   A voluntary deed in lieu of foreclosure avoids foreclosure proceedings and possible deficiency judgments.

42. A   A mortgage secured by personal property is a chattel mortgage. Judicial foreclosure is not required.

43. B   An installment contract in default may be judicially foreclosed. The vendee may not rescind the contract.

44. 1st yr int: $100,000$ bal $\times 10.5\% = 10,500$
2nd yr int: $90,000$ bal $\times 11.0\% = \$9,900$
3rd yr int: $80,000$ bal $\times 11.5\% = \$9,200$
4th yr int: $70,000$ bal $\times 12.0\% = \$8,400$
5th yr int: $60,000$ bal $\times 12.5\% = \$7,500$
Total Interest = **$45,000**

45. $1,200 payment $\times$ 12 mos = $14,400 total

$14,400 − $12,000 interest = $ 2,400 prin.

$120,000 loan − $2,400 prin = **$117,600** bal.

46. $88,000 − $3,000 exp. and tax = $85,000 avail

   1st mortgage gets $70,000 = $15,000 avail

   2nd mortgage gets $15,000 = $0 avail

   3rd mortgage gets 0 = $0 avail

   4th mortgage gets 0 = $0 avail

CHAPTER 10

1. D A deed of trust is an instrument which transfers title to a trustee as security for a loan. A mortgage does not transfer title to a third party.

2. C Title held by a trustee is reconveyed to the borrower by the trustee upon request of the beneficiary.

3. B The power of sale clause empowers the trustee to sell the property upon the borrower's default on the terms of the note or deed of trust.

4. C Naked title, which is necessary to protect the note, is conveyed by a deed of trust.

5. D A deed of trust delivers bare, or naked, title to the trustee.

6. C The borrower conveys a bare title to the trustee when a deed of trust is recorded.

7. D Title is conveyed by the trustee to the purchaser at foreclosure when a deed of trust is foreclosed.

8. A A reconveyance clause is found in a deed of trust, but not in a mortgage. A power of sale clause is used in trust deeds and, in some states, in mortgages. Acceleration and defeasance clauses are common in both documents.

9. A Both the canceled note and a request for reconveyance must be delivered to the trustee to get a reconveyance, which is then recorded to clear the public records.

10. B A reconveyance must be recorded in the public records to clear the deed of trust.

11. B The successful bidder at a deed of trust foreclosure sale will get a trustee's deed, which conveys whatever right, title, and interest had been deeded to the trustee.

12. C A lender would normally like to have an assignment of rents clause. The absence of statutory redemption and court-ordered foreclosure are advantages to the lender.

13. B Nationwide, mortgages are more commonly used as security instruments for real estate loans than any other form of instrument. Trust deeds or deeds of trust are the next most popular.

14. A The shortened period of time between default and foreclosure favors the lender and contributes to the popularity of trust deeds where state law favors their use. Other advantages include no statutory redemption period, provision for assignment of rents and the fact that title is already in the name of the trustee.

15. B A debt secured by a deed of trust becomes an obligation of the trustor's estate if death occurs before it is satisfied.

16. B The beneficiary is empowered to name a substitute trustee by the language of the deed of trust.

17. B A trustee can be appointed by automatic form where the trustee is not personally notified of the appointment, or by accepted form where the trustee is notified and accepts the assignment.

18. C Both an existing deed of trust and a mortgage can be assumed by a buyer, provided the lender does not object.

19. A To subordinate is to accept a position of lower lien priority; therefore, a deed of trust which has been subordinated cannot be a senior deed of trust.

20. C A land contract does not require a buyer to give a promissory note to the lender. Both a mortgage and a deed of trust need the execution of a promissory note.

21. D A mortgage, a land contract, or deed of trust can be foreclosed by judicial foreclosure, although only mortgages are commonly foreclosed in this manner.

22. C With a mortgage or deed of trust, the seller delivers a deed immediately. With a land contract, title is delivered when the property has been paid for.

23. A An assignment of rents clause allows the lender to take possession of the property, manage it, and collect the rents while the trustor is in default and before the foreclosure sale occurs.

24. A Courts watch carefully when foreclosure is conducted outside the courtroom. Thus, the loan must clearly be in default, all foreclosure rules followed to the letter of the law, and the property sold at public auction.

25. Claims against the proceeds of the sale would be paid in the following order: (1) expenses of the sale, (2) the unpaid loan balance, (3) claims of junior lien holders. The (4) trustor would receive any surplus money.

CHAPTER 11

1. A The terms "straight loan" and "term loan" are both used in reference to a loan wherein the principal is repaid in a lump sum at the end of the loan term.

2. B The maturity date is the day on which the final payment on a loan is due, i.e. the last day of the loan's scheduled life.

3. B There is no repayment of principal until the maturity date on a straight or term loan. The borrower signs a note or bond, hypothecates the real property as collateral, and agrees to repay the loan balance at maturity.

4. A The use of an amortization table does not require knowledge of the loan-to-value ratio, but does require knowledge of the frequency of payments, interest rate and amount of loan.

5. B An amortization table shows the amount of each periodic payment necessary to amortize a loan in a given time. A loan balance table shows the loan balance after given periods of time.

6. B To fully amortize a loan, payments are calculated so that the entire principal will be repaid by the maturity date, with each payment applied first to interest due, then to the reduction of the principal balance.

7. B An amortized loan with a five-year maturity would require less in interest payments than either of the other examples given because it repays faster.

8. A A loan that calls for the amortized payments of principal and interest plus prorated payments of taxes and insurance is called a budget loan or PITI loan.

9. B A balloon note is one which calls for a final payment larger than the preceding payments, in order to pay the remaining loan balance. It may or may not call for equal monthly payments of principal and interest prior to the final payment.

10. A The possibility that the borrower may have difficulty meeting the final payment when it becomes due, and that the borrower may have trouble refinancing when the final payment becomes due are negative aspects of balloon financing.

11. B A balloon loan calls for a final payment substantially larger than the previous payments. A partially amortized loan is a balloon loan because of its larger final payment.

12. B A loan balance table shows the balance owed on a loan at certain intervals during the loan's life. This is not shown in an amortization table.

13. D The higher the interest rate, the more effective earlier mortgage loan repayment would be in reducing interest payments.

14. B Biweekly payments of one-half of the monthly payments will substantially reduce the amount of interest paid over the life of the loan, and will shorten the life of the loan.

15. A Lenders calculate the loan-to-value ratio on price or appraised value, whichever is lower. The loan will be calculated as follows:

$96,000 price × 80% LVR = $76,800 max.

$96,000 price − $76,800 loan = $19,200 down

16. B Equity is the market value of the property less the debts against it. Loan-to-value ratio is the amount a lender will lend on a property divided by the appraised value or sale price, whichever is lower.

17. C As used in real estate, a "point" is one percent of the loan amount.

18. B Loan origination fees may be stated as a percentage of the loan or an itemized billing for expenses incurred by the lender.

19. B When a lender charges discount points to make a loan, the yield to the lender will increase.

20. A Discount points on mortgage loans tend to increase when money is tight and will decrease when money is loose.

21. D The FHA considers both the borrower's capability of repaying the loan and the value of the property as collateral for the loan when evaluating an application for mortgage insurance.

22. D The FHA does not operate at taxpayer expense. It charges borrowers a mortgage insurance premium.

23. B FHA mortgage insurance premiums are based on the loan amount and paid by the borrower. The premiums may be paid in cash or added to the loan amount, at the borrower's option.

24. A A nonmilitary borrower desiring an FHA-insured loan must make a down payment. The borrower may not borrow the down payment using a second mortgage against the property.

25. B Maximum FHA-insured loans change from time to time as average sale prices increase, and vary from one city to another depending on average sale prices in the area.

26. A Through its insurance programs the FHA has been instrumental in bringing about acceptance of long-term amortized loans. Its minimum (no maximum) construction standards

have led to standardized construction techniques.

27. A FHA mortgage insurance programs are available for single family or owner-occupied one-to-four unit residential properties.

28. C Both FHA-insured and VA-guaranteed loans are fully assumable without any increase in the interest rate.

29. C Both FHA-insured and VA-guaranteed loans can be repaid in full ahead of schedule without penalty.

30. D A conventional loan is one which is not insured or guaranteed by a government agency.

31. D FHA does not allow a junior mortgage at the origination of an FHA-insured loan. Since late 1983, interest rates are allowed to float with the market, points are negotiable between buyer and seller, and the seller may pay the borrower's MIP.

32. A See p. 215 in *Real Estate Principles*.

33. A The FHA has played an important role in the formulation of loan qualification criteria and the imposition of minimum construction standards.

34. B The FHA does NOT lend any money. It insures lenders against a loss brought about by the borrower's default on an FHA-insured loan.

35. B The VA-guaranteed loans are available without a down payment, and the VA loan guarantee substitutes for the protection normally provided to a lender by a down payment.

36. C A certificate of eligibility, a certificate of reasonable value, and income verification are all required for a veteran to secure a VA-guaranteed loan.

37. A VA-guaranteed loans are available for house and mobile homes.

38. B New financing, which would pay off the existing VA loan, would relieve the selling veteran of financial responsibility to the VA. Selling "subject to" would not, nor would a wraparound mortgage. "Freely assuming" the loan,

which was available years ago, does not relieve the original borrower.

39. C Veteran borrowers must pay a one-time funding fee to the VA at the time of origination of a VA-guaranteed loan.

40. A Private mortgage insurance covers only the top 20 to 25 percent of the loan, whereas the FHA insures the entire loan amount.

41. A. $90,000 price × 90% = $81,000 loan $81,000 loan × .005 = $405 MIP for 1st year

    B. Mortgage insurance premiums are paid by the borrower, not the lender.

    C. The first year premium is $405 not $450.

    D. The first year's premium is paid at closing; payments toward the following year's premium are then paid monthly.

42. A FmHA guarantees loans on farms and rural homes, and also makes loans on farms and rural homes.

43. B See page 215 in *Real Estate Principles.*

44. D See page 218 in *Real Estate Principles.*

45. C See page 219 in *Real Estate Principles.*

46. D See page 220 in *Real Estate Principles.*

Finance Problems and Situations

1. Interest = $5,000 × 10% × 7 years = **$3,500**
   Principal & Int. = $3,500 ÷ $5,000 = **$8,500**

2. Yearly interest = $12,000 × 9% = $1,080
   Monthly interest = $1,080 ÷ 12 = $90
   Daily interest = $90 ÷ 30 = $3
   Total ($1,080 × 3) + (90 × 10) + (3 × 20) = **$4,200**

3. All produce the same result:
   $60,000 × 10% ÷ 12 × 2 = $1,000
   $ 5,000 × 10% × 2 = $1,000
   $10,000 × 10% = $1,000

4. $115.50 × 4 ÷ $4,200 = **11%**

5. ($900 − $80) × 12 ÷ $120,000 = **8.2%**

6. $40,000 × .08 ÷ 12 × 7.5 months = **$2,000**

7. $9.15 × 80 = $732 monthly P & I payment

Property taxes are $1,320 ÷ 12 = $110 per month.
Insurance is $240 ÷ 12 = $20 per month
Thus monthly PITI is $732 + $110 + $20 = **$862**

8. A 15-year loan at 11.5% interest that is 10 years old has a remaining balance of $531 per thousand. Therefore $531 × 50 = **$26,550**

9. $27,500 ÷ 25% = **$110,000**

10. Mo. #1 = $10,000 × 12% ÷ 12 mos = **$100.00**
    Principal reduc. = $120 − $100 = **$20.00**
    Mo. #2 = $9,980 × 12% ÷ 12 mos = **$99.80**
    Principal reduc. = $120 − $99.80 = **$20.20**
    Principal bal. = 10,000 − 40.20 = **$9,959.80**

11. Loan-to-value ratio is 80%
    Down payment = $78,000 × 20% = $15,600.00
    Mortgage debt = $78,000 × 80% = $62,400.00
    Monthly P + I is $9.00 per thousand
    $9.00 × 62.4 (thousands) = **$561.60**

12. Down pmt = 10% × $86,000 = $8,600 . . . + $4,000 *appraisal to purch price* = **$12,600.00**
    Loan amt = 90% × $86,000 = **$77,400.00**

13. Purchase price = $120,000 ÷ .75 = $160,000
    Down pmt. = $160,000 − $120,000 = $40,000

14. $500 less 20% for taxes and insurance leaves $400 for principal and interest payments. A 30-year, 9% loan has monthly payments of $8.05 per thousand, thus, $400 per month can support a $400 ÷ $8.05 = **$49,689** loan. Adding their cash down payment gives a maximum purchase price of **$58,189**

CHAPTER 12

1. D Truth-in-Lending Act requires that, in loans covered by the Act, the borrower be advised of the cost of borrowing, and that the borrower be given the right of rescission within three days after signing loan papers, amount borrowed and the financing fee. Appraisal fees do not need to be disclosed nor closing costs, disclosure of which are covered by RESPA.

2. D Consumer loans to natural persons are covered by the TIL Act, but commercial loans, personal property loans in excess of $25,000, and business loans are exempt.

3. D APR is the "annual percentage rate."

4. A The TIL laws require a creditor to disclose the full cost of obtaining credit, and allow credit transactions to be rescinded within three days in certain instances. TIL does not regulate the cost of credit and RESPA mandates closing costs disclosures.

5. B Regulations for the Truth-in-Lending Simplification Act are issued by the Federal Reserve Board and are contained in Revised Regulation Z.

6. B The annual percentage rate is made up of the interest rate combined with the other costs of the loan. It is usually higher than the interest rate alone.

7. D The loan on the automobile is a personal property loan in excess of $25,000 and is therefore exempt from the requirements of the TIL act.

8. A Advertisements offering real estate for sale may state the price and interest rate, but if any "trigger terms," such as down payment or monthly payment are stated, the ad must include other specific disclosures. Advertising may also be in general terms, such as those given in responses B, C, and D.

9. D The lender's net yield from the loan need not be shown, but the number of payments, computation of early payment credits, and the amount of any balloon payments must be stated.

10. D The penalties defined in responses A, B and C may all be imposed for a violation of the TIL laws. A penalty of $10,000 per day results for each day that the violation continues.

11. B The right to rescind applies to consumer loans but not to a loan for the acquisition of the borrower's principal dwelling.

12. D The value of the property, condition of the title, and the ability to repay the loan are all considered in evaluating a

loan application. Occasional part-time and/or overtime earnings are generally not considered.

13. D There is no term for an 8-unit building.

14. B Redlining is refusing to make loans in certain neighborhoods.

15. A As equity increases, the probability of default diminishes. Insured loans are generally made at higher LVRs than uninsured loans. Previous defaults or repossessions are considered indications of a poor credit risk.

16. B Generally, before loan approval, a borrower must have sufficient funds for the down payment and state if he intends to occupy the property.

17. A The lowest interest rate would be given to owner-occupied dwellings. Also, the lower the LVR, the lower the interest rate.

18. D Income adequacy is considered in evaluating a loan application. Race, marital status and sex are not considered.

19. A Total fixed monthly expenses may be up to 33% to 38% and include alimony and child support payments. Housing expenses include taxes and insurance, and in some instances, utility costs as well.

20. A U.S. Savings Bonds are much more liquid assets than a recreational lot, and would be more favored by a lender in evaluating a loan application.

21. D A lender may consider the applicant's intention to occupy the property in evaluating a loan application, but may NOT consider religion, marital status, or race.

22. B The Fair Credit Reporting Act gives an individual the right to inspect his or her file at a credit bureau.

23. D By law, he may pursue options A, B, and C. Applying to another lender won't change the information contained in the reports used by most lenders.

24. C A bankruptcy is considered obsolete information after 10 years; general credit data after 7 years.

25. A   Responses B, C, and D are considered vague and therefore not misleading. "For only $699 a month" requires other disclosures, i.e., number of payments, finance charges, amount borrowed, down payment.

26. B   Cash value is useful NOW, but the greater face value will assist the survivors in paying off the loan. A will can be altered at any time, so is of little value.

27. A   The lower the loan to value, i.e., 70%, the greater the equity the borrower has in the property. It is less likely that he will default, losing all his invested equity. A 95% loan is generally insured by FHA or PMI while a 100% loan is most likely a guaranteed DVA loan.

28. B   ECOA protects borrowers from discrimination. TILSRA is a form of consumer protection regarding the advertising of financial terms and RESPA deals with closing costs.

29. D   A lender may not discriminate on the basis of the age of a building, racial and income composition of neighborhoods. A lender may refuse to loan money in a known geological hazard area, or a property that is in violation of zoning or deed restriction.

30. B.   The most important factor in evaluating credit is payment history(35%).

CHAPTER 13

1. A   Lenders in the primary mortgage market accept loan applications, make and administer loans. The secondary market investors purchase existing loans.

2. D   Savings and loan associations have historically been the largest source of funds for residential mortgage loans in this country.

3. B   Certificates of deposit carry higher rates of interest than passbook accounts in order to compete with higher yields from other investments and thereby prevent disintermediation.

4. B   Disintermediation occurs when large amounts of money are removed from thrift institutions for investment in government or corporate securities. This results in a decrease in activity in the real estate market.

5. B   S&Ls combat problems of rising interest rates by enforcing due-on-sale clauses in mortgages and by encouraging borrowers to accept adjustable rate loans.

6. D   The FSLIC was placed under the control of the FDIC to help restore the savings and loan system in 1989, long after decline of S&L residential activities.

7. B   Deposits in commercial banks exceed those in S&Ls and they are largely in demand accounts. Commercial banks tend to be less active in long-term real estate loans, but are often active in construction loans.

8. A   Primarily located in the Northeast area, mutual savings banks are quite similar to savings and loans. They are owned by their depositors who receive "interest" depending on the success or failure of their loans.

9. B   Their ability to calculate payoffs from actuarial tables and receipt of premiums in predictable amounts make life insurance companies ideally suited to long-term investments.

10. B   Life insurance companies invest premium dollars in corporate bonds, real estate loans and government bonds, but do not invest in personal property loans.

11. D   Generally, life insurance companies prefer industrial, multi-family or corporate real estate loans.

12. C   Participation loans are those in which the lender receives both interest and any percentage of the profits from the rental income from a property, and are designed as a protection against inflation.

13. C   Mortgage companies locate and qualify borrowers and then originate loans and service the loans which they have sold on the secondary mortgage market.

14. A   Commercial banks, S&Ls, and mutual savings banks regularly carry on mortgage banking activities. Insurance companies do not engage in this activity.

15. B Mortgage brokers neither lend their own money nor service loans. Their fee is generally paid in points by the borrower.

16. D Mortgage brokers do not ordinarily service loans. This activity is engaged in by commercial banks, S&Ls and mortgage companies.

17. B Municipal bonds provide a good source of below-market-rate real estate loans by paying tax-free interest income to investors.

18. A The secondary mortgage market provides a means for lenders to sell real estate loans, and a means for investors to acquire these loans without origination and servicing facilities.

19. B Standardized, not customized, loan procedures and government and private mortgage insurance programs all have contributed substantially to the success of the secondary mortgage market. Lenders do make higher loan-to-value loans because of the insurance programs.

20. C FNMA (Fannie Mae) is a privately held corporation which is active in buying (primarily) VA and FHA mortgage loans. It is not managed by the federal government.

21. A Once Fannie Mae issues a commitment to purchase a specified dollar amount of loans within a fixed time, it must buy all loans delivered under the agreement, but participating lenders are not obligated to sell their loans to Fannie Mae.

22. B FNMA-approved forms must be used, limits on the size of loans are set annually, and FNMA does not buy third mortgages and does not exceed 70% or 80% loan-to-value on seconds.

23. B FNMA will purchase only first or second mortgage loans, government-insured or guaranteed loans and conventional loans; not third or fourth mortgage loans.

24. B FNMA buys carryback mortgages which meet the criteria for its Home Seller Program. This loan meets these criteria.

25. C GNMA is a federal agency, not owned by stockholders. It deals in FHA, VA and FmHA mortgages and operates a mortgage-backed securities program.

26. B Under Ginnie Mae's mortgage-backed securities program, principal and interest are passed through to investors, and the pool as a whole is guaranteed by Ginnie Mae.

27. D FHLMC deals primarily in conventional mortgages, serves as a secondary market for members of the Federal Home Loan Bank System, and issues securities on its own mortgage pools. It is not an agency of the federal government.

28. B Participation certificates issued by Freddie Mac can be sold for cash, may be used as collateral for loans, and are often held as investments. The minimum investment is $25,000.

29. D Freddie Mac guarantees that interest and principal on participation certificates will be paid in full and on time. Any losses from a default are not passed on to investors.

30. B Mortgage-backed securities are of unpredictable maturity, but yields are predictable.

31. B Private financial institutions serving the secondary mortgage market avoid competing with Fannie Mae, Ginnie Mae and Freddie Mac by specializing in the markets not served by these institutions. They will continue to thrive since they meet needs not met by the Big Three.

32. A Computers and mortgage networks serve as conduits between lenders and real estate brokerage offices.

33. D Business, government, and consumer credit borrowers compete strongly with home buyers for investment capital.

34. D The interest rate charged to a home buyer is determined by the cost of money to the lender, reserves for default and all loan servicing costs, and available interest alternatives. Usury laws have little, if any, effect on the rate.

35. B Due-on-sale clauses in mortgages are used by lenders to refuse loan assumption by uncreditworthy borrowers. They are also used to increase the rate of interest when the property is sold by requiring repayment or renegotiation.

36. A The provisions of the Garn Act apply to mortgage loans made after October 15, 1982, by any deposit institution.

37. C Enforcement of a due-on-sale clause can result from an installment sale contract, a lease with option to buy, or foreclosure of a junior lien. It cannot result from a lease of one year's duration.

38. A Prepayment clauses discourage borrowers from shopping for new loans at a lower interest rate unless there has been a substantial drop in rates.

39. C Individuals can invest in real estate mortgages by purchasing Ginnie Mae or Freddie Mac participation certificates or buying junior mortgages at a discount.

40. A Historically, financing methods have always changed to meet the current market conditions, and can be expected to continue to do so.

41. C. There are many sources of financing readily available to most consumers, but a lot of consumers lack the knowledge to evaluate lending practices, and they are often preyed upon be unscrupulous lenders who are taking advantage of that lack of knowledge.

42. C. It's purpose is to ensure the capital adequacy and financial soundness of Fannie Mae and Freddie Mac and has regulatory authority over them.

CHAPTER 14

1. A Lenders increase the attractiveness of adjustable rate mortgage loans by offering lower initial interest rates than on fixed-rate loans.

2. A The purpose of ARM loans is to more closely match the lender's loan yield to the lender's cost of funds.

3. C ARM loans do not lower settlement costs, but do increase the borrower's ability to qualify for a larger loan, decrease the monthly payments if market interest rates fall, and allow prepayment without penalty.

4. D ARM loans may be indexed to one-year U.S. Treasury securities, or six-month Treasury bills, or the cost of funds to thrift institutions.

5. A A one percent lower margin would result in reduced loan payments because the monthly interest charge would be lower.

6. D A payment cap on monthly mortgage amortization payments can result in negative amortization, an increase in the loan balance, and a loan balance in excess of the property value by continual addition of unpaid interest to the loan balance.

7. A The lender must explain the worst-case scenario to a buyer who is considering an ARM loan.

8. C ARM loans with teaser rates are avoided by most mortgage lenders and secondary mortgage market buyers because they can lead to early foreclosure when rates are increased. Lenders expect the yield to increase during the life of the loan.

9. C See page 262 in *Real Estate Principles*.

10. C See page 267 in *Real Estate Principles*.

11. D The loan will be a package mortgage, with the refrigerator included in the loan. The refrigerator may not be sold without the lender's permission, but the interest rate will be the same as that on the real property.

12. B Blanket mortgages include more than one property as security for a single loan, and the sale of either property could invoke a due-on-sale clause. If the mortgage contained a partial release clause, it would be possible to sell a property before the entire mortgage debt was repaid.

13. C Under the terms of a reverse mortgage, no payment is made of interest or principal prior to maturity. All of the other responses are correct.

14. B Advances on the construction loan are disbursed as construction progresses.

A take-out loan is secured from another lender to pay off a construction loan. Construction loans are considered high risk, and usually cost a higher interest rate than the less risky, permanent loan.

15. B A blended loan incorporates an existing loan at a low interest rate with a new loan at a rate of interest between the old rate and current market rate.

16. D The owner occupant sells his property in a sale leaseback and then remains as a tenant.

17. D A loan of $112,500 would exceed their equity of $100,000 in the property. The equity loan will still be junior to the first even if it is larger; priority is determined by date and time of recording. They can draw against the loan amount as needed.

18. A Carryback mortgages, when sold to any investors, are usually sold at large discounts. Terms are negotiated between the seller and buyer and income taxes can be calculated on the installment reporting method when payments extend beyond two years.

19. C Wraparound mortgages cannot be used if there is a due-on-sale clause.

20. C Subordination occurs when a mortgage holder agrees to accept a position of lower lien priority, thus allowing another mortgage to advance in priority.

21. B A sale may be made under a contract for deed by using wraparound financing provided there is no due-on-sale clause in the existing mortgage. It is not necessary for the property to be owned free and clear. Contract for deed may be used on any type property and the seller can approve the buyer without following any guidelines.

22. A A lease with option to buy eliminates the need for immediate financing of the full purchase price of the property. A right of first refusal does not accomplish this objective as it lacks possession. The other choices are also incorrect.

23. B A real estate agent who participated in creative financing which resulted in an over-encumbered property could be penalized by the loss of his/her license.

24. B One year is most common; six months is too often for most borrowers.

25. C An amendment to Regulation Z in 1988 requires creditors to provide more extensive information about the variable rate feature of ARMs.

26. D Young professionals are likely to see increases in their incomes so that they can more easily afford the increasing payments. Likewise, the GPM allows them to buy "more" house, the kind that their future income will support. Retired persons and "empty nesters" are usually cutting back, earning less so would not seek increasing payments. Earnings of military personnel generally do not rapidly increase.

27. A A package mortgage is secured by both real and personal property.

28. D A reverse mortgage could be used by an elderly couple who are living in a fully paid for home and who seek to pull money out of their residence to help with living expenses.

29. B The payment cap protects the borrower from hefty payment increases but does not make up the difference in what is owed and what is being paid. That difference is added to the principal and it earns interest just like the principal does. The balance owed rises. Responses A, C, and D are often seen as advantages.

CHAPTER 15

1. A Real property taxes are the main source of revenue for local governments.

2. C "Ad valorem" is Latin for "according to value" (of the property, not the neighborhood), and are levied annually.

3. C Local services are paid for by real property taxes, but interstate highways are not paid for from local revenues.

4. B An increase in the tax rate, assessment ratio, or assessed value will increase the taxes to be levied on a property.

5. A The assessment ratio may be equal to, or less than, the property value, but may not be greater than its value.

6. A $75,000 × .75 = $56,250
$90,000 × .50 = $45,000
$50,000 × 1.00 = $50,000
$130,000 × .35 = $45,500

7. D Taxes may be expressed as a millage rate, dollars of tax per $100 of assessed value, or dollars of tax per $1,000 of assessed value.

8. D $600,000 taxes divided by $24,000,000 total assessed value of all property = .025 = 25 mills. Therefore 2.5 mills is wrong.

9. B Failure to pay real property taxes will result in the loss of the property, but the owner's other assets, including his salary, will not be attached.

10. C Property named in a tax certificate may be redeemed by the owner or by a lien holder (especially the first mortgagee), but not by anyone willing to pay the taxes and interest.

11. B Tax deeds are issued following the expiration of the redemption period.

12. C Tax deeds are issued upon the sale of the property in those states wherein the sale of the property for delinquent taxes follows the expiration of the redemption period.

13. A Before bidding on a parcel of real estate being offered at tax sale, a bidder should do a title search to determine what, if any, other encumbrances exist against the property.

14. B The holder of a tax deed can enhance the marketability of the property by purchasing title (not homeowners) insurance or conducting a quiet title suit.

15. C Ad valorem taxes have lien priority over all other liens against a property.

16. A The assessment of land and buildings in a community is a matter of public record.

17. D The assessment rolls are public records of the assessed valuations of all properties in a jurisdiction.

18. B A property owner may demand a review of the assessed value of his property by pursuing the appeals process.

19. B The Board of Equalization's functions include the equalization of assessments between counties (not states), and also between individual property owners. It can review assessments, does not settle disputes nor determine tax rates.

20. A City officials may offer property tax exemptions to business on the basis that the cost to the public is outweighed by the economic benefits.

21. B Residences owned by the elderly may get certain benefits but are not exempt from taxation. Government-owned utilities, property owned by charitable organizations, and hospitals are usually exempt.

22. D Homes of the same value may bear different tax burdens because of delays in reassessment, because of different governmental services provided in different neighborhoods, or because the revenue sources vary from city to city.

23. B The ability of the owner to pay taxes does not influence the taxes levied on the property.

24. A Improvements which benefit a limited number of property owners are paid for by special assessments on the properties which benefit from the improvements.

25. B Extension of sewer lines to a privately owned industrial park would benefit a limited number of property owners and would likely be paid for by a special assessment.

26. B The cost of improvements in an improvement district is met by assessments on properties within the district.

27. C Special assessments are apportioned according to the value of benefits received.

28. A Special assessments covering the cost of improvements are levied against individual properties according to the benefits received.

29. D $90,000 sale price
$\underline{-5,400}$ commission
$84,600 net sale
$65,000 purch price
$\underline{+2,500}$ improvements
$67,500 net cost

$84,600 sale − $67,500 cost = **$17,100** gain

30. A Federal capital gains tax would apply to profit from the sale of land, but the gain is not taxed by all state governments. Only the sale of primary residences qualify for tax deferment provided another home is purchased within 24 months. (Refer to question 33.)

31. D Both the cost of legal services and fees or commissions paid to help find the property may be included in determining the cost basis of a home.

32. A In order to qualify for inclusion in the adjusted sales price, fix-up expenses for the sale must be done within 90 days prior to sale, and paid for within 30 days after the signing of a contract of sale, not the closing.

33. A See page 292 in *Real Estate Principles*.

34. B $100,000 price − $30,000 loan = $70,000 new
$70,000 ÷ $100 = 700 × $.55 = **$385** tax

35. A Taxes on capital gains are due on the portion of the gains received in any given year, and interest on mortgages is taxed as ordinary income. Another option is to pay all the taxes due at one time.

36. C A homeowner who files an itemized income tax return may take deductions for property taxes, mortgage interest on a personal residence loan as well as interest paid on an improvement bond. Since loan points to assist a VA or FHA buyer are not a seller's debt, they are not deductible, but can be deducted from the sale price as a settlement cost.

37. C The income tax laws of 1984 and 1985 discourage the charging of below-market rates on carryback mortgages. A seller is not subject to penalties if the rate charged is at least equal to the rate on federal securities of similar maturity.

38. C A real estate licensee should have enough general knowledge of tax laws to be able to answer basic questions and should know when to warn clients that tax problems could exist or result.

39. B A real estate agent has a responsibility to alert clients to seek tax counsel and for the quality and accuracy of any information given by the agent to clients.

40. B Conveyance taxes on real property title transfers are levied by certain state and local governments, but not by the federal government.

Property Tax Problems

Q. The order is 1, 3, 2, 4.

1A. $6,000,000 ÷ $240,000,000 = .025 = **25** mills

1B. $40,000 × .025 = **$1,000**

2. $100,800 ÷ $240,000 = .42 = **42%**

3. $70,000 × .50 × (.020 + .010 + .005) = **$1,225**

4. $3.50 per $100 = .035 mills tax rate
$1,365 ÷ .035 = $39,000 assessed value
$39,000 ÷ $60,000 = **65%** assessment ratio

5. $65,000 ÷ .52 = **$125,000**

6. $21.00 × 12 × 4 = **$1,008**

7. $450 ÷ .025 ÷ .60 = **$30,000** increase

8. 100 × $150 + $32,000 = $47,000
$47,000 ÷ 100 × 4 = **$1,880**

9. $102,000 × .022 = $2,244 before increase
$2,244 × .30 = **$673.20** tax increase

10. $5,040 m ÷ $120,000 m × $350,000 = **$14,700**
tip - 000's cancel out on the division

11. $100,000 × .30 × (.012 1 .025) ÷ 12 = **$92.50**

12A. $80,000 × .026 × (.98 discount) = **$2,038.40**

12B. $80,000 × .026 × .18 ÷ 12 = $31.20 per month charge
$80,000 × .026 ÷ (2 × $31.20) = **$2,142.40**

12C. $2,142.40 − $2,038.40 = **$104.00** difference

Gain on Sale Problems

April 1, 1965	Basis: $19,000
May 1, 1967	Cum. Basis: $19,350
July 1, 1970	Cum. Basis: $19,350
June 1, 1972	Cum. Basis: $20,850
Sept. 1, 1975	Cum. Basis: $21,650
April 1, 1976	Cum. Basis: $22,650
June 1, 1986	Cum. Basis: $27,650
Aug. 10, 1995	Realized: $139,000
Calculation of gain:	Realized $139,000
	Cum. Basis −27,650
	Gain $111,350

First Situation:

August 1, 1995	$151,000
August 1, 1995	$111,350
Basis for New Home	$ 39,650

CHAPTER 16

1. D Local custom determines whether the day a sale is finalized is referred to as the settlement date, the closing date or close of escrow. It is never referred to as the completion date.

2. D Title search, deed preparation, and loan arrangements must all be completed between the signing of the purchase contract and closing of the sale. If the buyer desired repairs, those should have been included in his offer to purchase.

3. D The buyer's walk-through is made as a final inspection just prior to the closing of a sale.

4. A During a walk-through, the buyer should test the heating and air conditioning systems, and the plumbing.

5. B The buyer and seller do not meet during an escrow closing, so could not shake hands. They usually do meet at a settlement meeting. Both are rarely present when the offer is presented and when notified of offer acceptance.

6. D A settlement meeting may take place at any location acceptable to all parties.

7. A An escrow closing may be conducted by mail, and there is no closing meeting.

8. A The buyer will sign the mortgage and the promissory note. The deed is signed by the seller. The lender signs the satisfaction.

9. B The purchaser must hold title to the property before he can mortgage it, so the deed must be delivered before the mortgage is signed.

10. C A settlement statement provides an accurate accounting of all funds dispersed and identifies the parties who receive funds from the transaction.

11. D Recordation of appropriate instruments is the final step in a real estate transaction.

12. D At a dry closing neither the deed nor the funds are disbursed to the buyer or seller.

13. B The buyer and seller do not meet for the settlement when a sale is closed through escrow.

14. D The selection of an escrow agent is made by mutual agreement between the buyer and seller. The agent is not a party to this selection.

15. A Funds being held by an escrow agent are deposited in a trust account.

16. C The purchase agreement will have been completed before the escrow is opened.

17. D Settlement by an escrow agent does not eliminate the need for a real estate broker, an attorney, or title insurance. Closing is handled by a neutral third party so the buyer and seller need not meet.

18. C In an escrow closing, the funds are disbursed by the escrow agent after all necessary recordings have taken place.

19. B The closing, delivery of title and recordation take place at the same time in an escrow closing.

20. C The escrow agent serves as an agent for both buyer and seller.

21. A Escrow closings can eliminate personal confrontations between buyer and seller, but do not eliminate the need for an attorney.

22. D Escrow can be used when a property is being refinanced, a mortgage loan is

being paid off, or when a sale is being made by means of an installment contract; not when a lease is signed.

23. B Typically, the settlement will be scheduled for between 30 and 60 days after the signing of a purchase agreement.

24. D The law will usually tolerate reasonable delays for valid reasons, even if the contract contains a "time is of the essence" clause.

25. A The contract must be rescinded in writing in order to relieve the parties from potential future liability.

26. B The original contract is legally enforceable. However, the better offer could be accepted if both parties agree to rescind the original contract.

27. C Taxes, all rents from income producing properties, and an assumed homeowners insurance policy are among items prorated at the settlement or escrow closing. The buyer pays title insurance in full.

28. B Prorations are usually made as of the date of title transfer.

29. D The proration is a debit to the seller and credit to the buyer of $106.08, computed as follows:

$36,720 $\times$ .08 $\div$ 12 = $244.80 per month interest

$244.80 4 30 = $8.16 per day $\times$ 13 = **$106.08**

30. A The proration is a charge to the buyer and credit to the seller computed as follows:
$194.50 premium $\div$ 12 mos = $16.20/mo.
$16.20 per mo. $\div$ 30 days = $ .54/day
(4 mos $\times$ $16.20) + (25 days $\times$ $ .54)= **$78.30**

31. B Since the taxes have not been paid, the prorated amount would be a charge to the seller and computed as follows:
$662.40 per yr $\div$ 12 mos = $55.20 per month
$55.20 per month $\div$ 30 days = $1.84 per day
Jan. 1 to April 13 = 3 months, 13 days
(day of closing is charged to the buyer)

3 $\times$ $55.20 = $165.60; 13 $\times$ $1.84 = $23.92
$165.60 + $23.92 = **$189.52** charge to seller

32. D Prepaid taxes will result in a credit to the seller and a debit to the purchaser. The computation is as follows:
$1,320 per yr $\div$ 12 mos = $110 per month
August 16 to December 31 = 4.5 months *(taxes prepaid by the seller)*
$110 $\times$ 4.5 = **$495** credit seller, debit buyer

33. B The buyer will be charged interest for the remainder of December at closing. The first monthly payment will be due on February 1 for the month of January.

34. D Payment for the street assessment can be negotiated by the parties to the contract.

35. B Sales financed by means of an installment contract are not covered by the provision of RESPA.

36. C Because no federally related lender was involved, this sale is not covered by the provisions of RESPA.

37. A RESPA prohibits kickbacks or fees for services not actually performed during the closing process, but does not prohibit the buyer from selecting the title insurance company.

38. B RESPA limits tax and insurance escrows required by a lender at closing to the owner's share of accrued taxes prior to closing, plus 1/6th of the next year's estimated tax and insurance payments. Some lenders voluntarily pay interest, and some states require that they do so.

39. B RESPA requires that the buyer be given an estimate of closing charges and costs in advance of closing, but does not prohibit payments outside of escrow. The lender must use the HUD Uniform Settlement Statement, which must be available to the buyer the day before settlement.

Settlement Problems

1. 70% × $540 = $378 (seller pays)
   30% × $540 = $162 (buyer pays)
   $216 (answer)

2. $450 + $300 = $750 rent paid Nov 1 for Nov.
   $750 ÷ 30 = $25 per day
   $25 × 15 days = **$375;** debit seller, credit buyer

3. $500 ÷ 12 × 8 (mos after settlement) = $333.33
   $35,000 × .06 = $2,100 commission
   $35,000 − $22,790 − $2,100 + $333.33 = **$10,443.33**

4. $540 ÷ 12 mos = $45 mo. taxes and insurance
   $9,000 × .075 ÷ 12 = $56.25 loan interest for month
   $130 − $56.25 − $45 = $28.75 principal reduction
   $9,000 − $28.75 = **$8,971.25** (answer)

5. Seller owes buyer for the first 17 days of Nov.
   $12,000 × .10 interest ÷ 360 days per year × 17 days = **$56.67** (answer)

6. County taxes for Nov. and Dec., credit seller
   2 months = $300 ÷ 12 × 2 mos. = $50
   School taxes for Nov. thru June, credit seller
   8 months = $540 ÷ 12 × 8 mos. = $360
   $360 + $50 = **$410** (answer)

7. The seller has collected rent for 20 days in June on 9 units that now belong to the buyer.
   $600 ÷ 30 days = $20 per day per unit
   20 days × $20 per day × 9 units = $3,600. Credit the buyer and debit the seller $3,600

CHAPTER 17

1. D The landlord is the lessor and the tenant is the lessee. The landlord's right to regain control and possession of the premises at termination of the lease is called reversion. The tenant holds a nonfreehold estate.

2. A Any lease which contains a definite termination date is classified as an estate for years.

3. B A periodic estate continually renews itself until terminated by either lessee or lessor.

4. C A lease of more than one year must be in writing in order to be enforceable. As a rule, a two-week lease, a month-to-month lease, and a one-year lease are enforceable even though not in writing.

5. B In order to be enforceable, a lease for more than one year must be in writing.

6. B A month-to-month lease is enforceable even though it is not in writing, but a lease for more than one year must be in writing in order to be enforceable.

7. B A tenant's right to uninterrupted use of the leased premises is known as quiet enjoyment.

8. A A lease for one year commits the tenant to a full year's rent and the landlord to granting the tenant occupancy for the full year. Neither can terminate early; a new owner must honor existing leases.

9. D A valid lease must contain the names of all parties, the terms of the agreement between landlord and tenant, and description of the property in order to be legal. It is not necessary to have an assignment clause.

10. B A lease must contain a statement of the amount of rent to be paid but a security deposit is not essential.

11. D Unless the lease calls for rent to be paid in advance, it is not due until the end of the lease.

12. A A tenant is held responsible for damage to the premises, but not for normal wear and tear.

13. C The term "waive" means to surrender, abandon or relinquish.

14. A The burden of upkeep and repair of rented premises falls on the tenant in commercial leases but not in residential leases.

15. C The bookcases became fixtures when permanently installed and thus became the property of the landlord. The

tenant can be held responsible for expenses incurred in their removal, but their installation would not automatically cause forfeiture of the tenant's security deposit.

16. B State-enacted landlord-tenant laws tend to strike a reasonable balance between the rights and responsibilities of both parties.

17. D A gross lease is one in which the tenant pays a fixed rent and the landlord pays all the operating expenses.

18. A The terms "step-up lease" and "graduated lease" are both used to denote a lease which calls for specified rental increases at predetermined intervals.

19. A The terms "escalator clause" or "participation clause" refer to contract language whereby the landlord may pass increases in operating expenses to the tenant.

20. B Under a net lease, the tenant agrees to pay some or all of the operating expenses of the property in addition to a base rent.

21. A A percentage lease calls for rent to be paid all or in part in the form of a percentage of the gross sales made from the premises.

22. D Under the terms of a gross lease, a landlord has no automatic protection against rising operating costs, but could be so protected by the terms of a net lease, an escalator clause or an index clause.

23. B An option clause permits the tenant to renew the lease for an additional period at a predetermined rent.

24. A A lease is an executory contract and may be assigned unless it contains a nonassignment clause.

25. A When a contract is assigned, the assignor remains solely liable for its terms and obligations. The assignee is liable to the assignor.

26. A Typically, under a ground lease, the lessor holds fee simple title to the land, the lessee pays for and owns the improvements. Because they are often for long periods of time, 50 to 99 years, they are often recorded.

27. A While a lease for years may be terminated by constructive eviction, actual eviction, mutual agreement of the parties, or by eminent domain, it may only be terminated by the tenant when the landlord fails to provide essential services (constructive eviction).

28. B A gross rent lease for two years with an option to renew at the end of two years followed by an option to either renew or buy the property best fulfills the tenant's objective.

29. D The contract rent and the economic rent are usually the same at the beginning of a lease, but the economic rent may increase or decrease during the term of the lease.

30. B The landlord's inaction constituted constructive eviction and makes the lease terminable at the tenant's option. The tenant is not relieved of the obligation to pay rent if he continues to remain in possession of the premises.

31. A The landlord's actions constituted a retaliatory eviction and are illegal.

32. C The government's exercise of its power of eminent domain brought damage to both the landlord and the tenant and both are entitled to compensation, paid directly to them.

33. D Because the lease was recorded prior to the mortgage, it is not affected by a foreclosure of the mortgage, but remains binding upon the buyer at foreclosure.

34. B Rent controls often create more problems than they solve.

35. B Comparison of market rents with total operating costs and capitalization of net income to determine value are fundamental investment decisions in the purchase of income-producing properties.

36. C To promote rental housing, tenant referral fees, newspaper advertising, signs and arrows on and near the

property are more cost-efficient forms of advertising than radio or television advertising.

37. B A lengthy tenant application form tends to discourage marginally qualified tenants and also provides a basis for checking references.

38. B Rent reductions and/or concessions are used to attract tenants in a soft rental market.

39. A The treatment of tenants as permanent residents, even though turnover is expected, tends to increase tenant retention. If a manager has thoughts as expressed in responses C and D, he/she should look for a new profession.

40. B Good communication with tenants and prompt attention to repairs and maintenance are fundamental to good tenant relations.

41. B Careful tenant selection, good service and a businesslike policy of rent collection are more effective than threats of legal action in reducing losses from uncollected rents.

42. B An on-site resident manager serves both as a general superintendent of the property and as the eyes and ears of the property management company.

43. A Accounting is usually handled off-site; handling tenant complaints, showing vacancies to prospective tenants and maintenance are handled on-site.

44. D Successful property managers tend to be experienced in handling people, money and tools.

45. B The Institute of Real Estate Management (IREM) is a professional property management organization within the National Association of Realtors.

46. B The designation CPM is awarded by IREM. CAM is awarded by the National Apartment Association; RAM by the National Association of Home Builders and MAI is an appraisal designation.

47. A The Building Owners and Managers Institute confers the designation Systems Maintenance Administrator upon members who have completed required courses offered by the Institute.

Property Management Problems

1. ($1,100,000 − $600,000) × .04 = $20,000 rent on the overage. $5,000 × 12 months = $60,000 base rent. $60,000 + $20,000 = **$80,000** rent for year

2. ($600 + 3) + ($600 × .04 × 13 months) = **$512**

3. $2,000 × .0225 = $45.00 allowed increase
   $405 + $45 = $450 allowed new rent
   $455 − $450 = **$5** over what the law allows

4. (2 × $500 + $400) × .06 = $84 commission
   2 × $500 + $400 − $84 − $140 = **$1,176** (answer)

5. $8,000 × 12 months × 2 years × .03 = $5,760
   $9,000 × 12 months × 3 years × .03 = $9,720
   $1,200,000 × .03 = $36,000
   Total commission = **$51,480**

CHAPTER 18

1. A In addition to response A, other assumptions made by the appraiser include reasonable time must be allowed for market exposure, both purchaser and seller will be fully informed, and neither buyer nor seller should be under abnormal pressure to buy or sell.

2. A A comparable property sold in the past six months is usually valid and useful for estimating current market values.

3. B Comparables should be inspected personally by the appraiser in order to avoid errors in making the appraisal.

4. C A similar home with equal amenities which was sold under market conditions six months ago would be more indicative of current values than any of the other choices given.

5. B Comparables with fewer adjustments are of greater usefulness than those with many adjustments; several comparables are desirable, but the number

must be weighed against the effort involved.

6. D The owner's asking price probably sets the upper limit of the property's value, and the prospect's offer the lower limit of value.

7. B Adjustments are made to the comparable property because the appraiser cannot adjust the value of something for which he does not yet know the value.

8. C The value of improvements made after the property was sold would not be reflected in the selling price of a comparable. Thus, no adjustments for them are made.

9. C $80,000 value $\times$ 3% (one-half the annual rate of 6%) = $2,400.

10. A 240 sq. ft. $\times$ $80/sq. ft. $-$ 10% depreciation = $17,280. This would be deducted from the comparable.

11. D Acquisition cost to the present owner is not considered by an appraiser.

12. C If buyers will pay more for a garage, this must be considered by the appraiser.

13. A Adjustments for advantageous financing would be made in the market comparison approach, but not in the cost or income approaches.

14. A A comparable's adjusted market price reflects all adjustments made and is its comparable value for appraisal purposes.

15. B The process of weighing each of the comparables is known as the correlation process.

16. D Land is seldom valued on a square yard basis, but is commonly valued on a square foot, acreage or front foot basis.

17. D The lot with the greater depth is worth more than the other, but less than twice as much.

18. A Only lots of similar zoning should be employed when making an appraisal.

19. D Responses A, B, and C are all correct; a CMA will not be accepted by a lender.

20. D Seller motivation is considered most in the competitive market analysis method.

21. D A gross rent multiplier is more likely to produce only a rough estimate of a property's value because it considers only the gross income without considering expenses.

22. B

Sale Pr.	Mo. Rent	Yr. Rent
$ 450,000	$ 5,000	$ 60,000
$ 382,500	$ 4,250	$ 51,000
$ 427,500	$ 4,750	$ 57,000
$1,260,000	$14,000	$168,000

$1,260,000 \div $168,000 = **7.5** GRM.

23. C $450 monthly rent $\times$ 10 units $\times$ 12 months $\times$ 7.5 GRM = **$405,000** value.

24. C Land is not depreciated in an appraisal.

25. A Because the building is historic, reproduction cost would be appropriate.

26. D

40' $\times$ 45' $\times$ $60/sq. ft. = $108,000 house
20' $\times$ 20' $\times$ $30/sq. ft. = $\underline{\quad 12,000}$ garage
$120,000 total

27. D The building exhibits physical deterioration, and economic and functional obsolescence. The land (which is probably useful for industry) is not obsolete.

28. B The building suffers from incurable depreciation from its poorly designed floor plan (functional obsolescence).

29. C Economic obsolescence results from factors outside the property. Functional obsolescence, physical deterioration, and curable depreciation result from factors inside the property.

30. D The amount of income produced, the rate of return demanded by investors, and the length of the investment period are all considered in the income approach to appraisal.

31. A Capitalization is the conversion of future income into present value.

32. A The lower the capitalization rate used by the appraiser, the higher the indicated value of the property.

33. C $1,200 income × 12 mos ÷ 11% = $130,909, rounded to **$130,900.**

34. A Anticipated annual rents from a property on an annual basis are identified as either projected gross income or scheduled gross income.

35. B Actual income and expenses for the past three to five years will provide the best starting point for projecting future gross income and expenses.

36. A A small error in income projections is magnified into a larger error in the indicated value of a property.

37. C Capital improvements are not included in a projected annual operating statement.

38. B Reserves for improvement are established for items that must be replaced more than once in a building's life, but not annually.

39. C Total operating expense divided by the effective gross income equals the operating expense ratio.

40. C Not all appraisal approaches are suitable for all properties. Market comparison should be used for residential properties and income approach for an apartment building.

41. A The actual selling price of a property is determined by agreement between the buyer and the seller.

42 C The Appraisal Foundation is a private organization.

43. D The new FIRREA legislation dictates that appraisal reports meet all requirements mentioned in A, B, and C.

44. B The standards were set up by FIRREA.

45. D A real estate analysis is the act or process of providing information, recommendations, and/or conclusions on diversified problems in real estate.

46. C A property's highest and best use is that which gives its greatest current value.

47. D The principle of substitution holds that the maximum value of a property tends to be set by the cost of acquiring another equally desirable property.

48. B The broker could be held liable for civil damages and would be subject to disciplinary action by the real estate department for unprofessional conduct.

49. B The willingness of people to pay for land coupled with the relative scarcity of land is known as the principle of supply and demand.

50. D The principle of conformity holds that the maximum value is realized when a general degree of homogeneity is present in a neighborhood.

51. A Property may have more than one value, depending upon the purpose for which the valuation was performed.

52. A Assemblage is the process of combining two or more parcels of land into one larger parcel.

53. D Plottage value results from assemblage and is the added value over and above the sum of the smaller parcels.

54. A A buyer's market results from an excess of supply over demand.

55. B This is a thin market because of so few properties and slow turnover.

56. C The designation MAI stands for Member of the Appraisal Institute.

Appraisal Problems

1. $80,000 × 1.45 × .88 = **$102,080**

2. $76,000 − $63,080 = $12,920 dollar amount of depreciation ÷ $76,000 =.17 = **17%**

3. $29,250 ÷ 117 acres ÷ .10 = **$2,500** per acre

4. $90,000 + $150,000 + $1,935,000 + $135,000 = $2,310,000 loan

   $2,310,000 × 12% ÷ 12 mos × 10 mos = $231,000 interest

   $2,310,000 + $231,000 × 1.15 ÷ 25 units = **$116,886** per unit

5. $112,000 is 112% of what price? $112,000 = 1.12 × price = $112,000 ÷ 1.12 = **$100,000**

6. (110′ × 200′) − (80′ × 95′) × $5.00 = $72,000 landscaping

   80′ × 95′ × 2 stories × $38.00/sq. ft. = $577,600 building

$110' \times \$430 = \$47,300$ land

$\$72,000 + \$577,600 + \$47,300 = \textbf{\$696,900}$

7. $((\$400 \times 5 \text{ units}) + (\$350 \times 5 \text{ units})) \times 12$ months $= \$45,000$ gross income per year

$\$45,000 - (12 \times \$1,250$ operating expenses$) = \$30,000$ net annual income

$\$30,000 \div 8\% = \textbf{\$375,000}$

8. $\$900,000 \times .55\ 4\ .12 = \textbf{\$4,125,000}$

(Note that .55 is what remains of each dollar after deducting .45 of expenses)

CHAPTER 19

1. C Through real estate license laws, state governments try to ensure that persons licensed to do business in real estate are competent in real estate matters, including financing, and are of good reputation for honesty and truthfulness.

2. D Attorney, executors, and trustees are exempt from license requirements while acting as such. Appraisers are not exempt.

3. A A real estate broker may operate independently. A real estate salesperson may operate only under the supervision of an employing broker. Higher educational standards are required of brokers, but salespeople are also held accountable for their actions as well as their broker.

4. B The holder of any form of license is referred to as a licensee.

5. D Owners of real estate are usually exempt from license requirements in selling or otherwise dealing with their own real property.

6. A A real estate listing is a contract between the owner and the listing broker; salespersons act as subagents of the broker and are not principal parties to listing agreements.

7. B The employing broker is ultimately responsible for the acts of salespersons in his employ.

8. C Requirements for licensure as a real estate salesperson include completion of education requirements, passing an examination. He may not take a listing until he is licensed and employed by a licensed real estate broker.

9. D The employing broker must receive the salesperson's license before the agent may operate as a licensee.

10. B Licensees are not required to retake original license examinations in order to maintain or renew their licenses.

11. C License examinations given by the national testing services include questions on general real estate practices together with real estate laws, regulations and practices of the jurisdiction. A real estate licensee should be aware of general accounting principles insofar as they relate to real estate.

12. D A real estate broker may share a commission with salespersons licensed in his employ or with other licensed brokers in any state, but not with salespersons licensed with other brokers.

13. B A notice of consent must be filed in each state in which a broker maintains a nonresident license.

14. A A business operating under any name other than the proprietor's own name is considered to be operating under a fictitious name.

15. C The chief executive officer of a corporation must hold a real estate broker's license in order for the corporation to be licensed as a real estate broker.

16. B Most states require that a branch office hold a branch office license and be managed by a licensed real estate broker responsible for his trust account.

17. B Licensing requirements are set by statutes enacted by the state legislature.

18. D In most states, members of the real estate commission are part-time volunteers, some of whom are licensed real estate agents and some who are public members.

19. A Regulations covering license applicants are established by the real estate commission and state legislature, not

by staff members of the department or division.

20. D Generally, the real estate commission is empowered to revoke a licensee's license, may issue a public reprimand, and the revocation may be appealed to a court of competent jurisdiction. The licensee can hardly expect a commission for a transaction based on a violation of the law.

21. B Many states protect the public against financial losses suffered by a victim of a licensee's wrongful acts by bonding requirements or through state-sponsored recovery fund.

22. B A licensee who deals primarily in real estate investment contracts as opposed to the actual real estate itself may be required to get a securities license in addition to a real estate license.

23. A Persons who contemplate becoming real estate agents should be prepared to work irregular hours for uncertain earnings, basically using their own initiative.

24. D Neither response A nor B is the most effective way for a new real estate salesperson to utilize his/her time. Good sales training will probably be more useful than worrying about the best commission split.

25. D Independent contractors are responsible for their own income taxes and social security contributions.

26. A Generally, affiliation with a national network of franchised real estate brokerage firms appeals to firms having from 10 to 50 salespeople.

27. D In order to be identified as a Realtor, one must become a member of the National Association of Realtors.

28. D The Realtors' Code of Ethics deals with a Realtor's relations with his clients, the general public and with fellow Realtors.

29. B Memberships in Realtor institutes are restricted to members of the National Association of Realtors.

30. B Licensee law violations can result in both loss of commission and loss of license.

31. C A state's real estate department, division or board regulates licensees and license law application. As such, it has no jurisdiction over an unlicensed person who violates the fair housing laws.

32. A If there is compensation, or the promise of compensation, a license is required. The amount of compensation, or the fact that it was not in money or that they were friends is not the deciding factor.

33. B There is an exception to the licensing requirement for the executor of an estate.

34. D A telephone answering service cannot give information about listings or take a listing. Callers may leave their name and phone number and request a return call from a licensed salesperson.

35. D The state sets no minimum commission rate, and to imply that it does is a violation of law.

36. C Only the broker who takes the listing is authorized to advertise it. That is because only the broker has a contract with the property owner.

37. B The innocent salespeople will have to find another broker to work for if they wish to continue working as salespeople.

38. C A real estate salesperson must have an employing broker; therefore, the builder must obtain a broker's license.

39. B When a salesperson licensee no longer works for a broker, the broker must return that salesperson's license directly to the state.

40. B The state is not concerned with commission disputes between a broker and salesperson, or whether a broker refuses to take an overpriced listing or whether a licensee doesn't sell any property. But the state is concerned about continuing misrepresentations.

41. D No matter how tempting or pressing the situation, the law must be respected. Since she is not licensed, she cannot commit any act of selling, such as quote price and terms. She can, however, put the customer in contact

with a licensee who can answer those questions.

42. D The trade name used by minority members of NAREB is a Realtist.

CHAPTER 20

1. A A real estate listing is an employment contract between a property owner and a real estate broker. It does not authorize the broker to sell and convey title to the property, nor to authorize repairs.

2. A A listing is a contract between the owner and the listing salesperson's employing broker, not the owner and salesperson.

3. B The written listing agreement contains all the essential elements of a valid and enforceable listing contract.

4. D Typically, an exclusive right to sell listing requires the owner to exclude other brokers from advertising or placing a sign on the property, and to pay a commission if a buyer is found who is ready, willing and able to buy at the price and terms stipulated in the listing, even if the buyer is found by the owner.

5. A An advance fee listing is one where the broker charges an hourly fee plus reimbursement for out-of-pocket expenses.

6. D The amount of a broker's commission is negotiated at the time the listing is signed and is stated in the listing contract.

7. B An exclusive right to sell listing entitles the broker to a commission if the property is sold, but not regardless of whether the property is sold.

8. A An exclusive agency listing permits the owner to sell of his own efforts without liability for a commission to the listing broker, but does not allow the owner to list concurrently with other brokers.

9. D Under the terms of an open listing, only the broker who produces a buyer is entitled to a commission, but the owner retains the right to sell of his own efforts without liability for a commission to anyone.

10. C A net listing may be an open listing, exclusive right to sell listing or an exclusive agency listing.

11. B Either an exclusive agency listing or an open listing permits the owner to sell of his own efforts without liability for a commission. An exclusive right to sell listing does not permit this.

12. B The broker fulfilled the terms of the contract when he produced a ready, willing and able buyer.

13. A Under the terms of an advance cost listing, the broker receives compensation for out-of-pocket expenses and may also charge a commission based on the sales price.

14. D A multiple listing agreement requires the payment of only one commission which is divided between the listing and selling brokers. It does not permit the owner to sell of his own efforts without liability for a commission.

15. A A multiple listing offers greatest market exposure, and the possibility of a higher sales price and a quicker sale.

16. B The seller is liable for the commission because the cancellation was arbitrary on his part and violated the terms of a valid listing contract and a valid contract of sale.

17. A Since the broker was the procuring cause of the sale, he is entitled to a commission.

18. C Under the terms of an open listing, the commission is payable to the broker who made the sale.

19. B An exclusive listing contract is one between the owner and the broker who employs the listing salesperson and is not terminable by the death of the listing salesperson.

20. D Unless the purchase contract contains an agreement to the contrary, any forfeited earnest money deposits become the property of the owner/seller.

21. C Discount brokers must sell more prop-erties in less time to be successful, so they reject listings that will not sell quickly.

22. B Homeowners sometimes attempt to sell their property without a broker's aid because the payment of a sales commission would consume too much of their equity.

23. A The purchaser should reveal confiden-tial information to the broker since the broker represents the purchaser and can better meet his needs if he is aware of pertinent data and circumstances.

24. C 3% + 6% + 6% + 6% = 21% ÷ 4 = **5.25%**

25. B $120,000 × 8% = $9,600 total commis-sion

    $9,600 × .10 = $960 to the manager

    $9,600 − $960 = $8,640 remainder

    $8,640 − 45% to office = **$4,752** to agent

26. C $360 × 1/3 = $120 first month com-mission

    $360 × 3.5% × 11 mos = $138.60 next 11 months

    $120 + $138.60 = **$258.60** total com-mission

27. B $35,000 × 1.2 = $42,000 list price

    $42,000 − $3,000 = $39,000 accepted by seller

    $39,000 × .94 = **$36,660** after 6% com-mission

28. B $100,000 × .06 = $6,000 on first $100,000

    $100,000 × .05 = $5,000 on next $100,000

    $200,000 × .04 = $8,000 on next $200,000

    $600,000 × .03 = $18,000 on bal. $600,000

    $37,000 Total commission

29. B $100,000 ÷ .93 = **$107,527**

30. B $120,000 × .07 = $8,400

    $112,500 × .07 = $7,875

    $8,400 − $7,875 = **$525**

Commission Calculations

1. $94,500 × .06 = **$5,670**

2. $93,000 × .06 = **$5,580**

3. $88,000 ÷ .94 = **$93,617**

4. $94,000 × .06 = $5,640 commission before MLS fee and splits

    $5,640 − $100 MLS fee = $5,540 × .25 = **$1,385** for the listing sales associate

    $5,540 × .45 = **$2,493** for the sales associate

    $5,540 × .30 = **$1,662** for the broker (com-pany)

5. $94,200 × .06 = $5,652 − $100 MLS fee = $5,552 commission before splits

    $5,552 × .25 = **$1,388** each for the listing sales associate and the broker (company)

    $5,552 × .5 = **$2,776** for the selling broker

6. $2,776 × .50 = **$1,388** each for the cooper-ating broker and the sales associate

7. $3,927 ÷ .70 ÷ .06 = **$93,500** *(simply reverse the math used to calculate the commission)*

CHAPTER 21

1. C The broker is bound by fiduciary re-sponsibilities of obedience, accounting and loyalty. The principal (seller) is re-sponsible for maintaining the property.

2. C A universal agency authorizes the agent to transact all types of matters for the principal.

3. B A general agent is authorized to bind his employer in a trade or business.

4. D A real estate broker is a special agent of the owner of property listed for sale with the broker.

5. D A salesperson is an agent of the em-ploying broker (subagent of the seller), who is the agent for the principal un-der a listing contract.

6. A Agency authority which is derived from custom in the industry is identi-fied as implied authority.

7. A A broker's fiduciary responsibility is to his principal, not to third parties with whom he deals.

8. B A broker who lists a property in which he has an ownership interest holds an agency coupled with an interest.

9. D An agent does not have the fiduciary responsibility of giving legal advice,

and is prohibited from doing so unless the agent is a member of the bar.

10. B A dual agency exists when the broker acts as agent for both purchaser and seller in a single transaction.

11. C For a broker to act as a dual agent in a single transaction, both parties must agree to the dual agency.

12. B A middleman brings the parties of a transaction together but does not participate in negotiations.

13. B The buyer deposited the earnest money to show good faith toward the purchase. It should be returned to him. If the broker feels that he should receive a commission, he should look to the seller.

14. A Commingling is the illegal combining of the funds of others with those of the agent, and constitutes grounds for revocation of a broker's license.

15. C Misrepresentation by a broker can result in the loss of rights to a commission, revocation of license or civil suit for damages, but not in criminal prosecution.

16. C An owner who gives false information may be liable for a commission to the broker, cancellation of the sale, and money damages to the purchaser.

17. B An agent's failure to investigate the cause of an apparent underlying defect can result in civil liability for damages to the injured party.

18. B An agent may be held responsible for the competency of persons engaged by the agent to investigate a question raised by a purchaser.

19. C An "as is" sale does not free the agent from liability for withholding material facts about a property.

20. B The real estate department lacks jurisdiction over this matter and could not take any action against the principal. The broker should discourage the principal, but have no part of it.

21. A The purpose of errors and omissions insurance is to indemnify an agent against legal actions brought by those with whom he deals.

22. C Puffing or puffery is making an extravagant or nonfactual statement that would be recognized by a reasonable person as an exaggeration. Puffery should be used with extreme care because of the potential liability for misrepresentation.

23. C A breach of fiduciary responsibility by a broker may lead to disciplinary action by the real estate department including license revocation and civil action by the principal, but not to criminal prosecution.

24. D A principal owes the agent compensation, reimbursement, indemnification and performance. The agent owes the principal obedience of lawful instructions.

25. B A broker should always make clear to third parties his obligation of loyalty to the principal.

26. B A sales associate is a general agent for the employing broker, not a special agent, and the relationship is subject to all laws and rules of agency.

27. B A cooperating broker must make clear to all parties whether he is acting in the interests of the purchaser or seller.

28. C A buyer who employs a broker to represent him eliminates the problem of divided broker loyalty and can base his offers on the net amount the seller will receive from the sale.

29. D HUD property reports are given to prospective buyers of new subdivision lots offered to residents of another state.

30. B Property reports required by state or federal law do not indicate governmental approval of the property. These reports must be given to the prospective purchaser before a purchase agreement is signed.

31. B As stated in answer C, a buyer's broker can show any properties if agreed to by the owners of those properties.

32. D All of the penalties in answers A, B, and C are applicable. Substantial fines are also usually assessed.

33. C This practice, i.e. price fixing, as well as boycotting (avoiding cooperation with competitors) and allocation of markets, are all violations of the anti-trust laws. Steering is a Fair Housing violation, not anti-trust.

34. B If the mainstream brokers have agreed among themselves not to cooperate with the flat fee broker, this might be construed as boycotting, an illegal activity defined by anti-trust laws.

CHAPTER 22

1. A The Civil Rights Act of 1866 prohibits discrimination on the basis of race, but not on any other basis.

2. D The Fair Housing Act of 1968 prohibits discrimination in housing on the basis of religion, in terms or conditions for sale or rent or in advertising, but not on the basis of age.

3. A The 1988 Amendment to the Fair Housing Act of 1968 prohibits discrimination on the basis of physical handicap and familial status.

4. A Steering is the practice of directing home seekers to certain neighborhoods based on race, color, religion, sex, national origin, handicap or familial status and is prohibited by the 1968 Fair Housing Act.

5. C Block busting is not limited to the fear of loss of value because of the changing racial composition of a neighborhood and is prohibited by the Fair Housing Act of 1968.

6. D The Fair Housing Act of 1968 applies to single-family housing and to multiple dwellings.

7. C The Civil Rights Act of 1866 prohibits racial discrimination with no exemptions.

8. C The fair housing laws do not contain prohibitions against discrimination on the basis of marital status.

9. A The Fair Housing Act of 1968 permits discrimination in church-operated housing if membership in the church is open to anyone.

10. C The prohibitions of the Fair Housing Act of 1968 do not apply to housing operated by a private club if it is not operated for a commercial purpose.

11. D State real estate departments do not enforce the federal fair housing laws.

12. A The Civil Rights Act of 1866 is enforced by having the complainant file an action in federal court.

13. B The agent should refuse to accept the listing because to do so would violate the federal fair housing laws.

14. A The Fourteenth Amendment applies the Fifth Amendment rules to the states.

15. A Under the Fair Housing Act of 1968, owner-occupied dwellings of four or fewer units and a home being sold "For Sale By Owner" are exempt if the owners do not use discriminatory advertising. Also, religious organizations and private clubs are exempt if membership is not discriminatory and the lodging is not run commercially.

16. C See the discussion for question 15.

17. A The Equal Credit Opportunity Act prohibits age discrimination in determining ability to repay.

18. D Prohibited by the Fair Housing Act of 1968, steering is the practice of directing home seekers to or away from particular neighborhoods based on race, color, religion, sex, or national origin, handicap or, in this case, familial status.

19. C A fee may be charged. A person may not be turned down simply because of his/her age or marital status. Credit reports are private and not to be shown to or discussed with anyone.

20. B Redlining was the illegal practice of denying insurance and home loans to certain neighborhoods, most often because of racial composition. Underwriting is providing insurance or financial support. Block busting is breaking up a neighborhood, and steering is restricting entry into a neighborhood.

21. B The ADA deals primarily with commercial property and prohibits dis-

discrimination against people with disabilities.

22. C The ADA provides access requirements.

23. D The ADA is very detailed and there are still many gray areas in the statute.

24. B For individual actions, the damages are limited to $10,000. The court may also award court costs and reasonable attorney's fees to the aggrieved party.

25. A No law expects lenders to lower their credit standards; redlining is illegal, and the types of credit offered by the financial institutions must be made public.

26. D The Federal Home Loan Bank Board has listed guidelines that various federal examiners consider when assessing CRA performances.

27. B Protected class is any group of people that by law are protected from discrimination. It has nothing to do with numbers, which the word "minority" seems to imply.

28. D Familial status has been defined by HUD as in response D.

29. B Originally, under the Fair Housing Act of 1968, punitive damages were limited to $1,000, but that cap was removed by the 1988 amendments. Actual damages may be awarded to the complainant and an injunction may be made to stop the sale or rental to someone other than the complainant.

30. B The complainant must prove that discrimination did occur.

CHAPTER 23

1. D Scarcity of land, rising construction costs, desire for ownership and Section 234 of the National Housing Act have all contributed to the popularity of condominium ownership.

2. A Section 234 of the National Housing Act provides a legal model for condominium ownership and makes available FHA insurance on condominium unit mortgage loans.

3. B Condominiums are not covered by state laws governing cooperative ownership.

4. A A system of self-government and the existence of separate and common elements are distinguishing features of a condominium development.

5. A Individual units in a condominium are classed as separate property.

6. B Common elements in a condominium development are owned by all unit owners, who hold undivided interests in the elements.

7. C Limited common elements are those common elements the use of which is restricted to one unit owner.

8. A An enabling declaration or master deed is used to convert a single estate into separate property estates and an estate composed of the common elements.

9. A Bylaws provide the rules by which an owners' association operates.

10. D The condominium developer usually files the enabling declaration for condominium development.

11. A The purchaser of a condominium unit receives a deed from the seller.

12. B The enabling declaration cannot be altered by an owners' association, but the bylaws, CC&Rs or house rules may be changed.

13. D The role of the board of directors in a condominium compares to the city council in a local government.

14. A Day-to-day management of a condominium development may be provided by an on-site manager or by a property management company.

15. A A condominium development secures its budgeted maintenance funds from association dues assessed upon each unit owner, usually monthly.

16. A The board of directors of a condominium has authority to raise association dues.

17. D An owners' association should maintain reserves for maintenance of all the common elements listed in responses A, B, and C. A unit owner is responsible for replacing his old dishwasher.

18. A The owners' association of a condominium is responsible for hazard insurance on the common elements. Individual unit owners are responsible for maintenance within their units, property taxes and furnishings.

19. B Liability arising from injuries received on any of the common elements belongs to the condominium association.

20. D The deficiency judgment would be entered against any other property, real or personal, owned by K.

21. B Failure to pay condominium association dues will result in a lien against the delinquent owner's unit.

22. C In a condominium, taxes are assessed against each individual unit with a bill sent to each unit's owner.

23. B The purchase of a condominium unit can be financed by means of an FHA-insured loan, an installment contract, a conventional loan or carryback financing by the seller. There is no special form of financing for condominiums.

24. A A condominium unit purchaser surrenders personal freedoms to community rule and exchanges freedom of choice for the freedom from responsibility.

25. D Windows are common elements owned by all the unit owners. Any structural change is a violation of the CC&Rs; however, the owners' association can make an exception or change the CC&Rs.

26. A Condominium residents have ownership of the interior space of a unit (sometimes including a garage) plus an interest in the building structures, common areas and land area of the entire project.

27. C Cooperators do NOT hold a fee title to their units; they are shareholders in a nonprofit corporation which holds title to the property. Cooperatives are NOT regulated by horizontal property acts.

28. A A cooperative corporation does not foreclose on a delinquent cooperator but may terminate the cooperator as a shareholder, resell his shares, or bring civil action to recover the delinquent amount.

29. A Traditionally, the resale of cooperative shares has been financed by installment sales agreements because the underlying mortgage is a mortgage on the entire premises.

30. A Government of condominiums and cooperatives is very similar. An owner of a condominium has no liability for the mortgage debt against his neighbor's unit, and they own fee simple. Cooperators own a share of stock inseparable from a proprietary lease. Traditionally, cooperative units could not be financed separately from the rest of the building.

31. D A cooperative is governed by a board of directors elected by the cooperators.

32. D Cooperatives have been in existence in the United States for a much longer time than condominiums, PUDs or timeshared ownership.

33. C In a planned unit development, title to the common areas is held by the owners' association, of which all unit owners are members.

34. A In a PUD, the title to common areas is held by the owners' association and there are CC&Rs governing individual owners. PUD CC&Rs are not meant to be burdensome. They help maintain the attractiveness of the development.

35. B A PUD owners' association can control exterior paint colors and the number of persons who may occupy a dwelling unit. It has no control over financing or choice of buyers either in the initial sale or in subsequent resales.

36. D Rules governing the use of recreational facilities in a condominium, cooperative or planned unit development are found in the CC&Rs and house rules.

37. A Resort timesharing, the concept of selling divided shares in living units at a vacation facility, is a recent development in communal ownership of real estate.

38. B Approximately 70% of timeshared properties are owned in fee simple.

39. C The purchaser in a right-to-use time-share property does not hold title to the property and is not a tenant in common with other users of the unit. The buyer pays for possessory rights in advance.

40. B The purchaser of a timeshare in a unit under the fee simple format holds a fee simple estate, and so holds title in perpetuity and receives a deed to his share in the property. He may use a note and mortgage to finance his purchase.

41. A A right-to-use timeshare is usually less expensive than a comparable fee simple timeshare, and an off-season week is less expensive than an in-season week.

42. B The purchase of future vacations at a prepaid price and the ability to exchange are among the principal attractions of timeshare ownership. Generally, timeshare resales show little or no appreciation, and some people become bored returning to the same place year after year.

43. B As investments, timeshares are generally regarded as a high risk, low appreciation probability.

44. D About 25 states have enacted legislation regulating timeshare sales.

CHAPTER 24

1. A The concept of insurance is to reimburse the insured for financial losses. Insurance does not prevent loss-causing events from occurring.

2. D Flood insurance is not among the coverages provided by the New York fire form.

3. D The premium is the money paid by the insured for insurance coverage.

4. A An endorsement to an insurance policy is also known as a rider.

5. A Coverage for additional perils can be obtained by purchasing a separate policy or by adding an endorsement to an existing policy.

6. B Financial responsibility to others as a result of one's actions or negligence is known as personal liability (not slander or libel), or public liability.

7. C Flood damage is not covered by a homeowners' insurance policy; it is a separate coverage.

8. D A typical homeowner's insurance policy will not cover automobiles kept in a garage on the premises, but does cover the dwelling house, other structures, living expenses while damage is being repaired and personal property within the home.

9. D A comprehensive homeowner policy covers the most perils.

10. A An HO–1 policy will not cover damage caused by the weight of ice, snow and sleet. This would be covered by an HO–2, HO–3, or HO–5 policy.

11. D The HO–8 policy covers the same perils as an HO–1 policy and insures for actual cash value. It was designed especially for older homes.

12. D A typical HO–2 policy does not cover any earthquake damage, but does cover the damage from windstorms, vandalism or freezing water pipes.

13. B Damage from nuclear accident is not covered by an HO–5 policy, nor by any homeowner policy for that matter.

14. C The HO–4 policy is especially designed to meet the needs of a tenant in a rented dwelling by duplicating the coverage of an HO–2 policy without insuring the dwelling itself.

15. C A tenant's policy covers the renter's personal belongings, but not the building.

16. A An HO–6 policy insures a condominium unit owner's personal property within the unit. The association's policy covers the common elements, including buildings and pools.

17. B Medical payments can be paid only to guests of the insured on the premises or to others injured by the insured away from the property. The insured, family members, or claims arising

from business pursuits are not eligible for medical payments.

18. A Lenders will usually require the owner to provide fire and extended coverage on structures, but not on personal property.

19. B The lender on a condominium unit will usually require proof that the condominium association carries insurance on the common elements, but will not require a unit owner to carry liability insurance.

20. C $\dfrac{\$45{,}000 \text{ insurance carried}}{\$60{,}000 \text{ replacement cost } 3\ 80\%} = .9375$

$\$20{,}000 \text{ loss} \times .9375 = \textbf{\$18,750} \text{ recovery}$

21. B Lenders typically require the borrower to carry a replacement cost policy equal to the full amount of the loan.

22. C An "old for old" insurance policy fixes the insurance company's liability to the insured to the actual cash value of the insured property.

23. D Homeowner's insurance in the amount of 80% of replacement cost will pay full replacement cost up to the face amount of the policy in the event of a loss.

24. C Carryback financing does not normally require flood insurance or certification that a property is not in a flood zone. VA-guaranteed mortgages, all FHA-insured mortgages and conventional mortgages from federal S&Ls all require this.

25. B An insurer who cancels a policy which contains the New York fire form must give the insured a 5-day notice and a prorated refund of unused premiums.

26. D A landlord package policy provides coverage for damage to property, liability, medical expenses, loss of rents, but not for tenants' personal property.

27. D An insured may cancel a New York fire form policy without giving a 5-day notice. Any refunds will be based on short-rate premiums, which is less than a prorated refund.

28. A An insurance policy may be suspended by the insurer if the hazard exposure is allowed to increase beyond the risks contemplated when the policy was issued or if the property is left vacant beyond a specified time.

29. A New home buyers may protect against losses due to structural defects by having the home inspected before purchase and by purchasing insurance under the Home Owners Warranty Program.

Insurance Problems

1. $\dfrac{\$40{,}000}{\$80{,}000 \times 80\%} \times \$15{,}000 = \textbf{\$9,375}$

2. HO–2 coverage includes smoke damage, and since the homeowners carry over 80% of replacement cost, they will recover the full $800.

3. The building owners are responsible for damage caused by the sign falling off their building.

CHAPTER 25

1. D Deed restrictions are controls on private land-use.

2. D State governments, local governments and subdivision developers may all impose some form of land-use controls.

3. C The placement of interior partitions in a building is not regulated by zoning laws.

4. D Zoning laws may not be used to protect an existing land user from competitive business establishments.

5. D Authority to enact zoning laws is derived from a government's police power.

6. C Land-use designations are not uniformly used throughout the United States.

7. A Zoning laws tell a landowner how land may be used, but do not provide compensation for loss of value due to zoning.

8. A Checking the zoning on a parcel of land includes viewing the zoning maps and then consulting the zoning ordinances to see what is allowed. Nei-

ther the deed nor the survey will help determine permissible zoning.

9. C Building codes dictate construction standards; zoning laws do not.

10. B A landowner who developed land without first obtaining a building permit could be forced to tear down the building.

11. A A nonconforming use is one not in accord with present zoning laws. It may sometimes be permitted under a grandfather clause.

12. D Under the provisions of a grandfather clause, a building owner may perform all normal maintenance on the nonconforming building but may not remodel or enlarge the building or extend its life.

13. A A zoning variance allows an owner to deviate from an existing zoning law without a change in the zoning law.

14. C Because the use permit was granted conditionally, the inventory is restricted to those items permitted by the use permit.

15. B Spot zoning is the rezoning of a small area of land in an existing community.

16. A A change from apartment zoning to single-family residential zoning constitutes downzoning. The owners are not compensated for any loss of land value.

17. A Land zoned for multi-family residential that is located between single-family residential zoning and commercial or industrial zoning would be a buffer zone.

18. A Before a subdivider can sell lots in a new subdivision, all mapping requirements must be met and the subdivision plat must be recorded.

19. B Building codes set minimum standards for materials and construction methods for buildings.

20. B Building codes are employed to establish acceptable material and construc-construction standards for buildings.

21. D A certificate of occupancy must be obtained before a newly constructed building may be utilized by tenants.

22. B A restriction which limits occupancy on racial grounds would be against public policy and would be unenforceable. However, the conveyance would still be valid.

23. D A deed restriction would be used to limit the height of trees in a subdivision.

24. D Land uses may be regulated by deed restrictions, zoning laws or subdivision regulations, but not by building codes.

25. A A master plan should provide for a balance between social and economic functions and should include provisions for flexibility if future growth does not develop as expected. It should not define neighborhoods by racial and religious identities.

26. B An environmental impact statement sets forth the effect of a proposed development on the community.

27. B Environmental impact statements provide a means of estimating the impact of a proposed development on the environment and provide a means of making better decisions regarding land uses.

28. C An environmental impact statement will not reveal the effect of a planned development on property values.

29. A Before accepting the listing, the broker should determine the conversion's conformity to zoning requirements and whether proper permits were obtained.

30. D The prospect should make the offer to purchase contingent upon the rezoning of the property for residential use.

31. D The broker should accept the listing, check with the building department, and then advise the owner as to his options.

32. D As a rule, landowners who are denied proposed development of their land cannot force purchase of the land by the community or payment for loss of land value.

33. B Transferable development rights may be traded on the open market or pur-

chased by the government and sold to others.

34. D Transferable development rights have been used to protect historical buildings, agricultural land and environmentally sensitive land.

CHAPTER 26

1. D "Backbone Industries" is not a standard term for export businesses. Industries which produce goods and services for export are referred to as base industries, export industries or primary industries.

2. B Industries which produce goods and services for local consumption are known as service industries, secondary industries or filler industries.

3. B The real estate brokerage business is an example of a secondary or service industry.

4. B The loss of a community's largest employer can result in declining real estate values, a slow-down in new construction, population decline and the closing of some service industries.

5. A Base industries are essential to a community's economic health and to the maintenance of real estate values.

6. B Generally, one job in a base industry generates two jobs in service industries.

7. B A sudden increase in demand will cause existing housing prices to rise rapidly, then fall slightly as supply catches up with demand.

8. A An excess of supply works to the advantage of buyers.

9. C Most people's peak earning years occur between ages 45–55 years.

10. C Typically, the largest and most expensive housing is acquired between ages 45 and 55.

11. C The post-World War II baby boom spanned a period of 15 years, from 1946 through 1960. This would include persons aged 45 to 50 in 1995.

12. A A dramatic increase in the birth rate creates an immediate demand for bedrooms and a long-range demand for houses.

13. B Real estate values are affected by the federal government's tax rules, laws, deficits and monetary policies. Federal government is not involved in zoning.

14. B 12% interest minus 28% tax rate = 8.64% after-tax cost (or, 12% $\times$ .72 = 8.64%).

15. A Federal tax laws do not allow an owner to depreciate land.

16. C. Economists agree that there are three factors that establish criteria for home sales: (1) job growth, (2) low interest rates, and (3) rising home prices.

17. A Federal governmental borrowing has the greatest effect upon what an individual must pay for a real estate mortgage loan.

18. D An increase in the money supply equal to the rate of growth is needed to keep prices from falling in a growing economy.

19. A The printing of more money than is needed for economic growth will lead to a short-term drop in interest rates and a long-term increase in inflation.

20. B Creation of extra money by the Federal Reserve leads to inflation which makes home purchases by persons of modest income more difficult.

21. B The advent of the secondary mortgage market made previously untapped sources of real estate mortgage loans readily available and contributed to the real estate speculation and inflation of the late 1970s. All borrowers have been aided by the strong activity of the secondary money market.

22. A Cost-push inflation results from increased manufacturing costs.

23. A Demand-pull inflation results from too much money chasing too few goods, and has little to do with manufacturing costs.

24. B Demand-pull inflation results from too much money chasing too few goods.

25. B Real-cost inflation is brought on by the increased effort necessary to produce the same quantity of goods or services.

26. B The real cost of interest is the inflation-adjusted cost.

27. C In 1980 the Federal Reserve entered into a period of restrained monetary growth in order to curb inflation.

28. A Expectations about inflation tend to lag actual changes. This is true whether inflation is heating up or cooling down.

29. B An owner who occupies a property as a principal residence tends to be the least demanding of appreciation potential.

30. A Ultimately, the marketplace supply and demand determines the interest rates for real estate mortgage loans.

31. C The Federal Reserve Board's objectives for the American economy include high employment, stable prices, steady growth and a stable foreign exchange rate.

32. B The Federal Reserve Board influences the national economy by adjusting the money supply. This changes the supply-demand balance for money, and, in turn, interest rates. The Federal Reserve does not, and in fact cannot, alter interest rates directly; only indirectly through changes in the money supply.

33. B An increase in the monetary base at a rate faster than that of the GNP will lead to a temporary fall in interest rates and a temporary economic growth.

34. A. If the government increases taxes, it reduces private income and the consumer cannot spend as much (it lowers the consumer's disposal income).

35. B See page 525 in *Real Estate Principles*.

CHAPTER 27

1. D Cash flow refers to the income generated by a property in excess of operating expenses and mortgage payments.

2. D 4 units × $500 rent/unit − 5% vacancy rate − $700 operating expenses − $1,500 mortgage payment = ($300)/month (i.e., negative cash flow)

3. C 4 units × $500 rent/unit − 5% vacancy rate − $700 operating expenses − $1,400

interest payment − $1,000 depreciation = ($1,200) = $1,200/month taxable income

4. D $16,900 cash flow ÷ $130,000 down = .13

5. A Mortgage balance reduction is an out-of-pocket expense but not a reduction for tax purposes.

6. B Depreciation on a property is a deduction against income tax but is not an out-of-pocket expense to the investor.

7. C The higher an investor's tax bracket, the more valuable the depreciation on a property in terms of tax shelter.

8. A Tax laws permit depreciation to be started over each time the property is sold, but do not allow depreciation in excess of a building's value.

9. A Depreciation claimed in excess of actual loss in value is taxed upon sale of the property but may be deferred if the property is traded.

10. B Equity buildup can result from mortgage reduction or appreciation in the value of a property.

11. B The current property value is $120,000 − $75,000 loan balance = $45,000 current equity. Original equity was $20,000 down payment. Equity buildup is $25,000 ($45,000 current equity − $20,000 original equity)

12. A Negative leverage occurs when borrowed funds cost more than they produce in benefits.

13. B The "at risk" rule would limit depreciation to the original investment plus loan reduction.

14. B Taxes and interest are deductible in the year when the expenses are incurred.

15. A Houses and condominiums tend to be overpriced in relation to the rent they produce because their prices are influenced by the amenity value of home ownership.

16. B Because houses and condominiums can usually be resold for higher prices than would be justified by rents alone, they appeal to some investors.

17. A To be a good investment, when a property which generates a negative cash flow is sold, there must be a substantial appreciation to offset the negative cash flow.

18. C A 15-unit building usually will require a part-time resident manager. It cannot be managed on a couple of hours of spare time a week.

19. A A minimum of 25 units is usually needed to support a full-time resident manager.

20. D Management costs per unit drop as the number of units in an apartment building increase.

21. A The manager of a 20 to 30 unit apartment building may expect to interview prospective tenants, show vacant units, take rental applications and perform maintenance tasks. He should not expect to file the owner's tax returns.

22. B Office buildings usually yield a higher return on investment than do apartment buildings because even though they cost more to build, they bring a higher rent per square foot.

23. C Office buildings bring higher rents per dollar of investment than do one-to-four family buildings or vacant land.

24. A Tenants in office buildings demand more services and other amenities than do residential tenants.

25. A A change in office tenants can often result in a major vacancy loss and usually requires extensive remodeling. Therefore, tenant turnover is more costly than in residential properties.

26. B A long-term lease exposes the owner to possible difficulties in selling the building and exposes the owner to the possibility that operating costs may increase without an increase in rent.

27. A Location is more important to office tenants than to residential tenants, so there is greater risk in locating an office building.

28. D Risks are greatest early in a building's development, so the earlier an investor enters an investment, the greater the profit he expects to receive.

29. B Taxes on profits from a new real estate development are due when the property is sold.

30. D Tax benefits are slightly less rewarding after completion than in the early stages of development.

31. C Because of the building's reduced economic life, the older the building, the higher the return per invested dollar demanded by investors.

32. B Income often outpaces consumption during the second 20 years of life.

33. C High risks should be taken during the 25-45 year old period, followed by emphasis on moderate returns, moderate risks and tax shelters, followed by low risks and liquidation of assets in later years.

34. A Tax shelters have their greatest value during peak income years.

35. D The benefits of participation in a limited partnership include freedom from management decisions, limited financial liability, opportunity to diversify and tax benefits equal to sole ownership.

36. B The liability of a limited partner for the partnership's obligations is limited to the amount of the limited partner's investment in the partnership.

37. B By giving the organizers a percentage of the profits instead of a fixed fee, the organizers have a direct stake in the partnership's success.

38. A The risk of an investor losing his money is known as downside risk.

39. B An investor in a partnership should be prepared to stay with the partnership until the properties are refinanced or sold, and should be aware of the difficulties of selling shares for the proportional worth of the investor's interest. His investment is not liquid, not easily converted to cash.

40. B The Securities and Exchange Commission administers the federal laws which regulate limited partnerships.

41. A The disclosure statement given to prospective investors in a limited partnership is known as a prospectus.

42. B Blue-sky laws permit state governments to halt the sale of an investment opportunity.

Investment Problems

1. **Corporate executive:** III, IV

   Reasons: high tax bracket, substantial money available for investment, must have professional management.

2. **Married couple** 57 and 55 years old: II

   Reasons: This would comfortably fit their available assets, not too risky, and offer them part-time work as live-in managers.

3. **Young couple:** I, V

   Reasons: This couple does not appear to have enough money for a larger purchase. Also, they need professional management. With regard to V, a local real estate agent might be engaged to manage it. Both I and V provide tax shelter benefits.

4. **Group of doctors:** III, IV

   Reasons: large down payment available, need for tax shelter, need for professional management.

5. **Bachelor,** age 38: I, II, V

   Reasons: limited down payment (number II may require junior financing), probably has some time to manage the property, tax shelter is needed.

Glossary

Abstract of title: a summary of all recorded documents affecting title to a given parcel of land

Abstracter (conveyancer): an expert in title search and abstract preparation

Accelerated Cost Recovery System (ACRS): a rapid depreciation write-off method

Accelerated depreciation: a method of depreciation that achieves a faster rate depreciation than straight-line

Acceleration clause: allows the lender to demand immediate payment of the entire loan if the borrower defaults

Accession: the addition to land by man or nature

Accretion: the process of land buildup by waterborne rock, sand, and soil

Acknowledgment: a formal declaration by a person that he or she, in fact, did sign the document

Acre: a unit of land measurement containing 43,560 square feet

Actual cash value: the new price less accumulated depreciation

Actual eviction: the landlord serves notice on the tenant to comply with the lease contract or vacate

Actual notice: knowledge that one has gained based on what he has actually seen, heard, read, or observed

Addendums: *see* Rider

Adjustable rate mortgage (ARM): a mortgage loan on which the interest rate rises and falls with changes in prevailing rates

Adjusted market price: the value of a comparable property after adjustments are made for differences between it and the subject property

Adjusted sales price: the sales price of a property less commissions, fix-up expenses, and closing costs

Adjustment period: the amount of time that elapses between adjustments of an adjustable mortgage loan

Administrator: a person appointed by a court to settle an estate when there is no will

Ad valorem taxes: taxes charged according to the value of a property

Advance cost listing: a listing wherein the seller is charged for the out-of-pocket costs of marketing the property

Advance fee listing: a listing where the broker charges an hourly fee plus out-of-pocket expenses

Adverse possession: acquisition of land by prolonged and unauthorized occupation

Agency by estoppal: results when a principal fails to maintain due diligence over his agent and the agent exercises powers not granted to him

Agency by ratification: one that is established after the fact

Agency coupled with an interest: one that results when the agent holds an interest in the property he is representing

Agent: the person empowered to act by and on behalf of the principal

Air lot: a designated airspace over a parcel of land

Air right: the right to own and use the airspace above the surface of a parcel of land

Alienation clause: a clause in a note or mortgage that gives the lender the right to call the entire loan balance due if the property is sold or otherwise conveyed

Alienation of title: a transfer in ownership of any kind

Allodial system: one in which individuals are given the right to own land

All-risks policy: all perils, except those excluded in writing, are covered

Alluvion: the increase of land when waterborne soil is gradually deposited

Amendatory language: government required clauses in FHA and VA contracts

Amendment: the method used to change a zoning ordinance

Amortized loan: a loan requiring periodic payments that include both interest and partial repayment of principal

Amount realized: selling price less selling expenses

Annual percentage rate (APR): a uniform measure of the cost of credit that includes interest, discount points, and loan fees

Appraise: to estimate the value of something

Appreciation: an increase in property value

Appropriation process: the enactment of a taxing body's budget and sources of money into law

Appurtenance: a right or privilege or improvement that belongs to and passes with land

"As is": said of property offered for sale in its present condition with no guarantee or warranty of quality provided by the seller

Assemblage: the process of combining two or more parcels into one

Assessed value: a value placed on a property for purpose of taxation

Assessment appeal board: local governmental body which hears and rules on property owner complaints of over-assessment

Assessment roll: a list or book, open for public inspection, that shows assessed values for all lands and buildings in a taxing district

Assessor's map: one that shows assessor parcel numbers for all land parcels in a taxing district

Assessor's parcel number: a system for assigning numbers to land parcels to aid in property tax assessment and collection

Assign: to transfer to another one's rights under a contract

Assignee: one to whom a right, title, or interest is assigned (also called an assign)

Assignment: the total transfer of one's rights under a contract to another

Assignment of rents: establishes the lender's right to take possession and collect rents in the event of loan default

Assignor: one who assigns a right, title, or interest to another

Association: a not-for-profit organization that can own property and transact business in its own name

Assumption: the buyer is obligated to repay an existing loan as a condition of the sale

Attachments: *See* Rider

Attorney-in-fact: one who is authorized by another to act in his (her) place

Avulsion: the removal of land by the action of water

Balloon loan: a loan in which the final payment is larger than the preceding payments

Balloon payment: name given to the final payment of a balloon loan

Bare title: title that lacks the usual rights and privileges of ownership and possession

Bargain and sale deed: a deed that contains no covenants, but does imply that the grantor owns the property being conveyed

Bargain brokers: a term that refers to real estate brokers who charge less than most competing brokers in their area

Base industry: an industry that produces goods or services for export from the region

Base line: a latitude line selected as a reference in the rectangular survey system

Basis: the price paid for property, used in calculating income taxes

Bench mark: a reference point of known location and elevation

Beneficial interest: a unit of ownership in a real estate investment trust

Beneficiary: the lender in a deed of trust arrangement

Beneficiary statement: a lienholder's statement as to the unpaid balance on a trust deed note

Bequest: personal property received under a will

Bilateral contract: when a promise is exchanged for a promise

Bill of sale: a document that shows the transfer of personal property

Binder: a short purchase contract used to secure a real estate transaction until a more formal contract can be signed

Biweekly payment loan: a loan that calls for 26 half-size payments a year

Blanket mortgage: a mortgage that is secured by more than one real property

Blended-rate loan: a refinancing plan that combines the interest rate on an existing mortgage loan with current rates

Blind pool: an investment pool wherein properties are purchased after investors have already invested their money

Block busting: the illegal practice of inducing panic selling from buying into dubious investment schemes

Board of equalization: a governmental body that reviews property tax assessment procedures

Breach of contract: failure without legal excuse to perform as specified by a contract

Broad form (HO–2): an insurance term that describes a policy that covers a large number of named perils

Broad market: one wherein many buyers and many sellers are in the market at the same time

Budget mortgage: feature loan payments that include principal, interest, taxes, and insurance (often called PITI)

Buffer zone: a strip of land that separates one land use from another

Building codes: local and state laws that set minimum construction standards

Buy-down: a cash payment to a lender so as to reduce the interest rate a borrower must pay

Buyer's broker: a broker employed by, and therefore loyal to, the buyer

Buyer's market: one with few buyers and many sellers

Buyer's walk-through: final inspection just prior to settlement

Bylaws: rules that govern how an owners' association will be run

Call: lender's right to require early repayment of the loan balance

Capital gain: the gain (profit) on the sale of an appreciated asset

Capitalize: to convert future income to current value

Carryback financing: a note accepted by a seller instead of cash

Case law: individual court decisions

Cash flow: the number of dollars remaining each year after collecting rents and paying operating expenses and mortgage payments

Cash-on-cash: the cash flow netted by a property dividend by the amount of cash necessary to purchase it

Caveat emptor: let the buyer beware

CC&Rs: covenants, conditions, and restrictions by which a property owner agrees to abide

Certificate of deposit: a saver's commitment to leave money on deposit for a specific period of time

Certificate of occupancy: a government-issued document that states a structure meets local zoning and building code requirements and is ready for use

Certificate of reduction: a document prepared by a lender showing the remaining balance on an existing loan

Certificate of title: an opinion by an attorney as to who owns a parcel of land

Certified property manager (CPM): professional designation for property manager

Cession deed: deed conveying street rights to a county or municipality

Chain: a surveyor's measurement that is 66 feet long

Chain of title: the linkage of property ownership that connects the present owner to the original source of title

Characteristics of land: fixity, immobility, indestructibility, modification, nonhomogeneity, scarcity, and situs

Characteristics of value: demand, scarcity, transferability, and utility

Chattel: article of personal property

Chattel mortgage: a pledge of personal property to secure a note

Check: a 24-by-24 mile area created by guide meridians and correction lines in the rectangular survey system

Client: the agent's principal

Closing: the act of finalizing a purchase transaction

Closing meeting: a meeting at which the buyer pays for the property, receives a deed to it, and all other matters pertaining to the sale are concluded

Closing statement: an accounting of funds to the buyer and the seller at the completion of a real estate transaction

Cloud on the title: any claim, lien, or encumbrance that impairs title to property

Codicil: a written supplement or amendment to an existing will

Color of title: some plausible but not completely clear-cut indication of ownership rights

Commercial Mortgage-Backed Securities (CMBS): mortgage bank securities for commercial loan funding.

Commingling: the mixing of clients' or customers' funds with an agent's personal funds

Common elements: those parts of a condominium which are owned by all the unit owners as tenants in common

Common law: law that develops from custom and usage over long periods of time

Common law dedication: results when a landowner's acts or words show intent to convey land to the government

Community property: spouses are treated as equal partners with each owning a one-half interest

Community Solutions Program: Fannie Mae promotion of flexible mortgages for school employee, police officers, fire fighters, and health care workers.

Comparables: properties similar to the subject property that are used to estimate the value of the subject property

Competent parties: persons considered legally capable of entering into a binding contract.

Competitive market analysis (CMA): a method of valuing homes that looks not only at recent home sales but also at homes presently on the market plus homes that were listed but did not sell

Comprehensive insurance policy: an "all-risks" coverage

Concurrent ownership: ownership by two or more persons at the same time

Conditional sales contract: *See* Installment contract

Conditional use permit: allows a land use that does not conform with existing zoning

Conduits: Organizations that handle CMBS and originate commercial and multi-family housing loans for purpose of pooling them as collateral for the issuance or Commercial Mortgage Backed Securities.

Connection line: a survey line that connects a surveyor's monument with a permanent reference mark

Consequential damages: an award to a property owner whose land is not taken but which suffers because of a nearby public land use

Consideration: an act or promise given in exchange for something

Construction loan: a loan wherein money is advanced as construction takes place (also called an interim loan)

Constructive eviction: tenant breaks the lease because landlord does not keep the premises habitable

Constructive notice: notice given by the public records and by visible possession, coupled with the legal presumption that all persons are thereby notified

Continuing education: additional education required to renew one's license

Contour line: line on a topographic map that connects points having the same elevation

Contract: legally enforceable agreement to do (or not do) a particular thing

Contract for deed: a method of selling and financing property whereby the buyer gets possession but the seller retains the title

Contract rent: the amount of rent specified in the lease contract

Conversion: an agent's personal use of money belonging to others

Conveyance tax: a fee or tax on deeds and other documents payable at the time of recordation

Cooperating broker: a broker who, acting as an agent of the listing broker, procures a buyer

Cooperative: land and building owned or leased by a corporation which in turn leases space to its shareholders

Cooperator: individual shareholders in a cooperative

Corner lot: a lot that fronts on two or more streets

Corporation: a business owned by stockholders

Correction deed: a document used to correct an error in a previously recorded deed

Correction line: a survey line used to correct for the earth's curvature

Correlation process: a step in an appraisal wherein the appraiser weighs the comparables

Cost approach: land value plus current construction costs minus depreciation

Cost-push inflation: higher prices due to increased costs of labor and supplies

Counteroffer: an offer made in response to an offer

Covenant: a written agreement or promise

Covenant against encumbrances: grantor warrants that there are no encumbrances other than those stated in the deed

Covenant of further assurance: grantor will procure and deliver to the grantee any subsequent documents necessary to make good the grantee's title

Covenant of quiet enjoyment: grantor warrants that the grantee will not be disturbed

Covenant of seizin: grantor warrants that he is the owner

Cul de sac: a street closed at one end with a circular turnaround

Curable depreciation: depreciation that can be fixed at reasonable cost

Curtesy: the legal right of a widower to a portion of his deceased wife's real property

Customer: a person with whom the broker and principal negotiates

Datum: any point, line, or surface from which a distance, vertical height, or depth is measured

Dedication: the voluntary conveyance of private land to the public

Deed: a written document that when properly executed and delivered conveys title to land

Deed as security: a deed given to secure a loan and treated as a mortgage

Deed of trust: a document that conveys legal title to a neutral third party as security for a debt

Deed restrictions: provisions placed in deeds to control how future landowners may or may not use the property (also called deed covenants)

Deed tax: a tax on conveyances of real estate

Default: failure to perform a legal duty, such a failure to carry out the terms of a contract

Defeasance clause: a mortgage clause that states the mortgage is defeated if the accompanying note is repaid on time

Deficiency judgment: a judgment against a borrower if the foreclosure sale does not bring enough to pay the balance owed

Delayed exchange: a nonsimultaneous tax-deferred trade

Delinquent loan: a loan wherein the borrower is behind in payments

Demand-pull inflation: higher prices due to buyers bidding against each other

Deposit receipt: a receipt given for a deposit that accompanies an offer to purchase; also refers to a purchase contract that includes a deposit receipt

Depreciation: loss in value due to deterioration and obsolescence

Dereliction: the process whereby dry land is permanently exposed by a gradually receding waterline

Desktop Originator/Desktop Underwriter: Fannie Mae introduced service to help lenders identify and stop fraud in mortgage transactions before the loan is closed.

Devise: a transfer of real property by means of a will

Devisee: one who receives real property under a will

Disclosure liability: to buyers and sellers

Discount broker: a full-service broker who charges less than the prevailing commission rates in his community

Discount points: charges made by lenders to adjust the effective rate of interest on a loan (one point is equal to one percent of loan)

Disintermediation: the movement of money out of savings accounts and into corporate and government debt instruments

Distributees: those designated by law to receive the property of the deceased when there is no will

Divided agency: representation of two or more parties in a transaction by the same agent

Doctrine of capture: The first to use the water (evenunderground water) has a prior right to its use.

Doctrine of prior appropriation: a legal tenet that allows a first user to continue diverting water

Documentary tax: a fee or tax on deeds and other documents payable at the time of recordation

Dominant estate: the parcel of land which benefits from an easement

Dower: the legal right of a widow to a portion of her deceased husband's real property

Downside risk: the possibility that an investor will lose his money in an investment

Downzoning: rezoning of land from a higher-density use to a lower-density use

Dry closing: a closing that is essentially complete except for disbursement of funds and delivery of documents

Dry rot: decay of wood that usually results from alternate soaking and drying over a long period

Dual agency: representation of two or more parties in a single transaction by the same agent

Due-on-sale clause: a clause in a note or mortgage that gives the lender the right to call the entire loan balance due if the property is sold or otherwise conveyed (see alienation clause)

Duplex: structure with two dwelling units

Duress: the application of force to obtain an agreement

Earnest money deposit: money that accompanies an offer to purchase as evidence of good faith

Easement: the right or privilege one party has to use land belonging to another for a special purpose not inconsistent with the owner's use of the land

Easement appurtenant: an easement that runs with the land

Easement by necessity: an easement created by law usually for the right to travel to a landlocked parcel of land

Easement by prescription: acquisition of an easement by prolonged continuous use

Easement in gross: an easement given to a person or business affecting one property

Economic base: the ability of a region to export goods and services to other regions and receive money in return

Economic obsolescence: loss of value due to external forces or events

Economic rent: the amount of rent a property could command in the open market

Effective yield: a return on investment calculation that considers the price paid, the time held, and the interest rate

Emblement: annual planting that requires cultivation

Eminent domain: the right of government to take privately held land for public use, provided fair compensation is paid

Employment multiplier: the number of service-industry jobs created by each new base-industry job

Encroachment: the unauthorized intrusion of a building or other improvement onto another's land

Encumbrance: any impediment to a clear title, such as a lien, lease, or easement

Endorsement: a policy modification (also called a rider or attachment)

Entry and possession: the borrower moves out and the lender moves in, which is witnessed and recorded

Environmental Impact Statement (EIS) or report (EIR): a report that contains information regarding the effect of a proposed project on the environment

Equitable mortgage: a written agreement that is considered to be a mortgage in its intent even though it may not follow the usual mortgage wording

Equitable title: the right to demand that title be conveyed upon payment of the purchase price

Equity: the market value of a property less the debt against it

Equity build-up: the increase of one's equity in a property due to mortgage balance reduction and price appreciation

Equity mortgage: line of credit made against the equity in a person's home

Equity of redemption: the borrower's right prior to foreclosure to repay the balance due on a delinquent mortgage loan

Equity sharing: an agreement whereby a party providing financing gets a portion of the ownership

Errors and omission (E&O) insurance: designed to pay legal costs and judgments against persons in real estate brokerage business

Escalator clause: provision in a lease for upward rent adjustments

Escheat: the reversion of a person's property to the state when death occurs and there is no will or heir

Escrow agent: the person placed in charge of an escrow

Escrow closing: the deposit of documents and funds with a neutral third party along with instructions as to how to conduct the closing

Escrow company: a firm that specializes in handling the closing of a transaction

Estate: the extent of one's legal interest or rights in land

Estate at will: a leasehold estate that can be terminated by a lessor or lessee at any time

Estate for years: any lease with a specific starting time and a specific ending time

Estate in severalty: owned by one person; sole ownership

Estoppel certificate: a document in which a borrower verifies the amount still owed and the interest rate

Exclusive agency listing: a listing wherein the owner reserves the right to sell the property himself, but agrees to list with no other broker during the listing period

Exclusive right to sell: a listing that gives the broker the right to collect a commission no matter who sells the property during the listing period

Execute: the process of completing, performing, or carrying out something

Executed: means that performance has taken place

Executive director: the person in charge of real estate regulation in a state

Executor: a male named in a will to carry out its instructions

Executor's deed: a deed used to convey the real property of a deceased person

Executrix: a female named in a will to carry out its instructions

Expressed contract: a contract made orally or in writing

Face amount: the dollar amount of insurance coverage

Faithful performance: a requirement that an agent obey all legal instructions given to him by his principal

Fair, Isaac & Company (FICO): Developed scores in evaluations in approvals and processing credit applications.

Familial status: one or more individuals (who have not obtained the age of 18 years) living with a parent or another person having legal custody of such individual or individuals or the designee of such parent or other person having such custody, with the written permission of such parent or other person

Fannie Mae: a real estate industry nickname for the Federal National Mortgage Association

Fannie Mae Property GeoCoder: A free, on-line application to determine whether a property qualifies for the Fannie Neighbors option.

Farmer Mac: a real estate industry nickname for Federal Agricultural Mortgage Corporation

Fannie Neighbors: A nation-wide, neighborhood based mortgage program designed to increase home ownership and revitalization in areas as underserved by HUD, in low to moderate incomeminorities censustracts of in central cities.

Federal clauses: refers to government-required clauses in real estate contracts

Federal Home Loan Mortgage Corporation (FHLMC): provides a secondary mortgage market facility for savings and loan associations

Federal National Mortgage Association (FNMA): provides secondary market for real estate loans

Federal Reserve Board: governing board of the nation's central bank

Fee simple: the largest, most complete bundle of rights one can hold in land; land ownership

Fee simple determinable estate: a fee estate limited by the happening of a certain event

Fee simple subject to condition subsequent: the grantor has the right to terminate the fee estate

Fee simple upon condition precedent: title does not take effect until a condition is performed

Feudal system: all land ownership rests in the name of the king

Fiat money: money created by the government; printing press money

Fictional depreciation: depreciation deductions as allowed by tax law

Fictitious business name: a name other than the owner's that is used to operate a business

Fiduciary: a person in a position of trust, responsibility, and confidence for another such as a broker for his client

Financial liability: the amount of money one can lose; one's risk exposure; investing

Financing statement: a recorded document designed to protect the rights of a chattel lienholder

First mortgage: the mortgage loan with highest priority for repayment in event of foreclosure

Fiscal policy: government policy to balance or not balance budgets

Fixity: refers to the fact that land and buildings require long periods of time to pay for themselves

Fixture: an object that has been attached to land so as to become real estate

Flag lot: a lot shaped like a flag on a flagpole

Flat-fee broker: a broker who for a fixed price will list a property and help the owner sell it

Foreclose: to terminate, shut off, or bar a mortgagee's claim to property after default

Foreclosure: the procedure by which a person's property can be taken and sold to satisfy an unpaid debt

Formal will: a will that is properly witnessed

Fourplex: a structure with four living units

4-3-2-1 rule: a depth adjustment for valuing vacant lots

Four unities of a joint tenancy: time, title, interest, and possession

Franchisee: the party who has a franchise

Franchiser: the party giving the franchise

Fraud: an act intended to deceive for the purpose of inducing another to give up something of value

Freddie Mac: a real estate industry nickname for the Federal Home Loan Mortgage Corpo-ration

Freehold estate: an estate in land that is held in fee or for life

Front foot: one linear foot along the street side of a lot

Functional obsolescence: depreciation that results from improvements that are inadequate, overly adequate, or improperly designed for today's needs

Funding fee: a charge by the VA to guarantee a loan

Gain on the sale: the net difference between the amount realized and the basis

General agency: an agency wherein the agent has the power to bind the principal in a particular trade or business

General lien: a lien on all of a person's property

General partnership: a form of co-ownership for business purposes wherein all partners have a voice in its management and unlimited liability for its debts

General plan: a comprehensive guide for land development

Gift deed: a deed that states "love and affection" as the consideration

Ginnie Mae: a real estate nickname for the Government National Mortgage Association

Good consideration: consideration without monetary value such as love and affection

Government National Mortgage Association (GNMA): government agency that sponsors a mortgage-backed securities program and subsidizes low-income housing

Government survey: a system for surveying land that uses latitude and longitude lines as references

Graduated payment mortgage: a fixed interest rate loan wherein the monthly payment starts low and then increases

Grant: act of conveying ownership

Grant deed: a deed that is somewhat narrower than a warranty deed with regard to covenants and warranties

Grantee: the person named in a deed who acquires ownership

Grantor: the person named in a deed who conveys ownership

Grantor-grantee indexes: alphabetical lists used to locate documents in the public records

GRI (Graduate, Realtors Institute): a designation awarded to Realtors who complete a prescribed course of real estate study

Grid system: state-sponsored survey points to which metes and bounds surveys can be referenced

Gross lease: the tenant pays a fixed rent and the landlord pays all property expenses

Gross rent multiplier (GRM): a number that is multiplied by a property's gross rent to produce an estimate of the property's worth

Ground lease: the lease of land alone

Ground rent: rent paid to occupy a plot of land

Groundwater level: the upper limit of percolating water below the earth's surface

Growing equity mortgage: a fixed-rate loan with increasing monthly payments that pays off early

Guaranteed replacement cost: full replacement cost insurance protection as required by lenders

Guardian's deed: used to convey property of a minor or legally incompetent person

Guide meridian: a survey line running north and south that corrects for the earth's curvature

Habendum clause: the "To have and to hold" clause found in deeds, part of the words of conveyance

Heirs: those designated by law to receive the property of the deceased

Highest and best use: that use of a parcel of land which will produce the greatest current value

Holdover tenant: a tenant who stays beyond his lease period and who can be evicted or given a new lease

Holographic will: one that is entirely handwritten and signed by the testator but not witnessed

Home buyer's insurance: protection for structural defects and faulty workmanship

Homeowner policy: a combined property and liability policy designed for residential use

Home seller program: a plan whereby the FNMA will buy mortgages from home sellers

Homestead Act: allows persons to acquire fee title to federal lands

Homestead protection: state laws that protect against the forced sale of a person's home

Hundred percent commission: an arrangement whereby the salesperson pays for office overhead directly rather than splitting a commission with the broker

Hypothecate: to use property to secure a debt without giving up possession of it

Illiquid asset: an asset that may be difficult to sell on short notice

Illiquidity: the possibility that it may be difficult to sell on short notice

Implied authority: agency authority arising from industry custom, common usage, and conduct of the parties involved

Implied contract: a contract created by the actions of the parties involved

Impound or reserve account: an account into which the lender places monthly tax and insurance payments (escrow account)

Improvement: any form of land development, such as buildings, roads, fences, pipelines, etc.

Improvement district: a geographical area which will be assessed for a local improvement

Income approach: a method of valuing property based on the monetary returns that a property can be expected to produce

Incurable depreciation: depreciation that cannot be fixed and simply must be lived with

Indenture: an agreement or contract

Independent contractor: one who contracts to do work according to his own methods and is responsible to his employer only for the results of that work

Index lease: rent is tied to an economic indicator such as inflation

Index rate: the interest rate to which an adjustable mortgage is tied

Indicated value: the worth of property as shown by recent sales of comparable properties

Inflation guard: an insurance policy endorsement that automatically increases

Informal reference: method of identifying a parcel of land by its street address or common name

Innocent misrepresentation: wrong information but without the intent to deceive

Inquiry notice: information the law presumes one would have where circumstances, appearances, or rumors warrant further inquiry

Installment contract: a method of selling and financing property whereby the seller retains title but the buyer takes possession while he makes his payments

Installment method: the selling of an appreciated property on terms rather than for cash so as to spread out the payment of income taxes on the gain

Insurable interest: the insured financial interest in a property

Insurance premium: the amount of money one must pay for insurance coverage

Insured: one who is covered by insurance

Interest rate cap: the maximum interest rate change allowed on an adjustable loan

Interim loan: a loan that is to be replaced by a permanent loan, a construction loan

Intermediate theory: the legal position that a mortgage is a lien until default, at which time title passes to the lender

Interspousal deed: used in some states to transfer real property between spouses

Inter vivos trust: a trust that takes effect during the life of its creator

Intestate: without a last will and testament

Intestate succession: laws that direct how a deceased's assets shall be divided when there is no will

Inverse condemnation: a legal action in which an owner demands that a public agency buy his land

Investment strategy: a plan that balances returns available with risks that must be taken in order to enhance the investor's overall welfare

Involuntary lien: a lien created by operation of law

Jointly and severally liable: enforceable on the makers as a group and upon each maker individually

Joint tenancy: a form of property co-ownership that features the right of survivorship

Joint venture: an association of two or more persons or firms in order to carry out a single business project

Judgment lien: a claim against property in favor of the holder of a court-ordered judgment

Judgment roll: a publicly available list of court-ordered judgments

Judicial foreclosure: foreclosure by lawsuit

Junior mortgage: any mortgage on a property that is subordinate to the first mortgage in priority

Key lot: a lot that adjoins the side or rear property line of a corner lot

Landlord: the lessor

Landlord policy: an insurance policy designed to protect owners of rental property

Land patent: a government document used for conveying public lands in fee to miners and settlers

Land trust: a real estate trust wherein the person who creates the trust (the trustor) is also its beneficiary

Land-use control: a broad term that describes any legal restriction that controls how a parcel of land may be used

Latitude line: an east-west reference line that circles the earth

Lawful objective: to be enforceable, contract cannot call for the breaking of laws

Lease: an agreement that conveys the right to use property for a period of time

Leasehold estate: an estate in land where there is possession but not ownership

Lease with option to buy: (lease-option) allows a tenant to buy the property at present price and terms for a given period of time

Legacy: personal property received under a will

Legal consideration: the requirement that consideration be present in a contract

Legal notice: information the public is charged with knowing

Legatee: a person who receives personal property under a will

Lender's policy: a title insurance policy designed to protect a lender

Letter of intent: a document that expresses mutual intent but without liability or obligation

Leverage: the impact that borrowed funds have on investment return

License: a personal privilege to use land on a non-exclusive basis

Licensee: one who holds a license

Lien: a hold or claim which one person has on the property of another to secure payment of a debt or other obligation

Lienee: the party subject to a lien

Lienor: the party holding a lien

Lien theory: the legal position that a mortgage creates a charge against property rather than conveying it to the lender

Life estate: the conveyance of fee title for the duration of one's life

Life estate pur autrie vie: a life estate created for the life of another

Life tenant: one who possesses a life estate

Lifetime cap: the maximum interest rate adjustment permitted over the life of a loan

Limited common elements: common elements whose use is limited to certain owners

Limited partner: a partner who provides capital but does not take personal financial liability or participate in management

Limited partnership: composed of general partners who mainly organize and operate the partnership and limited partners who provide the capital

Liquid asset: an asset that can be converted to cash on short notice

Liquidated damages: an amount of money specified in a contract as compensation to be paid if the contract is not satisfactorily completed

Listing: contract wherein a broker is employed to find a buyer or tenant

Littoral right: the lawful claim of a landowner to use and enjoy the water of a lake or sea bordering his land

Loan balance table: shows the balance remaining to be paid on an amortized loan

Loan commitment letter: a written agreement that a lender will make a loan

Loan escrow: an escrow opened for the purpose of repaying a loan

Loan origination fee: a charge for making a loan

Loan points: a charge, expressed in percentage points, to obtain a loan; one point is one percent of loan

Loan servicing: the task of collecting monthly payments and handling insurance and tax impounds, delinquencies, early payoffs, and mortgage lending

Loan-to-value ratio: a percentage reflecting what a lender will lend divided by the market value of the property

Longitude line: a north-south reference line that circles the earth

Loose money: means that lenders have adequate funds to loan and are actively seeking borrowers

Loyalty to principal: a requirement that an agent place the principal's interests above his own

MAI: Member of the American Institute of Real Estate Appraisers

Maintenance fees: fees paid by a condominium or PUD unit owner to the owners' association for upkeep of the common elements

Majority: the minimum age required for legal competency (in most states 18 years)

Maker: the person who signs a promissory note

Mapping requirements: regulations a subdivider must meet before selling lots

Margin: the amount added to the index rate that reflects the lender's cost of doing business

Marginal release: a notation on the recorded mortgage that shows the book and page location of the mortgage release

Market approach: a method of valuing a property based on the prices of recent sales of similar properties

Market value: the cash price that a willing buyer and a willing seller would agree upon, given reasonable exposure of the property to the marketplace, full information as to the potential uses of the property, and no undue compulsion to act

Marketable title: title that is free from reasonable doubt as to who the owner is

Marketable Title Act: state law aimed at cutting off rights and interest in land that has been inactive for long periods

Masking: to cover over something that may be illegal or unethical

Master plan: a comprehensive guide for a community's physical growth

Maturity: the end of the life of a loan (also called the maturity date)

Mechanic's lien: a claim placed against property by unpaid workmen or materials suppliers

Meeting of the minds, mutual agreement: means that there must be agreement to the provisions of a contract by all parties involved

Menace: threat of violence to obtain a contract

Meridian: north-south line that encircles the earth and is used as a reference in mapping land

Metes and bounds: a method of land description that identifies a parcel by specifying its shape and boundaries and distance and directions

Middleman: a person who brings two or more parties together but does not conduct negotiations

Mile: 5,280 feet or 1,760 yards

Mill rate: property tax rate that is expressed in tenths of a cent per dollar of assessed valuation

Minor, infant: a person under the age of legal competence (in most states under 18 years)

Mistake: refers to ambiguity in contract negotiations and mistake of material fact

Modification: the influence on land use and value resulting from improvements made by man to surrounding parcels

Monetary base: the legal reserves of banks at the Federal Reserve

Monetary inflation: price rises due to the creation of excessive amounts of money by government

Monetary policy: action by the Federal Reserve to create and destroy money

Monetize the debt: the creation of money by the Federal Reserve to purchase Treasury securities

Money damages: compensation paid in lieu of contract performance

Monument: an iron pipe, stone, tree, or other fixed point used in making a survey

Mortgage: a document which makes property secure for the repayment of a debt

Mortgage broker: a person who brings borrowers and lenders together, a loan broker

Mortgage company: a business firm that makes mortgage loans and then sells them to investors

Mortgage Electronic Registration System: (MERS) is a computerized book registration system of tracking the beneficial interest of "bundle of rights" connected with both residential and commercial real estate loans.

Mortgage insurance: insures lenders against nonrepayment of loans

Mortgage networks: the use of computers to search and apply for mortgage loan money

Mortgage pool: a common fund of mortgage loans in which one can invest

Mortgage-backed securities (MBS): certificates that pass through principal and interest payments to investors

Mortgage-equity technique: a method for valuing income-producing property that takes into consideration the price and availability of money

Mortgagee: the party receiving the mortgage, the lender

Mortgagee's policy: a title insurance policy designed to protect a lender

Mortgagee-mortgagor indexes: the alphabetical lists used to locate mortgages in the public records

Mortgagor: the party giving the mortgage, the borrower

Multiple Listing Service (MLS): an organization that enables brokers to exchange information on listings

Municipal bond: a source of home loans that in turn is financed by the sale of municipal bonds

Mutual agreement, mutual consent: means that there must be agreement to the provisions of the contract by all parties involved

Mutual rescission: voluntary cancellation of a contract by all parties involved

Naked title: title lacking the usual rights and privileges of ownership

National Association of Realtors: the dominant real estate industry trade association in the U.S.

Negative amortization: occurs when a loan payment is insufficient to pay the interest due and the excess is added to the balance owed

Negative cash flow: a condition wherein the cash paid out exceeds the cash received

Negative leverage: occurs when borrowed funds cost more than they produce

Net lease: tenant pays a base rent plus maintenance, property taxes, and insurance

Net listing: a listing wherein the commission is the difference between the selling price and a minimum price set by the seller

Net operating income (NOI): gross income less operating expenses, and collecting losses

Net spendable: the number of dollars remaining each year after collecting rents and paying operating expenses and mortgage payments

Net worth: total assets minus total debts

New for old: insurance policy pays replacement cost of damaged property

Nonconforming use: an improvement that is inconsistent with current zoning regulations

Nonfungible: not substitutable

Nonhomogeneity: no two parcels of land are not alike

Nonjudicial foreclosure: foreclosure is conducted by the lender

Notary public: a person authorized by the state to administer oaths, attest and certify documents, and take acknowledgments

Note: a written promise to repay a debt

Notice of consent: allows the secretary of state to receive legal summonses for nonresidents

Notice of default: public notice that a borrower is in default

Notice of lis pendens: notice of a pending lawsuit

Novation: substitution of a new contract or new party for an old one

Nuncupative will: will made orally

Obligee: the person to whom a debt or obligation is owed; the lender

Obligor: the person responsible for paying a debt or obligation; the borrower

Offeree: the party who receives an offer

Offeror: the party who makes an offer

Offset statement: a statement by an owner or lienholder as to the balance due on existing lien

Office of Federal Housing Enterprise Oversight (OFHEO): established by HUD to ensure the capital adequacy and financial soundness of Fannie Mae and Freddie Mac.

Off-site management: refers to those property management functions that can be performed away from the premises being managed

Old for old: insurance policy pays only the depreciated value of damaged property

On-site management: refers to those property management functions that must be performed on the premises being managed

Open listing: a listing that gives a broker a nonexclusive right to find a buyer

Operating expense: expenditure necessary to maintain the production of income

Operating expense ratio: total operating expenses divided by effective gross income

Opinion of title: an attorney's opinion as to the status of the title

Option: the right at some future time to purchase or lease a property at a predetermined price

Optionee: the party receiving the option

Optionor: the party giving the option

Origination fee: a charge for making a loan

Ostensible authority: results when a principal gives a third party reason to believe that another person is his agent even though that person is unaware of the appointment

Outside of the closing: means that a party to the closing has paid someone directly and not through the closing (also called outside of escrow)

Overall rate: a mortgage-equity factor used to appraise income-producing property

Overencumbered property: occurs when the market value of a property is exceeded by the loans against it

Owners' association: an administrative association composed of each unit owner of a condominium

Owner's policy: a title insurance policy designed to protect the fee owner

Package mortgage: a mortgage secured by a combination of real and personal property

Parol evidence rule: permits oral evidence to augment a written contract in certain cases

Partially amortized loan: a loan that begins with amortized payments but ends with a balloon payment

Partial release: a release of a portion of a property from a mortgage

Participation certificate (PC): a secondary mortgage market instrument whereby an investor can purchase an undivided interest in a pool of mortgages

Participation loan: one that requires interest plus a percentage of the profits

Partition: to divide jointly held property into distinct portions so that each co-owner may hold his or her proportionate share in severalty

Party (plural, parties): a legal term that refers to a person or a group involved in a legal proceeding

Party wall: a fence or wall erected along a property line for the mutual benefit of both owners

Pass-through securities: certificates that pass mortgage principal and interest payments on to investors

Payment cap: a limit on how much a borrower's payments can increase

Percentage lease: rent is based on the tenant's sales

Percolating water: underground water not confined to a defined underground waterway

Perfecting the lien: the filing of a lien statement within the required time limit

Periodic estate: a tenancy that provides for continuing automatic renewal until canceled, such as a month-to-month rental

Perjury: willful lie made under oath

Personal property: a right or interest in things of a temporary or movable nature; anything not classed as real property

Personal representative: a person named to settle an estate

Physical deterioration: deterioration from wear and tear and the action of nature

PITI payment: a loan payment that combines principal, interest, taxes, and insurance

Planned unit development (PUD): individually owned lots and houses with community ownership of common areas

Plat: a map that shows the location and boundaries of individual properties

Pledge: to give up possession of property while it serves as collateral for a debt

Plottage value: the result of combining two or more parcels of land so that the one large parcel has more value than the sum of the individual parcels

Point: one percent of a loan amount; one-hundredth of the total amount of a mortgage loan

Point of beginning or point of commencement: the starting place at one corner of a parcel of land in a metes and bounds description

Police power: the right of government to enact laws and enforce them for the order, safety, health, morals, and general welfare of the public

Positive cash flow: a condition wherein cash received exceeds cash paid out

Positive leverage: occurs when the benefits of borrowing exceed the costs of borrowing

Possession: the day on which the buyer can move in

Power of attorney: a written authorization to another to act on one's behalf

Power of sale: allows a mortgagee to conduct a foreclosure sale without first going to court

Predatory Lending: unscrupulous lenders preying upon consumers by taking advantage of their lack of knowledge.

Preliminary title report: title search without a commitment to insure the title

Prepayment penalty: a fee charged by a lender for permitting a borrower to repay his loan early

Prepayment privilege: allows the borrower to repay early without penalty

Prescriptive easement: easement acquired by prolonged continuous use

Primary market: where lenders originate loans

Principal: a person who authorizes another to act for him

Principal broker: the broker in charge of a real estate office

Principal meridian: a longitude line selected as a reference in the rectangular survey system

"Principals only": means the owner wants to be contacted by persons who want to buy and not by agents

Probate court: a court of law with the authority to verify the legality of a will and carry out its instructions

Procuring cause: the broker who is the primary cause of a transaction

Pro forma statement: a projected annual operating statement that shows expected income, operating expenses, and net operating income

Projected gross: expected rentals from a property on a fully occupied basis

Promissory note: a written promise to repay a debt

Property disclosure statement: government-required information that must be given to purchasers in subdivisions

Proprietary lease: a lease issued by a cooperative corporation to its shareholders

Prorating: the division of ongoing expenses and income items between the buyer and the seller

Prospectus: a disclosure statement that describes an investment opportunity

Public grant: a transfer of land by a government body to a private individual

Public improvement: one that benefits the public at large and is financed through general property taxes

Public liability: a financial responsibility one has toward others as a result of one's actions or failure to take action

Public recorder's office: a government operated facility wherein documents are entered in the public records

Public trustee: a publicly appointed official that acts as a trustee in some states

Puffing: statements a reasonable person would recognize as nonfactual or extravagant

Purchase money loan: a loan used to purchase the real property that serves as its collateral

Quadrangle: a 24-by-24 mile area created by the guide meridians and correction lines in the rectangular survey system

Qualified fee estate: a fee simple estate subject to certain limitations imposed by its grantor

Quiet enjoyment: the right of possession and use of property without undue disturbance by others

Quiet title suit: court-ordered hearings held to determine land ownership

Quitclaim deed: a legal instrument used to convey whatever title the grantor has; it contains no covenants, warranties, or implication of the grantor's ownership

Range: a six-mile-wide column of land running north-south in the rectangular survey system

Ready, willing, and able buyer: a buyer who is ready to buy at price and terms acceptable to the owner

Real-cost inflation: higher prices due to greater effort needed to produce the same product today versus several years ago

Real estate: land and improvements in a physical sense as well as the rights to own or use them

Real estate commission: a state board that advises and sets policies regarding real estate licenses and transaction procedures

Real estate commissioner: a person appointed by the governor to implement and carry out laws enacted by the legislature that pertain to real estate

Real estate department: a state office responsible for such matters as license examinations, license issuance, and compliance with state license and subdivision laws

Real estate investment trust (REIT): a method of pooling investor money using the trust form of ownership and featuring single taxation of profits

Real estate listing: a contract wherein a broker is employed to find a buyer or tenant

Real Estate Settlement Procedures Act (RESPA): a federal law that deals with procedures to be followed in certain types of real estate closings

Real property: ownership rights in land and its improvements

Real savings: savings by persons and businesses that result from spending less than is earned

Realtist: member of the National Association of Real Estate Brokers

REALTOR®: a registered trademark owned by the National Association of Realtors for use by its members

Realtor-Associate: membership designation for salespersons working for Realtors

Reasonable care: a requirement that an agent exhibit competence and expertise, keep his client informed, and take proper care of property entrusted to him

Receiver: a manager to take charge of property during the redemption period

Reconveyance: the return to the borrower of legal title upon repayment of the debt against the property

Recording act: law that provides for the placing of documents in the public records

Recovery fund: a state-operated fund that can be tapped to pay for uncollected judgments against real estate licensees

Rectangular survey system: a government system for surveying land that uses latitude and longitude lines as references

Red flag: something that would warn a reasonably observant person of an underlying problem

Redlining: the practice of refusing to make loans or insurance in certain neighborhoods

Referee's deed in foreclosure: a deed issued as the result of a court-ordered foreclosure sale

Regulation Z: a federal law requiring lenders to show borrowers how much they are paying for credit

Reissue rate: reduced rate for title insurance if the previous owner's policy is available for updating

Release deed: a document used to reconvey title from the trustee back to the property owner once the debt has been paid

Release of mortgage: a certificate from the lender stating that the loan has been repaid

Reliction (dereliction): the process whereby dry land is permanently exposed by a gradually receding waterline

Remainder interest: a future interest in real estate held by a remainderman

Remainderman: one who is entitled to take an estate in remainder

Remaining balance table: shows the balance remaining to be paid on an amortized loan

Remise: to give up any existing claim one may have

Renegotiable rate mortgage: a loan that must be renewed periodically at current interest rates

Rental Listing Services: firms that specialize in finding rental units for tenants

Rent control: government-imposed restrictions on the amount of rent a property owner can charge

Replacement cost: the cost, at today's prices and using today's construction methods, of building an improvement having the same or equivalent usefulness as the subject property

Reproduction cost: cost, at today's prices, of constructing an exact replica of the subject improvements using the same or very similar materials

Reserve account (impound account): an account into which the lender places the borrower's monthly tax and insurance payments (escrow account)

Reserves for replacement: money set aside each year for the replacement of items that have a useful life greater than one year

Resort timesharing: exclusive use of a property for a specified number of days each year

RESPA: Real Estate Settlement Procedures Act

Restrictive covenants: the clauses placed in deeds and leases to control how future owners and lessees may or may not use the property

Retaliatory eviction: landlord evicts tenant because tenant has complained to authorities about the premises

Reverse mortgage: the lender makes payments to homeowner who later repays in a lump sum when they sell or die (also called a reverse annuity mortgage or RAM)

Reversion: the right to future enjoyment of property presently possessed or occupied by another

Revoke: recall and make void

Rider: any annexation to a document made part of the document by reference

Right of first refusal: the right to match another offer and get the property

Right of survivorship: a feature of joint tenancy whereby the surviving joint tenants automatically acquire all the right, title, and interest of the deceased joint tenant

Right-of-way: the right or privilege to travel over a designated portion of another person's land

Right-to-use: a contractual right to occupy a living unit at a timeshare resort

Riparian right: a nonexclusive right of a landowner whose land borders a river or stream to use and enjoy that water

Rod: a survey measurement that is 16 feet long

Sale and leaseback: owner-occupant sells his property and then remains as a tenant

Sale by advertisement: allows a mortgagee to conduct foreclosure sale without first going to court

Salesperson: a person employed by a broker to list, negotiate, sell, or lease real property for others

Salvage value: the price that can be expected for an improvement that is to be removed and used elsewhere

Satisfaction of mortgage: a certificate from the lender stating that the loan has been repaid

Scheduled gross (projected gross): the estimated rent a fully occupied property can be expected to produce on an annual basis

S Corporation: allows limited liability with profit-and-loss pass-through

Seal: a hot wax paper, or embossed seal, or the word "seal," or L.S. placed on a document

Second mortgage: one which ranks immediately behind the first mortgage in priority

Secondary mortgage market: a market where loans can be sold to investors

Section: a unit of land in the rectangular survey system that is 1 mile long on each of its four sides and contains 640 acres

Section 203(b): FHA's popular mortgage insurance program for houses

Security deed: a loan deed with a reconveyance clause

Seller financing: a note accepted by a seller instead of cash

Seller's closing statement: a detailed accounting of the seller's money at settlement

Seller's market: one with few sellers and many buyers

Senior mortgage: the mortgage against a property that holds first priority in the event of foreclosure

Separate property: property that a spouse owns that is not subject to community property

Service industry: an industry that produces goods and services to sell to local residents

Service the loan: to collect monthly payments and impounds, handle payoffs, releases, and delinquencies

Servient estate: the land on which an easement exists in favor of a dominant estate

Settlement: the day on which title is conveyed

Settlement meeting: meeting at which the buyer pays for the property, receives a deed to it, and all other matters pertaining to the sale are concluded

Settlement statement: an accounting statement at settlement that shows each item charged or credited, to whom and for how much

Severalty ownership: owned by one person, sole ownership

Severance damages: compensation paid for the loss in market value that results from splitting up property in condemnation proceeding

Shared Appreciation Mortgage (SAM): a mortgage loan wherein the borrower gives the lender a portion of the property's appreciation in return for a lower rate of interest

Sheriff's deed: a deed issued as a result of a court-ordered foreclosure sale

Situs: refers to the preference by people for a given location

Sole ownership: owned by one person

Special agency: an agency created for the performance of specific acts only

Special assessment: a charge levied to provide publicly built improvements that will benefit a limited geographical area

Special lien: a lien on a specific property

Special warranty deed: grantor warrants title only against defects occurring during the grantor's ownership

Specific performance: performance of a contract according to the precise terms agreed upon

Spot zoning: the rezoning of a small area of land in an existing neighborhood

Square-foot method: appraisal technique that uses the square-foot construction costs of similar structures as an estimating basis

SREA: Senior Real Estate Analyst

Standard parallel: a survey line used to correct for the earth's curvature

Statute of Frauds: a law requiring that certain types of contracts be written in order to be enforceable in a court of law

Statute of limitations: a legal limit on the amount of time one has to seek the aid of a court in obtaining justice

Statutory dedication: conveyance through the approval and recordation of a subdivision map

Statutory estates: estates created by law and including dower, curtesy, community property, and homestead rights

Statutory law: law created by the enactment of legislation

Statutory redemption: the right of a borrower after a foreclosure sale to reclaim his property by repaying the defaulted loan plus expenses

Steering: the illegal practice of directing minority members to or away from certain neighborhoods

Step-up rental: a lease that provides for agreed-upon rent increases

Straight-line depreciation: depreciation in equal amounts each year over the life of the asset

Strict foreclosure: when the lender acquires absolute title without the need for a court ordered foreclosure sale

Subagent: an agent appointed by an agent to act for the principal's benefit

Subject property: the property that is being appraised

Subject to: said of property that is bought subject to the existing loan against it

Sublease: a lease given by a lessee

Sublet: to transfer only a portion of one's lease rights

Subordination: voluntary acceptance of a lower mortgage priority

Subsurface right: the right to use land below the earth's surface

Sunk cost: a cost already incurred that is not subject to revision

Surface rights: the right to use the surface of a parcel of land

Surplus money action: a claim for payment filed by a junior mortgage holder at a foreclosure sale

Surrogate court: a court of law with the authority to verify the legality of a will and carry out its instructions

Suspend: temporarily make ineffective

Syndication (syndicate): a group of persons or businesses that combines to undertake an investment

Tacking: adding successive periods of continuous occupation to qualify for title by adverse possession

Take-out loan: a permanent loan arranged to replace a construction loan

"Taking back paper": said of a seller who allows a buyer to substitute a promissory note for cash

Tax basis: the price paid for a property plus certain costs and expenses

Tax certificate: a document issued at a tax sale that entitles the purchaser to a deed at a later date if the property is not redeemed

Tax deed: a document that conveys title to property purchased at a tax sale

Tax deferred exchange: a sale of real property in exchange for another parcel of real estate, to affect a nontaxable gain

Tax lien: a charge or hold by the government against property to ensure the payment of taxes

Tax shelter: the income tax savings that an investment can produce for its owner

Teaser rate: an adjustable loan with an initial short-term rate below the market

Tenancy at sufferance: occurs when a tenant stays beyond his legal tenancy without the consent of the landlord

Tenancy by the entirety: a form of joint ownership reserved for married persons; a right of survivorship exists and neither spouse has a disposable interest during the lifetime of the other

Tenant: one who holds or possesses property, the lessee

Tenant's form (HO–4): an insurance policy designed for residential tenant's personal property

Tenants in common: shared ownership of a single property among two or more persons; interests need not be equal and no right of survivorship exists

Term loan: a loan requiring interest-only payments until the maturity date (due date) at which time the entire principal is due

Testamentary trust: a trust that takes effect after death

Testate: to die with a last will and testament

Testator: a person who makes a will (masculine), testatrix (feminine)

Testimony clause: a declaration in a document that reads, "In witness whereof the parties hereto set their hands and seals" or a similar phrase

The Nehemiah Program: was founded with a $500,000 grant from a local Baptist church in 1994, with the intentions of rebuilding parts of Sacramento, California, It has now grown into a national program handling over $150 Million Dollars a year.

Thin market: a market with few buyers and few sellers

Third party: a person who is a party to a contract but is not the client or the agent

Thrifts: a term applied to savings and loan associations and mutual savings banks

Tight money: means that loan money is in short supply and loans are hard to get

"Time is of the essence": a phrase that means that the time limits of a contract must be faithfully observed or the contract is voidable

Timesharing: the exclusive use of a property for a specified number of days each year

Title: the right to or ownership of something; also the evidence of ownership such as a deed or bill of sale

Title by descent: laws that direct how a deceased's assets shall be divided when there is no will

Title by prescription: acquisition of real property through continuous, prolonged and unauthorized occupation (also called adverse possession)

Title closing: the process of consummating a real estate transaction

Title cloud: a title defect

Title insurance: an insurance policy against defects in title not listed in the title report or abstract

Title plant: a duplicate set of public records kept by a title company

Title report: a statement of the current condition of title for a parcel of land

Title search: an inspection of publicly available records and documents to determine the current ownership and title condition for a property

Title theory: the legal position that a mortgage conveys title to the lender

T lot: a lot at the end of a T intersection

Torrens system: a state-sponsored method of registering land titles

Townhouse: a dwelling unit usually with two or three floors, shared walls; usually found in PUDs

Township: a 6-by-6-mile square of land designated by the intersection of range lines and township lines in the rectangular survey system

Tract index: a system for listing recorded documents affecting a particular tract of land

Trade fixture: a business or trade-related article attached to a rental building by a business tenant

Transferable development right (TDR): a legal means by which the right to develop a particular parcel of land can be transferred to another parcel

Trigger terms: credit advertising that requires compliance with Truth-in-Lending rules

Triplex: a structure with three dwelling units

Trust: ownership by a trustee for the benefit of another

Trust account: a separate account for holding clients' and customers' money

Trust deed (deed of trust): a document that conveys title to a neutral third party as security for a debt

Trustee: one who holds property in trust for another

Trustee's deed: given to the successful bidder at a deed of trust foreclosure sale

Trustor: the borrower in a deed of trust, one who creates a trust

Truth-in-Lending Act: a federal law that requires certain disclosures when extending or advertising credit

Undivided interest: ownership by two or more persons that gives each the right to use the entire property

Undue influence: unfair advantage to obtain a contract

Unilateral contract: results when a promise is exchanged for performance

Unilateral rescission: innocent party refuses to perform contractual duties because the other party has not performed

Unity of interest: all joint tenants own the same percentage of interest together

Unity of person: the legal premise that husband and wife are an indivisible legal unit and a requirement of tenancy by the entirety

Unity of possession: all co-tenants must enjoy the same undivided possession of the whole property

Unity of time: each joint tenant must acquire his or her ownership interest at the same moment

Unity of title: all joint tenants must acquire their interest from the same deed or will

Universal agency: an agency wherein the principal is empowered to transact matters of all types for the principal

U.S. Public Lands Survey: a system for surveying land that uses latitude and longitude lines as references

Usury: charging a rate of interest higher than that permitted by law

Valid contract: one that meets all requirements of law, is binding upon its parties, and is enforceable in a court of law

Valuable consideration: money, property, services, forbearance, or anything worth money

Variable Rate Commission: retains the lower commission for the bargain broker but allows the commission to increase (i.e. to a full 3%) to the broker in order to give other brokers an incentive to help market their properties.

Variable rate mortgage: a mortgage on which the interest rate rises and falls with changes in prevailing interest rates

Variance: waiver to an individual landowner from zoning requirements

Vendee: the buyer

Vendor: the seller

Voidable contract: a contract that binds one party but gives the other the right to withdraw

Void contract: a contract that has no binding effect on the parties who made it

Voluntary lien: a lien created by the property owner

Waive: to surrender or give up

Walk-through: final inspection of a property just prior to settlement

Warranty: assurance or guarantee that something is true as stated

Warranty deed: a deed that usually contains the covenants of seizin, quiet enjoyment, encumbrances, further assurance, and warranty forever

Warranty forever: the grantor's guarantee that he will bear the expense of defending the grantee's title

Waste: abuse or destructive use of property

Water right: the right to use water on or below or bordering a parcel of land

Water table: the upper limit of percolating water below the earth's surface

Words of conveyance: the grantor's statement that he is making a grant to the grantee

Worker's compensation: insurance for injuries to workers while on the job

Worst-case scenario: shows what can happen to the borrower's payments if the index rises to its maximum in an adjustable loan

Wraparound mortgage: a mortgage that encompasses existing mortgages and is subordinate to them

Writ of execution: a court document directing the county sheriff to seize and sell a debtor's property